1008088815

Queen of Heaven

ReFormations

MEDIEVAL AND EARLY MODERN

Series Editors:
David Aers, Sarah Beckwith, and James Simpson

QUEEN
of HEAVEN

The Assumption and Coronation of the Virgin
in Early Modern English Writing

LILLA GRINDLAY

University of Notre Dame Press
Notre Dame, Indiana

University of Notre Dame Press
Notre Dame, Indiana 46556
undpress.nd.edu

Library of Congress Cataloging-in-Publication Data

Names: Grindlay, Lilla, author.
Title: Queen of Heaven : the assumption and coronation of the Virgin in early
   modern English writing, 1558/?1625 / Lilla Grindlay.
Description: Notre Dame, Indiana : University of Notre Dame Press, [2018] |
   Series: Reformations: Medieval and Early Modern | Includes bibliographical
   references and index. |
Identifiers: LCCN 2018036114 (print) | LCCN 2018045262 (ebook) | ISBN
   9780268104115 (pdf) | ISBN 9780268104122 (epub) | ISBN 9780268104092
   (hardback : alk. paper) | ISBN 0268104093 (hardback : alk. paper) | ISBN
   9780268104108 (pbk. : alk. paper) | ISBN 0268104107 (pbk. : alk. paper)
Subjects: LCSH: Mary, Blessed Virgin, Saint—In literature. | English
   literature—Early modern, 1500–1700—History and criticism.
Classification: LCC PR428. M367 (ebook) | LCC PR428. M367 G75 2018 (print) |
   DDC 820.9/38232914—dc23
LC record available at https://lccn.loc.gov/2018036114

For Bruce, Jess, and Sam

CONTENTS

ACKNOWLEDGMENTS

This book began its life as a doctoral thesis at University College London, where I had the immense privilege of being supervised by Helen Hackett. Helen's support, friendship, and guidance have been immeasurable. I am also indebted to Alison Shell, who as secondary supervisor went way above and beyond and whose expertise has considerably shaped my research.

Many of the chapters I have written have grown out of papers given at conferences. I am grateful for the comments and suggestions from a range of scholars who have heard me air my views, particularly Robert Miola, Arthur Marotti, Susannah Brietz Monta, Susan Signe Morrison, and Gary Waller. Anne Dillon, René Weis, Gerard Kilroy, Jeanne Shami, and Alexander Samson have also offered invaluable advice. Fr. Peter McGeary, Serenhedd James, and Fiona Porter generously gave their time to proofread sections of the book, while Tristan Franklinos provided expert help with Latin translations. I also owe a debt of thanks to the University of Notre Dame Press, especially Stephen Little and Matthew Dowd, for their support. Particular thanks must go to Elisabeth Magnus for her sharp-eyed and sensitive copy editing and to the anonymous readers of the manuscript, whose invaluable corrections and suggestions have vastly improved the finished product. Any remaining errors are entirely my own.

I have also been fortunate to have many friends and colleagues who have lifted me out of the solitude of writing. There are too many names to mention them all, but particular thanks go to Lorna Dolan and Catherine Mangan for the interest they have shown. As always in my life, I owe a huge debt to Alice Merino for her intellectually stimulating conversations and emotional sustenance, given in equal measure over tea and cake in venues across London. My parents, Julie and George Ruck, and in-laws, Pat and Colin Grindlay, have also shown immense support throughout the project.

My final—and biggest—thank-you is to my husband and children, whose love and belief in me have made writing and researching possible. My children, Jess and Sam, have dealt patiently with my mental and physical absences. I have written this book over a number of years, during which they have grown into young adults, and throughout this time their wit and spark have dragged me—just occasionally—out of Elizabethan and Jacobean England and back to reality. My husband, Bruce, is the busiest person I know and yet has still found the time to read my work, discuss ideas, and offer unerring support. He is my rock, and I could not have completed the book without him.

NOTES ON THE TEXT

When referencing early modern editions, I have retained original spellings, with the exception of *i/j* and *u/v*, which have been modernized.

All biblical references have been taken from the Geneva Bible, unless stated otherwise: *The Geneva Bible*, introd. Lloyd E. Berry, facs. of 1560 ed. (1969; repr., Peabody, MA: Hendrickson, 2007).

All biographical information is from the *Oxford Dictionary of National Biography Online*, unless stated otherwise, http://www.oxford dnb.com, which is abbreviated as *ODNB* in the text.

All references to the works of Shakespeare are from *The Complete Works of Shakespeare*, ed. Stanley Wells, Gary Taylor, John Jowett, and William Montgomery (Oxford: Clarendon Press, 1986).

All references to *The Faerie Queene* are from Edmund Spenser, *The Faerie Queene*, ed. A. C. Hamilton with Hiroshi Yamashita and Toshiyuki Suzuki, 2nd ed. (Harlow: Pearson Longman, 2007).

In bibliographical references, ESTC refers to the English Short Title Catalogue, http://estc.bl.uk.

A&R refers to A. F. Allison and D. M. Rogers, *The Contemporary Printed Literature of the English Counter-Reformation between 1558 and 1640*, vol. 2, *Works in English* (Aldershot: Scolar Press, 1994).

Introduction
The Vanishing Virgin?

> In the wrackes of walsingam
>   Whom should I chuse,
> But the Queene of walsingam,
>   to be guide to my muse
> Then thou Prince of walsingam
>   graunt me to frame,
> Bitter plaintes to rewe thy wronge,
>   bitter wo for thy name.[1]

The opening lines of "The Walsingham Ballad" take the reader to a desolate landscape. In the Middle Ages, the Shrine of Our Lady of Walsingham was a popular English pilgrimage site, visited by countless pilgrims who sought assistance from the Virgin Mary. The shrine was
despoiled by Henry VIII in 1538, and "The Walsingham Ballad" powerfully evokes its ruined state. Attributed to the Catholic nobleman
Philip Howard, Earl of Arundel, the poem is a plaintive, melancholy
elegy to a lost world, in which the speaker is guided through the
"wrackes of walsingam" by the Virgin Mary. Theirs is a mournful pilgrimage with a tearful, bleak destination:

> Weepe weepe o walsingham
>   Whose dayes are nightes

Blessinges turned to blasphemies
  Holy deedes to dispites,
Sinne is wher our Ladie sate
  Heaven turned is to Hell.
Sathan sittes wher our Lord did swaye
  Walsingam oh farewell.

The Virgin's presence within this poem is as evasive as it is alluring. As "Queene of walsingam," she is regal and powerful, the glorious, triumphant figure of medieval iconography. She is also described as a guide to the poet's muse, an allusion to Mary as the mesmerizing idealized beloved of the courtly love tradition, and the inspiration of myriad sacred love poems. We soon realize, however, that hers is an impotent queenship. Her realm is the barren landscape of the ruined shrine; she is an elusive, disembodied presence who by the poem's end appears to have vanished away, usurped by the "Sinne" of the Reformation. The poem seems to be an elegy to a vanishing Virgin.

Does "The Walsingham Ballad" truly encapsulate the effect that England's Reformation had on perceptions of the Virgin Mary? As statues were torn down, shrines despoiled, and walls whitewashed, did the influential, devotional symbol of Mary really vanish from the nation's incipient Protestant consciousness, just as she vanishes from the poem? The answer cannot be an unequivocal yes. Even within this one ballad, the Virgin's representation is one of tensions and contradictions. My initial reading looked on the poem's surface to find a vanishing Virgin: a usurped queen and a lonely speaker who weeps over her absence. An image of the Virgin is conceptualized that is bound to a sense of loss and regret. Yet it is also possible to see the Virgin Mary as a figure of protest, a muse who guides the poet as he frames "bitter plaintes" to the "Prince of walsingam." If the prince in question is read as Henry VIII, Walsingham's despoiler, the reactionary nature of the poem intensifies. The lines "Bitter plaintes to rewe thy wronge, / bitter wo for thy name" can be interpreted as an ominous prediction of Henry's ruin—either earthly or spiritual.[3] The frequent repetition of the word *bitter* shifts the tone of the poem, and it is the Virgin who has given the poet both the inspiration and the courage to frame his hostile protest.

It is perhaps unsurprising that the Virgin's presence in this poem is one of tensions and contradictions. The Virgin Mary is a protean, multi-layered figure who frequently evades definitive statements. Appearances of the Virgin in the Gospels themselves are relatively rare; with the exception of St. Luke's Magnificat, Mary is in the main a mute figure whose acquiescence to God's will leads to a reversal of the Fall.[4] Virtually silent and barely present, Mary has fascinated artists, writers, and musicians for centuries. The gaps in the text of the Virgin's life have not only been filled by artistic representation; ideological and cultural concerns have also had an important part to play. The Virgin's image has also often been a site of polemic, shaped and reshaped by influential members of society throughout history. A Freudian approach to the Virgin Mary finds an overdetermined symbol—a composite figure onto which different, often conflicting, features are projected.[5] In the words of the anthropologist Simon Coleman, "In social scientific terms, we might describe Mary as a powerful symbol that is able to sustain a range of referents within the same form."[6] The result is an image that has adapted over time and frequently brings insights into the age in which each of its creators lived and worked. The image of the Virgin is one of paradoxes: she is simultaneously regal and domestic, submissive and militaristic, warmly human and impossible to reach.

This book focuses on one of the most evocative—and the most controversial—of Mary's many roles: the Queen of Heaven. The Virgin's bodily assumption into heaven sets her apart from the saints and confirms her place toward the top of the hierarchy of heaven. Enthroned and crowned in splendor, the Queen of Heaven serves as mediatrix between man and God. This powerful and alluring image of the Virgin inspired devotion in the Middle Ages, but during the Reformation it became a site of resistance. Mary's assumption and coronation are both extrascriptural in origin and thus struck a discordant note with Reformation Protestantism's emphasis on the Word. "What assurance have wee that the blessed Virgin Mary was in body rapt up into Heaven, and there crowned Queene of Heaven? There ought to be some very assured testimonie of the same," demanded reformist thinker Pierre Du Moulin in 1614.[7] The result of such mistrust was an obliteration of the Virgin's assumption and coronation from Protestant liturgy. This act of eradication can be seen as one of periodization. It is an attempt to confine the Queen of Heaven in a box labeled "medieval symbol" as England marches toward its brave new Reformation world. But a protean, adaptable image is difficult to confine. The Queen of Heaven did not simply vanish but remained a culturally significant figure who continued to arouse powerful and complex responses in spite of—and sometimes because of—attempts to eradicate her presence. Instead of disappearing, the "Catholic" figure of the Queen of Heaven became a focal point for vitriol in Protestant writing, constructed in diametric opposition to another of Mary's many roles, the humble and acquiescent handmaid of the Annunciation. The Queen of Heaven, or *Regina Coeli*, became a wholly separate figure from the *ancilla Domini*, the handmaiden of the Lord. Conversely, Counter-Reformation writing often rallied around the Virgin as heaven's queen, representing her as an active and often militaristic figure.

"Some out of vanity will call her the Queene of heaven" was the withering observation of the clergyman Thomas Tuke in 1614.[8] His words encapsulate the extent to which the image of the Queen of Heaven had become polemical, bound up for many with anti-Catholic sentiment. Embedded in Tuke's statement is also an admission of the incompleteness of England's Reformation, an admission that voices of dissent and rebellion existed and that the forbidden title of Queen of Heaven was still very much in currency. This implicit admission of a divergence of religious identity encapsulates the second aim of this book, which is to hold something of a mirror up to the confessional instability that existed in postmedieval England. My study is of a range of responses to the Queen of Heaven and therefore attends to writers who represent many different religious identities. Attitudes to the Queen of Heaven range from the devotional to the vitriolic—what is very rarely seen is a neutral response. One might presume that the Virgin's assumption and coronation could be deployed as a clear delineating marker between Protestant and Catholic. This is not always the case. A study of the attitudes of different writers to the Queen of Heaven thus gives us an insight into the pluralistic nature of religious belief in England during the reigns of Elizabeth and James, as well as revealing the extent to which the potent image of the Queen of Heaven was impossible to eradicate.

The feminist writer Sally Cunneen has described Mary as "a power-ful and changing presence for millions of men and women for two thousand years" and as "the most flexible of symbols."[9] Because the symbol of the Virgin Mary possesses an almost exhaustive capacity for adaptation and change, it is able to cross the boundaries that are often arbitrarily set between eras. The Queen of Heaven is a powerful, po-lemical, and politicized symbol, which evokes emotional and often con-tradictory responses. These words can be applied to medieval and early modern representations alike: through this one statement about the Queen of Heaven, a porousness between medieval and postmedieval is revealed. Scholars including Brian Cummings and James Simpson are challenging preconceptions that the medieval and early modern periods are neatly "divisible into detachable segments of time."[10] My own study of early modern representations of the Queen of Heaven reinforces this view, as it is frequently situated in dialogue with medieval iconography of the Virgin.[11]

Returning to "The Walsingham Ballad," we find that this porous-ness exists within the figure of the "Queene of walsingam" itself. In the mid-fourteenth century, the Lollard movement attacked excessive devo-tion to the statue of Our Lady of Walsingham, nicknaming the shrine's statue of the Virgin "the wyche of Walsingham."[12] The prophetic signifi-cance of this reshaping of the Virgin's image was not immediately real-ized. Henry VIII was extremely devoted to Our Lady of Walsingham: he made frequent pilgrimages to Walsingham in the early years of his reign, presenting the statue with a lavish collar of rubies.[13] By 1538, how-ever, the monarch's attitude had undergone a radical reversal. As the Walsingham shrine and priory were despoiled in this dramatic icono-clastic year, the statue of the Virgin was carried to London and ritually burnt. There is a macabre poetry to this story: the statue was stripped of its finery like a discarded wife and then burnt as a heretic.

The statue of Our Lady of Walsingham was burnt so that its sup-posed wonder-working elements were destroyed; because it did not sur-vive in altered form, fragments could not be remotivated as relics. Yet this physical destruction did not lead to obliteration. Instead, there was a shift from material matter to poetic representation. In the ballad, the presence of "the Queene of walsingam" is an extraordinarily resonant example of this. It becomes a symbol with many referents: of outlawed Catholic doctrine; of a once beloved woman scorned by a capricious monarch; and finally, retrospectively, of the "wyche" of Lollard excori-ation. The full potency of this reference is revealed only if one appreci-ates the way in which the conflicted image of the Virgin of the medieval pilgrimage tradition seeps into the texture of a poem that on the surface expresses an outrage and despair that seem to belong exclusively in a recusant world. The Virgin of this poem has not vanished but has been transformed.

RETHINKING THE VIRGIN MARY

Although this is not a chronologically structured book, it has chrono-logical limits set by the reigns of Elizabeth and James, with sources from a period spanning from 1558 to 1625. I use the word *limits* with an element of self-consciousness: one of the overarching philosophies of this study is that the past seeps into the present and that medieval views should be set in dialogue with those of England's Reformation. This view maintains it is reductive to establish a terminus ad quem. To give an arbitrary cutoff point of the end of James's reign may seem strange, therefore, given the flowering of Marian devotional books in the 1630s, when the Catholic queen Henrietta Maria was often equated to the Vir-gin Mary.[14]

There are a number of reasons for the chronological limits I have set. As the following chapters will show, there is a rich body of material written during the Elizabethan and Jacobean periods that deserves de-tailed focus and attention. This was the period of England's history where Protestantism was embedded, as it were, as the official national dogma, and it is the period most associated with a reading of Mary's image fading away. To encompass the years leading to England's Civil Wars would be to enter an era that constitutes a whole new body of re-search. It is an era that should be seen as marking a further re-formation of the Virgin's image, as the controversies and polarities that existed within the reigns of Elizabeth and James seep into the Caroline period and are invested with a new urgency. In itself, this forms a cogent example of the raison d'être of my study's ideology, that the contentious image of the Queen of Heaven was re-formed and reshaped in light of England's continuing confessional struggles.

Axiomatic to this investigation, therefore, is an awareness that England's Reformation was incomplete; my study of the Queen of Heaven in Elizabethan and Jacobean England maintains a focus on religious instability and pluralism. Elizabeth's ascension to the throne in 1558 marked the commencement of a period of time when, following the pendulum swings of the earlier sixteenth century, Protestantism can be viewed as the established religion of the state. Of course this is a statement that requires a number of provisos. Revisionist history has posed a credible challenge to previously accepted historiographical maxims that the late medieval era was one of decline and decay, where the English Catholic Church was a morally crumbling structure that easily collapsed when kicked.[15] The picture of confessional complexity painted by scholars including Eamon Duffy, Patrick Collinson, John Bossy, Christopher Haigh, and Alexandra Walsham is both nuanced and well developed.[16] To engage fully with the effects of a protracted Reformation upon the image of the Virgin, this study acknowledges the breadth of confessional standpoints initiated by such profound religious change.

An awareness of what Gillian Woods has termed "the complexity of denominational difference" within early modern England has led to an impressive body of work evaluating the effect of protracted Reformation struggles on imaginative literature.[17] With this has come a deepening understanding of what the early modern Catholic aesthetic actually *is*. Until the end of the twentieth century, our understanding of this aesthetic encompassed Catholic writing only, and knowledge today of the richness of this area owes a huge debt to some remarkable Catholic scholarship.[18] Catholic writing itself is a diverse field: one only has to look at Robert Miola's incisively edited anthology of Catholic writing, *Early Modern Catholicism*, to be reminded of this.[19] However, scholarly understanding of the Catholic aesthetic as a whole has widened to encompass not only literature by Catholic writers but also works that deploy imagery relating to Catholicism.

Alison Shell's trailblazing *Catholicism, Controversy and the Literary Imagination* epitomizes this approach: as well as recovering "the voices of the silenced" Catholic writers, Shell shows how anti-Catholicism can be viewed as an imaginative stimulus to Protestant writing. The work of Arthur Marotti, Sophie Read, and Brian Cummings, among others, has further developed our view of how imaginative writing from all confessional positions responds to controversies, doctrinal and otherwise, between Protestants and Catholics.[20] Particularly pertinent to my own interconfessional approach is Susannah Brietz Monta's examination of both Protestant and Catholic martyrologies: this reveals both a "conflict and overlap" that served to destabilize religious identities.[21] Issues of gender are integral to this discourse and, as Frances Dolan has shown, are often expressed through a relationship between the feminized Catholic Church and the trope of the disorderly Catholic woman.[22] Scholarship on Shakespeare and sectarianism has also played an important part. Although we are no longer at the mercy of exhaustive hunts for coded Catholic messages in Shakespeare's works, the contribution made by Shakespeare studies to our awareness of the sheer muddiness of confessional standpoints in Reformation England is profound.[23] A particularly influential body of work on the religious context of Shakespeare's work has addressed themes of nostalgia, loss, and memory, creating a powerful picture of the reappearance of the rituals of Catholicism on the Shakespearean stage.[24]

Views of the fate of the Virgin Mary in early modern England are often expressions of similar tropes of nostalgia, memory, and displacement. This has manifested itself in a number of ways. The most extreme conceptualization is an often-repeated claim that as England became a Protestant country the image of the Virgin simply faded away. Diarmaid MacCulloch describes, for example, "a general Protestant silence falling over Mary," while feminist theologian Tina Beattie comments that "by the seventeenth century, Mary had been all but eradicated from Protestant consciousness."[25] The belief that the Virgin faded into obscurity is the driving force behind a body of scholarly opinion, pioneered by Frances Yates and Roy Strong, that as the Virgin disappeared from cultural consciousness Elizabeth I filled the psychological and cultural gap that she had left behind. The words of Yates, once read, are difficult to forget: "The bejewelled and painted images of the Virgin Mary had been cast out of churches and monasteries, but another bejewelled and painted image was set up at court, and went in progress through the land for her worshippers to adore."[26] Although this is not a view to be dismissed out of hand, it does need to be treated with a degree of caution and qualification, and some weighty research has problematized this all-too-symmetrical theory. Louis Montrose retains a sense of skepticism about the extent to which any subject of Queen Elizabeth had a "flatly idolatrous attitude towards her image," while Helen Hackett has examined in depth the fault lines in the theory that one Virgin Queen filled the cultural and psychological gap left by another.[27] An acceptance that Elizabeth I appropriated the sacred iconography of the Virgin exists in some studies of the Virgin Mary: it is a way of referencing Elizabeth's reign in explorations where Reformation England is part of a much wider time scale.[28]

My own study will at various points enter a discussion that links the Virgin Mary with secular queenship, but its intention is to widen the debate. This was a period that produced what David Underdown has termed "an unusual concentration of women rulers," all of whom represented a potential flouting of patriarchal control.[29] Within the reign of Elizabeth herself, the spectral presence of Mary Queen of Scots, the recent traumatic memory of Mary I, and an awareness of the queenly matriarchal figure of Catherine de Medici just over the channel in France should be taken into consideration. There are also two queens of England in my own time frame: Elizabeth I, a queen regnant, and Anna of Denmark, James I's queen consort, a particularly interesting figure in terms of religious identity. Representations of the Queen of Heaven's image both reflected and refracted anxieties about female authority engendered by these very different secular queens.

A more nuanced approach to the tropes of nostalgia and displacement has been to position Mary as a powerful but fragmented part of the literary detritus of the Reformation. In *The Pathology of the English Renaissance*, Elizabeth Mazzola uses the phrase "symbolic residue" to suggest how repressed cultural memories such as purgatory and transubstantiation often surfaced in early modern literature.[30] A number of influential studies have viewed the presence of the Virgin similarly as a "symbolic residue," examining the significance of oblique echoes or references to aspects of Marian iconography in imaginative literature. A collection of essays edited by Regina Buccola and Lisa Hopkins entitled *Marian Moments in Early Modern British Drama* explores the variety and richness of oblique Marian references on the early modern stage, which the volume positions as evidence of a residual Catholic culture within the emergent, eventually dominant Protestant one.[31] Ruben Espinosa's monograph *Masculinity and Marian Efficacy in Shakespeare's England* extends the discussion through an exploration of the symbolic hold of oblique references to the Virgin as intercessor and compassionate mother in Shakespeare's work.[32] This is a fruitful methodology, but it can be susceptible to optimism. There is danger that a reading of a text is reduced to "Mary spotting" possible allusions to Marian iconography that may not always be of significance. At its most successful, this scholarship has unearthed valuable evocations of Marian echoes in early modern writing, showing how these can function as expressions of often unconscious survivals in the cultural mainstream. Gary Waller's study *The Virgin Mary in Late Medieval and Early Modern English Literature and Popular Culture* effectively deploys the language of psychoanalysis to demonstrate how images of the Virgin resurfaced in translated or fractured form. Waller's argument is that "the Virgin may indeed have faded from the emotional and spiritual life of Protestant England but traces of her liminal suggestiveness have remained."[33] The word *faded* here encapsulates the dominant terminology of this critical discourse (a whole section of Waller's monograph is entitled "Fades and Traces").

This important scholarship has served to dislodge a tendency to give Mary's role in Reformation England short shrift, but it leaves an overriding impression of a vanishing Virgin, of an image dissolving into echo and memory. This is certainly a beguiling picture, but it should be seen as representing only a part of a much bigger whole. In a brilliant foreword to the volume *Marian Moments*, Arthur Marotti sets the identification of oblique Marian echoes into the broader context of a rich range of references to the Virgin in early modern culture, including conscious polemical preservations of, or statements of allegiance to, Mariology by both Catholic and Protestant writers. Elsewhere, Marotti has himself explored the significance of confrontational references to the Virgin, arguing that expressions of Marian devotion in Elizabethan verse can be viewed as politically oppositionist acts, but there is an urgent need to redress the balance still further.[34] Oblique or fragmented references to the Virgin's image cannot tell the full story.

My own engagement with the image of the Queen of Heaven in Elizabethan and Jacobean England is influenced by these critical methodologies. This study fully acknowledges the significance of oblique references to the Virgin, but, in focusing on the Queen of Heaven, I am taking as my subject a controversial aspect of Mary's image that is far too strident to be contained as a mere echo. My main emphasis is therefore on how the image of the Queen of Heaven is overtly deployed in polemical and devotional writing and how it is related to apostasy and conversion. In privileging overt and not covert or fragmented representations of the Virgin, my intention is to disrupt the sense of fading away that is so often the dominant term of discourse about the Virgin's place in early modern writing. The very nature of the image of the Queen of Heaven means that it was frequently the site of conflict and controversy that became the impetus of a powerful creative spark. It was an image that provoked antipathy, fear, devotion, and evasion. But there was connection as well as conflict. My study aims to undo further a sense that "Protestant" and "Catholic" exist as monolithic entities.

A SPECTRUM OF FAITH

The reigns of Elizabeth I and James I encompassed a dramatic sweep of events, many of which originated in sectarian conflict. This study does acknowledge that texts can reflect particular moments in time, but it is not chronological in structure. Instead, it moves back and forth in time in a series of chapters that commences, broadly speaking, with the views of the hotter sort of Protestant and ends with the devotional standpoint of the Jesuit Catholic. In between, I examine work from a range of writers who, through their deployment of images of the assumption and coronation of the Virgin, provide an insight into different—and frequently elusive—confessional standpoints. I see this as moving across a spectrum of faith, though underpinning my acknowledgment of confessional complexity is an awareness of just how difficult it is to create a window into men's souls and how attempts to categorize people's belief systems can ultimately be reductive.

Chapter 1 turns to the history of the Virgin's image itself, examining some of the developments in iconography of Mary's assumption and coronation from the patristic period to the Reformation. The emphasis here is on England's Middle Ages, on evocations of the assumption and coronation that find new expression in later years. After this, the study is divided into two parts. Part I, "Some Out of Vanity Will Call Her the Queene of Heaven," comprises two chapters exploring polemical and pejorative images of the Queen of Heaven in Protestant writing. Chapter 2 examines the frequent mocking references to the Queen of Heaven in printed religious discourse, particularly sermon literature. This derision took a number of forms. The Virgin's powerful position as heaven's queen and man's intercessor led to complaints about her role as an overbearing mother who exercised too much control over her son. Christ here became literally infantilized by the Queen of Heaven's overpowering presence. Other Protestant polemicists used the story in Jeremiah 44 about the disobedient women of Pathros, who worshipped a pagan queen of heaven, as a direct link to Catholic veneration of the Virgin as Queen of Heaven. These repeated polemical references served the ironic function of keeping the Virgin's image alive rather than eradicating it. The vitriolic tone that many of these religious commentaries strike also creates an uneasy balance between veneration of the Virgin as a humble servant of God and misogynistic attacks on her as an authoritative and empowered woman.

Chapter 3 focuses on the way in which Reformation thinking engendered a bifurcation within iconography of the Virgin between the "Catholic" Queen of Heaven and the "Protestant" humble handmaid. It shows how iconoclastic destruction of statues of the Virgin was often validated via the creation of an alternative, "sham" version of the Virgin as Queen of Heaven, a figure that was viewed as ripe for satire. This iconoclastic discourse found its way into early modern writing. *Pasquine in a Traunce* by the reformer Curione presents two completely different versions of the Virgin Mary: the true, humble "Protestant" model and the meretricious "Catholic" Queen of Heaven, who appears in the text both as an animated statue of highly dubious morals and as the shadowy queen of a false, visionary "Catholic" heaven. I will argue that this discourse underpins the creation of Lucifera, Una, and Duessa in book 1 of *The Faerie Queene*, a text that was possibly influenced by Curione's work. The creation of sham Queens of Heaven is integral to the polemical trope of a feminized Catholic Church, and in its most radical manifestations the lines between the Catholic Queen of Heaven and the Whore of Babylon become shockingly blurred.

In part II, "Voices from the Shadows," my focus is more on individual personalities, whose writing reveals shifting perceptions of the image of the Queen of Heaven in an age of religious pluralism. The shadows that these voices speak from are those of gender, apostasy, and recusancy, as well as the margins of the court. In chapter 4, I interrogate further the relationship between the polarized models of humble handmaid and Queen of Heaven through an examination of early modern discourses on female behavior. For the male writers of several conduct books, the Virgin as *ancilla Domini* was a prototype for the ideal silent, godly, and obedient Protestant woman. The work of two Protestant women writers subtly disrupts this. In her "mother's advice" book, *The Mother's Blessing*, Dorothy Leigh criticizes worship of the Queen of Heaven, but her descriptions of the Virgin implicitly suggest a woman in a position of power. More radical still is the view expressed by Aemilia Lanyer in her extended Passion poem, *Salve Deus Rex Judaeorum*. This disrupts the binaries of humble handmaid and Queen of Heaven: Lanyer's Virgin Mary is an obedient godly figure, but her queenly state is also frequently alluded to.

Chapter 5 explores confessional complexity as expressed by the poet and politician Henry Constable, who converted to Catholicism in the 1590s. Constable's secular poetry bears all the hallmarks of the fashionable courtier poet, and he frequently wrote poems of love and service to Queen Elizabeth herself. Upon his conversion to Catholicism, the addressee of his love poetry became the Queen of Heaven, a representation of the Virgin that encapsulated a subtle criticism both of secular love poetry and of Elizabeth herself. Constable's presentation of the Virgin as a triumphant queen places her in opposition to earthly queens such as Elizabeth, but like other Catholic poets of his time he stresses that Mary is below Christ and God in a clearly defined heavenly hierarchy. Nevertheless, his repeated adoration of the Queen of Heaven should be viewed in oppositional terms, particularly his presentation of the Virgin as both Queen of Heaven and *Virgo Lactans*. The depiction of the maternal agency of the Virgin and the dependency of Christ made the *Virgo Lactans* a contentious image in Reformation writing, and Constable's deployment of this image is as confrontational as it is devotional. Chapter 6 takes the study further into the shadows of recusant England through a focus on the rosary books that were distributed to England's recusant community. For the Jesuit movement in particular, the rosary was more than a medieval memory: it was a proselytizing tool and a way to disseminate Tridentine values. The representation of the Virgin in these books epitomizes this: she becomes a politicized construct, reflecting not only Counter-Reformation ideologies but also the struggles and sorrows of recusant England. The Virgin is a polyvalent presence in the pages of rosary books, but the most powerful of her many roles is that of the intercessory Queen of Heaven, who as conduit to God becomes almost a replacement for an absent priest. The second part of this chapter returns to the margins of the court, introducing the idiosyncratic and often evasive confessional position of one man: the courtier poet Sir John Harington. Harington presented both King James and the young Prince Henry with a rosary poem in Latin and English. The poem formed part of a gift-book of his *Epigrams*, satirical and often scabrous poems of court gossip that are threaded through with a heartfelt plea for religious toleration. Like the Catholic writers of rosary books, Harington politicizes the image of the Virgin, though in his case this appears to be part of a personal—and risky—quest both for preferment and for religious toleration.

The final chapter is devoted to Robert Southwell, the Jesuit poet and martyr. It argues that although the Virgin was integral to Southwell's poetic attack on secular verse, her image is frequently characterized by a sense of absence. It begins by examining Southwell's polemical Latin poem "Poema de Assumptione BVM." Although this presents the Virgin as a warrior figure, she is a strangely evasive presence in a poem dominated by the repellent female figure of Death. This sense of an absence of female beauty also reveals itself in Southwell's frequent vicious satires on Petrarchan love poetry, which do not leave the reader with a strong sense of the Virgin as beauty's sacred archetype. Although Southwell's English poem "The Assumption of Our Lady" does express love for the Virgin, it too ultimately reveals a sense of absence, particularly in its depiction of her coronation. A possible reading of this elusiveness and absence is as an expression of the isolation of the English Catholic experience. The chapter also discusses the way in which Southwell's iconography of the Virgin's intact body at her assumption forms part of discourses on Catholic martyrdom, as it can be set in stark contrast to images that connote his own anticipated death.

The analysis of Southwell's poetry presents the biggest surprise of all. One could be forgiven for expecting to find in Southwell's work an unqualified devotion to the Virgin, but the reality is far more complex, a discovery that speaks volumes not only about the polyvalence of the Virgin's image but also about its ultimately elusive nature. The Queen of Heaven was a figure who elicited personal responses so emotive that they frequently resisted the constrictions that Reformation thinking attempted to impose upon them. The attempted polarization of Queen of Heaven and humble handmaid was ultimately unstable, and expressions of devotion to the Virgin were frequently politicized. The book's epilogue will demonstrate how some of these controversies still exist today.

CHAPTER 1

The Virgin's Assumption and Coronation through the Ages

That she can be represented in so many ways, thought about and imagined in so many forms, is an indication of how deeply she speaks to us about the hope for the world's transfiguration through Jesus; how she stands for the making strange of what is familiar and the homeliness of what is strange.

—Rowan Williams, *Ponder These Things*

A history of the assumption and coronation of the Virgin from patristic times to the early years of the Reformation would constitute a book—or several books—in itself.[1] Mine does not pretend to be an exhaustive account, but the narratives and examples I explore here articulate both the richness of this aspect of Mariology and its embedded presence in liturgy and popular culture. My main focus is on the Middle Ages, where I aim to show how representations of the Virgin's assumption and coronation function as more than mere prologues to the swelling act of the Reformation. The Bible itself gives scanty details of Mary's life, and there are no direct references to her assumption and coronation. From the second century onward, the gaps in the text of Mary's biblical story were filled by apocryphal writings, the most significant of which was the *Protoevangelium of James*.[2] This was an account of the childhood and life of the Virgin dating from around AD 150. Originally written in Greek, it was translated into several languages, including Latin, and was to have a profound influence on literary and artistic representations of the Virgin.[3] However, there is little concrete evidence of the existence of a uniform "cult" of Mary until the fifth century.[4] At the Council of Ephesus in AD 431, Mary was officially given the title *Theotokos* or "God bearer." The Council of Ephesus is often seen as the starting point of devotion to Mary, and from this time onwards comes the development of hymns, homilies, and feasts in her name. Twenty years later, the Council of Chalcedon affirmed Mary's virginity both *in partu* and *post partum*. By the end of the fifth century the main features of later Marian theology had thus been established.[5]

The accretion of doctrines surrounding the Virgin's assumption and coronation follows a slightly different course. In the fourth century, the empress Helena, mother of Constantine the Great, gave orders for excavations in Palestine to look for relics. The excavators unearthed what was believed to be the true cross but discovered nothing that could be associated with Mary's death. There were no bodily relics and no grave: these factors, together with the lack of narrative within the Gospels as to the death of Mary, meant that the story of her assumption grew from an entirely apocryphal corpus of traditions that emerged between the years 450 and 600.[6] These apocryphal texts often took the name of *Transitus* narratives. Within these early texts, distinctions can be made between narratives describing Mary's assumption, body and soul, into paradise and narratives—often referred to as Dormition narratives—where the Virgin's soul is taken to heaven, but her body is transferred to a hidden place to await reunion with the soul at the end of time. The most prominent early assumption text was the Latin *Transitus of Pseudo-Melito*, which dates from the end of the fifth century and which clearly stresses Mary's bodily assumption.[7] Apocryphal legends about the Virgin's assumption were also in currency in England in Anglo-Saxon times, when stories of Mary's bodily assumption were popularized by the circulation of a number of *Transitus* narratives.[8] My study will focus on Mary's bodily assumption, as this is the tradition that took the strongest imaginative hold in Western Christian traditions. The assumption of the Virgin came to be celebrated in a feast day, the Feast of the Assumption, on August 15. The official sanction of this feast date in the sixth century by Emperor Maurice established it as a celebration throughout the Christian world.[9] It was to become, in the words of Stephen Shoemaker, "perhaps the single most important Marian feast."[10]

Although there are many variants, the following tale of the Virgin's bodily assumption can be shaped from the Latin, Greek, and Syriac traditions.[11] It starts with a mirror image of the Annunciation, as Mary is visited by the angel Gabriel, who foretells her death. In many versions of the story, Gabriel presents the Virgin with a palm branch from paradise to be carried in front of her funeral bier. As Mary's death approaches, the apostles are summoned from their ministry throughout the world to be at her bedside. The Virgin's soul leaves her body in a moment of great beauty, accompanied by the singing of angels. The disciples carry Mary's body on the bier to the tomb, and there is often here an attack by angry Jews who wish to burn her body. In some versions, the high priest tries to overturn the bier. As he does so, his hands become fastened to it and he suffers great torment. He converts to Christianity and his hands are freed. The apostle Peter gives the high priest the angelic palm from the funeral bier, and he goes out into the city with it, miraculously giving sight to crowds of people who have been blinded. The narrative culminates with a second assumption as Mary's body joins with her soul to be transported into heaven by angels.

Iconography of the coronation of the Virgin is inextricably interlinked with the story of the Virgin's assumption: the Virgin rises to heaven to reign triumphantly by Christ's side as his queen. The first recorded image of the Queen of Heaven is from early in the sixth century, on the wall of the Church of Santa Maria Antiqua in Rome.[12] The coronation of the Virgin confirmed her hierarchical significance as higher than the angels and the saints, and this had significant implications on how the image of Mary was deployed.[13] To use Julia Kristeva's words, it made the Virgin "a repository of power."[14] But it also represented a paradox: here was a biblical woman who meekly obeyed the words of an angel, yet by her assumption into heaven she was elevated to a place above the angels. A further paradox was that in spite of this elevation many worshippers felt that they had a personal relationship with the Queen of Heaven because of her role as intercessor for man. Her bodily presence in heaven and the intimacy of her relationship with God meant that she could offer protection to every man and woman and became the personal focus of many of their prayers.

During the Middle Ages, the relationship between the Virgin and the Western poetic imagination truly crystallized, and the Queen of Heaven became a ubiquitous figure in Western devotional practice. Visual images played an important part in establishing the tradition of the Queen of Heaven, with paintings of the Virgin's assumption and coronation appearing in cathedrals and churches throughout Europe. In the seventh and eighth centuries, the Virgin and Child were increasingly presented as enthroned, and from the tenth century the popularity grew of statues known as "Virgin in Majesty" or "Seat of Wisdom."[15] This began with depictions of the Virgin and Child at the Magi's visitation but soon extended to a more generalized iconography of the Virgin in a posture of enthronement. Artists in the late Middle Ages often showed the Virgin being crowned not just by Christ but by the whole Trinity, as a visual indication of Mary's closeness to God.[16] There was also a political dimension to Mary's queenship. In the eleventh and twelfth centuries, Mary was increasingly viewed as a type of the church, or *Maria Ecclesia*. As Eva de Visscher has observed: "She represents the power of the Church in general and of the papacy in particular."[17]

The Virgin in the Middle Ages was not exclusively perceived as Queen of Heaven, however. The growth in popularity of the cult of the *Mater Dolorosa*, of Mary sorrowing at the foot of Christ's cross, can be read as a softening of the image from a queen to a mother. The *Mater Dolorosa* was particularly popular during the Black Death epidemic (1347–50), an indication of how the image of the Virgin became a figure with whom the laity could personally identify, as she had experienced similar trials in her earthly life.[18] Sarah Jane Boss sees this perception of Mary as a reflection of a change in the views of motherhood itself, which, thanks to the rise of the bourgeoisie, became linked with domesticity.[19] An increased emphasis on the cult of the Holy Family also added impetus to a late medieval emphasis on the humanity of both the Virgin and her son.[20] Paradoxes were once more revealed within the image of the

Virgin Mary—both humble mother and heavenly Queen appeared to coexist within the same imaginative space. As the anthropologist Victor Turner comments, the image of Mary can be seen as "a signifier meant to represent not only the historical woman who once lived in Galilee, but the sacred person who resides in heaven, appears at times to living persons, and intercedes with God for the salvation of mankind."[21]

THE VIRGIN'S BODILY ASSUMPTION IN THE VISIONS OF ELISABETH OF SCHÖNAU

Although Mary's role as Queen of Heaven became firmly established in Western Christian traditions, her bodily assumption was not initially accepted by all. In the 840s, for example, an influential letter entitled *Cogitis me*, which was attributed to Jerome, stressed Mary's spiritual, rather than bodily, assumption.[22] However, from the twelfth century, the concept that Mary's body as well as her soul was assumed into heaven became truly dominant. Integral to the development of this were the visions of the Benedictine nun Elisabeth of Schönau. Elisabeth was a well-born young woman from the Rhineland, Germany, who had been raised in the nuns' cloister of the Benedictine monastery in Schönau from the age of twelve. In 1152, at age twenty-three, she began to see terrifying visions of the devil. These apparitions of evil were overcome by the Virgin Mary, who came to dominate Elisabeth's visionary existence. Elisabeth's brother Ekbert joined the monastic community at Schönau in 1155 and took on the role of her amanuensis and editor, recording his sister's accounts of her visions. As Anne Clark has observed, Ekbert often coaxed the answers he wanted out of Elisabeth, seeking "to use her extraordinary gifts to resolve issues of current controversy."[23] This had a profound effect not only on the manner in which Elisabeth's visions were recorded but also on the nature of the visions themselves, which often seem more like theological debates than the reports of a seer-narrator.

One of the theologically tricky questions answered by Elisabeth's visions was whether the Virgin was bodily assumed into heaven. Elisabeth had several visions connected to the Virgin's assumption between

1156 and 1158, all of which were recorded by her brother in the text *The Resurrection of the Blessed Virgin*. During the first apparition, in 1156, Elisabeth asks the Virgin whether she has been bodily assumed into heaven, "just as I had been advised by one of our elders": it is clear that she has been prompted by others here (209). The Virgin is in this first vision evasive, but a year later in 1157 she appears to Elisabeth again and presents a more conclusive answer. While lying in bed, Elisabeth describes how she fell into a trance after a violent struggle:

And I saw in a far-away place a tomb surrounded by great light, and what looked like the form of a woman in it, with a great multitude of angels standing around. After a little while, she was raised up from the tomb and, together with that multitude standing by, she was lifted up on high. While I was watching this, behold, a man—glorious beyond all reckoning—came from the height of the heavens to meet her. In His right hand, He carried a cross on which there was a banner. I understood that this was the Lord Saviour, and there were countless thousands of angels with Him. Eagerly receiving her, they carried her with great acclamation to the heights of heaven. While I was watching this, after a short time, my Lady advanced to the door of light in which I usually saw her, and standing there she showed me her glory. (209–10)

The angel of the Lord who acts as Elisabeth's theological guide and interpreter explains the meaning of the vision: "This vision has shown you how our Lady was taken up into heaven in flesh as well as in spirit" (210). This clear affirmation of the Virgin's bodily assumption was influential: the visions of Elisabeth of Schönau were studied in France and England and were translated into French, Anglo-Norman, and Icelandic. They had all the immediacy of a firsthand account, so while they did not exactly eradicate doctrinal controversy surrounding Mary's bodily assumption they became a voice that could override the silence within scripture on the matter. The circulation of Elisabeth's visions gave impetus to an already widespread belief that the Virgin's body as well as her soul was assumed.[24] These visions of the assumption should be viewed as political as well as spiritual. Both Elisabeth and her brother were adversaries of Cathar heretics, who believed that the spirit was good and the flesh evil. Visions of the Virgin's bodily assumption were a way to counter the Cathars via the assertion that, on the contrary, flesh could be wholly pure.[25]

The emphasis on the Virgin's corporeal assumption in Western culture made Mary's ascent into heaven dramatic and active. As Julia Kristeva observes: "The fate of the Virgin Mary is more radiant even than that of her son."[26] Through her bodily assumption, the Virgin's body and soul are reunited, something that for the rest of humankind is reserved until the Last Judgment. On a deeper symbolic level, the assumption of the Virgin also presents her as an archetype of the risen body of Christ, a realization of the heavenly glory that Christ promised to the members of his church.[27] A belief in the Virgin's corporeal assumption can also be mapped onto preoccupations with the Virgin's sinless flesh; her body was saved from the putrefaction and decay that occurred to the sinful bodies of humankind. It became connected with the Immaculate Conception, a belief that Mary was conceived in her mother's womb free from original sin.[28] Because her assumption allowed her to escape this stench of human sin, Mary was often associated with sweet smells and fragrant flowers, particularly in the love poetry of the Middle Ages.[29] The doctrine of Mary's bodily assumption was also integral to the pilgrimage tradition, as it connected the Virgin with apparitions. In the words of Victor and Edith Turner: "Her body having disappeared from the world at the assumption, it is argued that she can reappear in the body, in a more concrete way than a saint whose body remains buried or whose relics are believed scattered in different places."[30]

THE WOMAN CLOTHED WITH THE SUN AND THE BRIDE OF THE SONG OF SONGS

One of Elisabeth of Schönau's visions showed a virgin crowned and surrounded by the blazing light of the sun:

> While we were celebrating the vigil of the birth of our Lord, around the hour of the divine sacrifice, I came into a trance and I saw, as it

were, a sun of marvellous brightness in the sky. In the middle of the sun was the likeness of a virgin whose appearance was particularly beautiful and desirable to see. She was sitting with her hair spread on her shoulders, a crown of the most resplendent gold on her head, and a golden cup in her right hand. A splendour of great brightness came forth from the sun, by which she was surrounded on all sides, and from her it seemed to fill first the place of our dwelling, and then after a while spread out little by little to fill the whole world. (123)

Repeatedly, the blazing light is blocked by a dark cloud, and repeatedly, the cloud passes and the earth is illuminated by the sun. Each time the world is plunged into darkness, the virgin who is sitting in the sun weeps copiously. Elisabeth received two explanations for this vision. In the first, which is an indication of the gender fluidity that existed in many medieval female relationships with Christ, the angel of the Lord tells her that the virgin she has seen represents Christ's sacred humanity, and the sun his divinity.[31] The darkness is mankind's iniquity, which blocks God's kindness and causes his anger, while the reappearance of the sun is the abundance of God's mercy. Three days later, however, a second vision offers Elisabeth a different way to read these symbols. This time, she is visited by John the Evangelist, accompanied by the Virgin, who is described as "the glorious Queen of Heaven." They tell her that the virgin of the vision signifies Mary as well as Christ: "For truly she too is the virgin sitting in the sun because the majesty of the most high God illuminated her fully, beyond all others who lived before her, and through her divinity descended to visit the shadows of earth. The golden crown that you saw on the virgin's head signifies that this illustrious virgin was born in the flesh from the seed of kings and rules with royal power on heaven and earth" (125). In this second interpretation of the vision, intended to complement rather than contradict the first, the woman Elisabeth has seen becomes the Queen of Heaven herself, in a description that underlines the full impact of the Virgin's constant intercessions for man. Her weeping signifies "the constant appeal of this most merciful mother who always importunes her Son for the sins of the people of God. . . . If she were not restraining the wrath of the Lord with her constant prayer, the whole world would already have passed into perdition due to the abundance of its iniquity" (125). The Virgin of Elisabeth of Schönau's Christmas visions appears in the center of a dazzling sun and thus recalls the Woman Clothed with the Sun of Revelation 12, a biblical passage frequently associated with the assumption of the Virgin: "And there appeared a great wonder in heaven. A woman clothed with the sunne, & the moone was under her feate, and upon her head a crowne of twelve stares" (Rev. 12:1). The Woman Clothed with the Sun is pursued by a dragon with seven heads and seven crowns. She gives birth to "a man childe, which shulde rule all nations with a rod of yron," and flees from the dragon into the wilderness (Rev. 12:5). Late in the fourth century, the early church father Epiphanius, bishop of Salamis, linked this biblical reference to Mary. Although Epiphanius was himself cautious about this interpretation, his observations were seized upon by other exegetes, and this entrancing biblical passage came to be seen as a typological reference to the Virgin. It was—and still is—one of the Bible readings used in the celebration of the Feast of the Assumption.[32]

Other biblical passages that came to be associated with the assumption and coronation of the Virgin came from the Old Testament book the Song of Songs. One of the many interpretations attached to this beautiful love poem was that its bride and bridegroom were typological representations of Mary and Christ. The bridegroom's invitation to the beloved to "arise my love, my faire one" (Song 2:10) thus became Christ the bridegroom's invitation to the Virgin to rise to heaven.[33] Expositions of Song of Songs 4:8 ("Come from Lebanon / come, you will be crowned") became manifestations of the celebration of the coronation of the Virgin. Liturgies for the Feast of the Assumption of the Virgin had begun to use the Song of Songs by the seventh century, and verses from the Song of Songs were sung as antiphons to celebrate the feast.[34] An influential exponent of this connection was the twelfth-century Cistercian abbot and mystic Bernard of Clairvaux, who wrote a series of sermons depicting the bridegroom and bride of the Song of Songs as allegorical representations of Christ and Mary as King and Queen of Heaven. His intense and passionate representation of the Virgin became almost a template for many subsequent representations of her image.[35]

Descriptions of the celebration of the Feast of the Assumption in twelfth-century Rome show the importance of the Song of Songs to this aspect of the liturgy. In what was known as the August procession, the whole populace would process to Santa Maria Maggiore on the night before the feast day itself for a spectacle that underlined the pope's significance as God's representative on earth and Rome's significance as the heavenly Jerusalem.[36] A full-length portrait of the Christ, the *Acheropita*, was removed from the pope's inner sanctum and processed through the city streets to the church. This procession was a visual reenactment of the Song of Songs, as it symbolized Christ the bridegroom leaving the residence of his earthly representative to enjoy a sacred reunion with his mother and bride.[37] The *Acheropita* ended its journey under a beautiful mosaic in the apse of Santa Maria Maggiore, in which Christ is seen crowning his mother Queen of Heaven. This mosaic is redolent with allusions both to the Song of Songs and to the Woman Clothed with the Sun: in it, the moon is placed below Mary's feet, while Christ holds an open book inscribed with the words "Veni Electa M[e]a et ponam in te thronu[m] meu[m]" (Come, my chosen one, and I shall place you on my throne), an echo of Song of Songs 4:8. The August procession in Rome was a lavish community celebration that was also adopted by the episcopal towns of Latium, where Hans Belting has described it as "the annual climax of the town's communal life."[38]

THE ENGLISH EXPERIENCE

This sense of community was translated onto English soil. In the late fourteenth century, the Augustinian priest John Mirk described the Feast of the Assumption as "an high day and an high fest yn all holy chyrch, þe highest þat ys of our lady." All men, women, and children over the age of twelve, Mirk advises, should fast on the evening before the festival and on the day itself and should come to church ready to "worscip oure holy lady wyth all your myght."[39] These words appeared in Mirk's *Festial*, an extremely popular collection of vernacular sermons written in the 1380s. Mirk's exhortations to worship with joy were to the ordinary men and women of his native Shropshire, but his

words were also used by priests who were not educated enough to com-
pose their own sermons. The *Festial* includes two sermons on the assumption. The first stresses Mary's bodily assumption and her freedom
from the stench of putrefaction and sin. It retells the palm assumption
narrative with great brio, culminating in Mary's glorious coronation as
Queen of Heaven: "And Criste sette hyre þer be hym in hys trone and
crowned hur quene of heven and emperas of helle and lady of alle þe
worlde, and hath ioy passyng alle other seyntus." Mirk's sermon on
the assumption glorifies Mary's powers as Queen of Heaven, as all in
heaven are "redy at hur commament" (203). However, his second sermon on the assumption lays great stress on Mary's humility and contemplative nature: "So hadde oure Lady þe deche of mekenesse so dep
doune in" (207). Mary is here presented as silent and frequently contemplative. John Mirk's celebratory descriptions of Mary's assumption
and coronation are a window into the polysemic nature of the Virgin's
image in medieval England. Mary is both humble handmaid and powerful Queen of Heaven in his highly influential sermons. This seemingly
paradoxical image was presented unequivocally to the uneducated of
medieval England. As Judy Ann Ford has commented, Mirk's sermons
are "an unrivalled opportunity to study late-fourteenth-century Christianity, as it was expounded to the ordinary rural men and women who
comprised the majority of the English population."[40]

At the other end of the social scale, many of England's influential women were drawn to the power associated with the figure of the
Queen of Heaven. In the Middle Ages, queens consort were often
linked to the Queen of Heaven because of the intercessory power of
both roles.[41] In the hammerbeam roof of the fifteenth-century Church
of St. Mary in Bury St. Edmunds, Suffolk, which is dedicated to the assumption of the Virgin, a carving of a procession of angels culminates
in a figure of a woman wearing a girdle to symbolize virginity, with a
crown in her hands. The figure has been identified not only as the Virgin Mary but also as Queen Margaret of Anjou, and the final figure of
the procession, a crowned king, represents her husband Henry VI as
well as Christ the King.[42] Margaret of Anjou's coronation pageants also
linked her with the Virgin as Queen of Heaven, underlining her role as
mediatrix between king and people.[43] In her coronation pageants, Anne

Boleyn too was lauded as a virgin crowned, and, in a nod to both her name and her pregnant state, she was linked to the Virgin's mother.[44] Visual images of the Queen of Heaven were also ubiquitous in England. When the statue of the crowned Virgin was the focal point of England's shrine in Walsingham, it was courted like a lady and at its heyday stood resplendent with votive offerings. It was perceived as having thaumaturgic powers and was frequently linked with miracles.[45]

Throughout England's Middle Ages the Virgin's assumption and coronation were sources of great joy in both liturgy and popular culture—but during this period these aspects of Mariology were also frequently associated with confrontation and debate. This can be seen in *The Golden Legend*, a popular collection of the lives of the saints taken from a variety of patristic and medieval sources by the thirteenth-century Italian preacher Jacobus de Voragine. The tales were translated and printed by William Caxton in 1483 and subsequently became something of a best seller. The *Legend*'s tale of the Virgin's assumption and coronation uses the *Protoevangelium* as its basis and is recounted with great vibrancy. At the end of her earthly life, "The Virgin's heart was aflame with desire to be with her Son; she was so deeply stirred in spirit that her tears flowed abundantly."[46] Her death is beautiful and painless: "Mary's soul went forth from her body and flew to the arms of her Son, and was spared all bodily pain, just as it had been innocent of all corruption" (466). There is rejoicing in heaven as Christ is seen bearing Mary's immaculate soul in his arms, and the apostles see a soul so white that they are unable to describe it. Mary's earthly body remains for three days in the earth, but it emits a light so bright that those washing the body are unable to see it. The apostles take Mary's body and lay it in the tomb: on the third day, Christ appears; the apostles urge him to bring his mother's body to life "and enthrone her at your right hand for eternity" (468). Christ concurs, and the language of the Song of Songs is echoed as Mary's body is assumed along with her soul: "Then the Savior spoke and said: 'Arise, my dear one, my dove, tabernacle of glory, vessel of life, heavenly temple! As you never knew the stain of sin through carnal intercourse, so you shall never suffer dissolution of the flesh in the tomb.' Thereupon Mary's soul entered her body, and she came forth glorious from the monument and was assumed into the heavenly bridal chamber, a great multitude of angels keeping her company" (468). The descriptions of the Virgin's body as shrouded in a light that is too bright for mortal man, and as too pure and sinless to decompose, indicate the preoccupation with the Virgin's sinless flesh that was frequently a consequence of belief in her bodily assumption. The text of *The Golden Legend* admits to its readers that its impassioned tale is an apocryphal one, but it adds the voices of many different sources to lend it weight. Elisabeth of Schönau's visions of the Virgin are quoted at length, as are the views of Bernard of Clairvaux, St. Augustine, and St. Jerome. The writer's sources are many, but the conclusions drawn create a unified voice: "It is noteworthy that the glorious Virgin Mary was assumed and exalted integrally, honorably, joyfully and splendidly. She was assumed integrally in soul and body, as the Church piously believes, and as many saints not only assert but make it their business to prove" (469). *The Golden Legend* constructs a dramatic and highly accessible narrative of the Virgin's assumption, but there is an interesting subtext to its impassioned words—that on some level the Virgin's bodily assumption needs to be justified.

This sense of joy mingled with an undercurrent of debate is present elsewhere in medieval popular culture. In the East Anglian N-Town cycle, a play entitled *The Assumption of Mary* dramatically brings the words of *The Golden Legend* to life.[47] The play incorporates the beautiful spectacle of the apostle John transported on a white cloud to be with Mary at her passing. Mary's soul is carried by Christ into heaven first; Christ then descends to earth once more, using the language of the Vulgate Song of Songs 4:8 to call his mother to his side: "Veni de Libano, sponsa mea; veni coronaberis."[48] The N-Town play is full of joy. As her soul rejoins her body, Mary praises her son, and they ascend together to "endles blysse" (519). The scene culminates in Christ uttering the following words as he crowns his mother as heaven's Queen:

Yow to worchepe, moder, it likyth the hol Trinyté.
Wherfore I crowne you here in this kyndam of glory.
Of alle my chosyn, thus schul ye clepyd be:
Qwen of Hefne and Moder of Mercy.

(409)

Before Mary's bodily assumption, Christ has asked the apostles what they think should happen to her body:

> What worschepe and grace semyth you now here
> That I do to this body, Mary that hytht is?
>
> (408)

The apostles, led by John, are in agreement that the Virgin's body should be assumed into heaven. One feels the weight of a collective agreement on the correct way to treat the Virgin's pure, sinless body. It is possible to glimpse here a subtext, similar to the one I have discussed in *The Golden Legend*, of the assumption and coronation as aspects of Mariology that may fuel controversy and debate and that need therefore to be validated by affirmations of their popularity. The very beginning of the N-Town play voices this through the character of the Doctor, who states:

> Ryht worchepful sovereynes, liketh yow to here
> Of the Assumpcion of the gloryous Moder Mary
> That Seynt Jhon the Evangelist wrot and tauht, as I lere,
> In a booke clepid apocriphum, wythoutyn dyswary.
>
> (387)

The Doctor not only names the source for the spectacle the audience is about to view but also reiterates that these events, although apocryphal, occurred "wythoutyn dyswary" (without doubt). The seeds were being unconsciously sown for what was to become a truism of the Reformation: that the Virgin's assumption and coronation constituted an argument to be won.

The dramatization of the Virgin's assumption in the York cycle of mystery plays presents an even stronger motif of overcoming skepticism and doubt. The York plays were a prestigious collection of pageants performed publicly on the streets of the city of York by members of various influential city guilds. At the end of the cycle come plays on the death of the Virgin, her assumption, and her coronation, performed respectively by the Drapers, the Weavers, and the Hostelers. The Weavers' play, *The Assumption of the Virgin*, incorporates a strand of the assumption story that is also found in *The Golden Legend*, in which Mary drops her girdle to doubting Thomas as physical proof of her assumption into heaven.[49] As she does so, she bids him to report exactly what he has seen to the other disciples. In great joy, Thomas does what he is told. The disciples initially do not trust his account of events. They need proof, and it is only when they have this, in the form of the girdle, that they believe Thomas's story.

As part of her dialogue with Thomas, the Virgin delivers a speech in which she looks forward to her forthcoming role as Queen of Heaven and man's mediatrix:

And in siȝtte of my sone þer [he] is sittand
Shall I knele to þat comely with croune.
Þat wh[o in] dispaire be dale or be doune
With pitevous playnte in perellis will pray me,
If he s[w]ynke or swete in swelte or in swoune,
I schall sewe to my soverayne sone for to say me
He shall graunte þame þer grace.

(430)

The Virgin's active and powerful role as man's intermediary and representative is encapsulated in the words "I schall sewe to my soverayne sone for to say me." The speech displays absolute confidence in the Virgin's salvific power: Christ will, upon her petition, grant grace to those whom his mother chooses to save. But the humility expressed in the line "Shall I knele to þat comely with croune" shows that although her role may be a regal one in which she will wield great authority, she is still in a submissive position before Christ. There are frequent allusions to the Virgin's meekness and humility in the York cycle of plays, which include speeches of thanks from the Virgin to Christ for deeming her worthy to be Queen of Heaven. In the subsequent Hostelers' play, *The Coronation of the Virgin*, Mary is described by an angel in two lines where humility and queenship coexist:

Of hevene and erþe þou arte quene;
Come uppe nowe lady, meke and mylde.[50]

(437)

The York cycle, like so many versions of the assumption story, sets Mary's triumphant rise into heaven as a mirror image of her annunciation. In both, she acquiesces to the will and words of others. As Christ leads his mother into heaven's bliss in *The Coronation of the Virgin*, the joy of her assumption is foregrounded with language that links the assumption with the Annunciation:

All aungellis bright þei schall þe bowe
And worschippe þe worþely iwis.
For mekill joie, modir, had þou
Whan Gabriell grette þe wele be þis,
And tolde þe tristely for to trowe
Þou schulde consayve þe kyng of blisse.
(439)

The paradox of the Queen of Heaven's position is perfectly encapsulated, as angels bow to a woman who herself has humbly placed her trust in an angel's words.

The N-Town play and the York cycle were popular spectacles that took the liturgy of the Virgin's assumption and coronation out into the city streets and marketplaces. Both plays used choral and instrumental music to enrich the audience's sense of miracle and wonder. As Joanna Dutka has commented, music in the mystery plays "vividly establishes the ritual setting."[51] When Mary's body is assumed to heaven in the N-Town play, a musical backdrop is formed by a celestial choir singing "Assumpta est Maria," a setting that is both an antiphon and an alleluia verse for the Feast of the Assumption.[52] Organ music is also played at this point: it is thought that portative organs or consorts of musical instruments were used for this, meaning that the play was not confined to performances in the nave but was performed in the open air.[53] In the York play, polyphonic music was included in the manuscript for the Weavers' assumption pageant, in what Richard Rastall has described as "musically the most important play in the cycle."[54] This included two settings of "Veni de Libano sponsa" from the Song of Songs.[55] Angel music in the play was written to be sung by the boy trebles, who were probably members of the choir of York Minster.[56]

It is to music I turn for a very different example of the joy and wonder associated with the figure of the Queen of Heaven in England's Middle Ages. This takes us from the streets and marketplaces of York and East Anglia and into Eton College, the chantry foundation and educational establishment founded in 1440 by Henry VI and dedicated to the Virgin Mary. Commemorations of the Virgin were a staple of English choral foundations such as these.[57] A book of polyphonic music, *The Eton Choirbook*, was produced in the early years of the sixteenth century. The Virgin is the muse and the inspiration for fifty-four motets of prayer, ravishing music in which she is constantly viewed as a figure of incomparable beauty of the courtly love tradition. One example of this is the motet "Gaude flore virginali," of which there are eleven settings in *The Eton Choirbook*. Here, she is "flore virginali" (the flower of all maidenhood) and "splendens vas virtutum" (a radiant vessel of goodness). The Virgin is more than a beautiful beloved here, however, as this florid motet also expresses obedience to the Queen of Heaven in her powerful role as man's intercessor. She is "sponsa cara Dei" (the dear spouse of God), a figure who surpasses all the hosts of angels in heaven and one on whose assent the whole government of heaven hangs, "cuius pendens est at nutum / Tota caeli curia." "Gaude flore virginali," like many of the motets of *The Eton Choirbook*, is a setting of antiphons to the Virgin that were frequently included in medieval primers, or Books of Hours. The nod to vernacular piety is clear here, as these intricate musical settings were celebrating words that were used in everyday prayer.

The motets of *The Eton Choirbook* were written for a ceremony that took place every evening in the college chapel. According to the college statutes, during this ceremony the sixteen choristers and their masters would assemble to perform antiphons before an image of the Virgin that was housed in a stone tabernacle in the nave of the chapel. Many of these motets require virtuosic singing; the ceremony has been described by the musicologist Magnus Williamson as "partly an act of prayer" and "also a spiritual concert."[58] During Lent, the choristers would sing a setting of the *Salve Regina*: there are fifteen different settings of this popular prayer in *The Eton Choirbook*. The *Salve Regina* pleads to the Virgin as Queen of Heaven, "Salve regina mater misericordie / vita, dulcedo, et spes nostra, salve"—(Hail, Holy Queen, Mother of Mercy / Hail our life, our sweetness, and our hope). Initially a Cistercian antiphon that was used in procession on the Feast of the Assumption in 1145, this melancholy prayer exhorts the Queen of Heaven to have mercy on "exules filli evae" (the banished children of Eve).[59] It depicts the Virgin as a merciful but also powerful figure, who is able to show the worshipper Jesus himself, "benedictum fructum ventris tui" (the blessed fruit of your womb). The Eton ceremony itself came to be known as the Salve Ceremony. It was not confined to this one chantry chapel alone; David Allinson has described it as lying "at the heart, not the margins, of late-medieval traditional religion."[60] By 1500, the Salve Ceremony was established throughout England, its popularity affirmed, perhaps, by the existence of many devotional confraternities, including the Salve Guild of the Church of St. Magnus the Martyr by London Bridge. The ceremony was abolished in 1547, but echoes of its structure can be found today in the Elizabethan tradition of choral evensong, something still preserved in churches and cathedrals in England, where prayers are followed by a musical anthem. The intricate motets from *The Eton Choirbook* are also still recorded and performed today, giving a privileged glimpse into the beauty of late medieval devotions to the Virgin.

THE MOVE TOWARD REFORM

By the time of the Reformation, it is clear that the assumption and coronation of the Virgin were firmly embedded in English literature, liturgy, and popular piety. However, as well as being of tremendous personal significance to individual worshippers, the Virgin's assumption and coronation were often associated with controversy and debate. In the years leading up to the Reformation, this sense of controversy became more marked, as it was possible to identify significant rumblings of discontent. In England, the Lollard movement of the late fourteenth century criticized excessive devotion to the Virgin. Mirk's *Festial*, the sermons that so exuberantly describe the Virgin's extrascriptural assumption and coronation, can themselves be set in the context of the Lollard challenge to the authority of church traditions in favor of the authority of the Bible.[61] The pilgrimage site at Walsingham was often a focal point for attacks on excessive devotion to the Virgin. Lollards were particularly scathing about the wonder-working elements of statues of Mary, nicknaming Our Lady of Walsingham "Our Lady of Falsyngham."[62] In his colloquy *The Religious Pilgrimage*, published in 1526, the humanist scholar Desiderius Erasmus ventriloquized Our Lady of Walsingham's voice, creating the character of a breastfeeding mother who is irritated by the presumption that she can wield power over her son: "Every Thing was asked of me, as if my Son was always a Child, because he is painted so, and at my Breast, and therefore they take it for granted that I have him still at my Beck, and that he dares not deny any Thing I ask of him, for Fear I should deny him the Bubby when he is thirsty."[63] This study will show the extent to which these anxieties about the dynamic between powerful Virgin and infantilized Christ were subsequently revisited by Protestant polemicists, particularly the controversies surrounding the *Virgo Lactans*. Erasmus himself was no schismatic, however. His was a tempering vision, which Diarmaid MacCulloch has persuasively argued gives an insight into an alternative future for Catholicism, had the Reformation not occurred: "There might have been a future for a Mariology drawing on the Christocentric theology of the Passion in a Catholicism which had not been traumatised by the Reformation."[64]

MacCulloch's view presents a very potent "what if," particularly when one considers Caroline Walker Bynum's pertinent observations about a greater emphasis on the humanity of Christ and the Virgin at this time.[65] Christine Peters has also identified an increasingly Christocentric focus within late medieval piety, arguing that there was an iconographical development of Mary as a mortal on whom the privilege of a coronation was being bestowed.[66] Representations of the Queen of Heaven were possibly on the threshold of a sea change by the end of the Middle Ages, but to conclude this is to remain in the realms of conjecture. However partial, however incomplete, England's Reformation did occur, and one result of this was a shift in perception of both the Virgin's assumption and her role as Queen of Heaven. An indication of this can be found in differing approaches to Song of Songs 4:8. As we have seen, the Vulgate words "Veni coronaberis" often denoted the coronation of the Virgin, who was figured as the Bride from the Song of Songs. These words were Englished by Gregory Martin in the Catholic Rheims-Douai Old Testament as "Come: thou shalt be crowned," a translation that allows for the reading of the Bride of the Song of Songs as the Queen of Heaven.[67] The Protestant Geneva Bible makes a startling omission at this point, however, as the Englishing of "Veni coronaberis" is omitted entirely. There is no mention of the Bride being crowned; instead, the spouse is invited simply to come and "loke from the top of Amanah." In the glossings of this verse there are no Marian references; instead, the Bride is purely a representation of the true church, as the verse is glossed as "Christ promiseth his Church" (281, n.d.). There is no scope at all here for links between the Bride of the Song of Songs and the Queen of Heaven. Through translation and commentary, battle lines are drawn. The work of reformers John Bale and John Foxe followed on from this repositioning of Marian paradigms within the Song of Songs. Instead of the Bride and Bridegroom from the Songs being read as Virgin and Christ, the Protestant Church became the true church, the Bride of both Song of Songs and Revelation.[68]

Prior to the Reformation, Mary as Queen of Heaven and Mary as humble handmaid were able to coexist within one polyvalent image. This study will show the extent to which these two aspects of Marian iconography were polarized by Reformation thinking. The teaching of Martin Luther gives a hint of this. Luther was devoted to the Virgin, and his commentary on the Magnificat, published in 1521, is evidence of this. In this, he did not eradicate the nomenclature of "Queen of Heaven," but he warned his followers against making too much of the phrase, which "does not make her a goddess who could grant gifts or render aid." Mary in this commentary is presented as a model of obedience and is placed in a humble, domesticated setting: "She is not puffed up, does not vaunt herself or proclaim with a loud voice that she is become the Mother of God. She seeks not any glory, but goes about her usual household duties, milking the cows, cooking the meals, washing pots and kettles, sweeping out the rooms, and performing the works of maidservant or housemother in lowly and despised tasks, as though she cared nothing for such great gifts and graces."[69]

As time went on, Luther—and particularly the Lutheran pastors who followed him—did eradicate the use of the term *Queen of Heaven* from sermons and written works. This effected, as Beth Kreitzer's research has shown, a transformation of the Virgin's role from active *Regina Coeli* interceding on mankind's behalf to *ancilla Domini*, a humble, submissive, and obedient peasant girl. Lutheran Mary thus becomes the perfect godly Protestant woman, serving as a role model to a pastor's female flock.[70] Bridget Heal describes this as a reworking of old established symbols that stripped Mary of her salvific power and instead exalted her as a model of right belief and conduct: "The humble and family-orientated Virgin who had featured in late medieval images of the Holy Kindred remained, but her domestic role was no longer offset by authority in the heavenly sphere."[71] This ideological shift is perfectly encapsulated by Merry Wiesner-Hanks as "a reduction of the female ideal from heavenly to housebound."[72] It was not a wholly successful change. Heal's monograph itself is a testament to the diversity of Marian devotional practice within Lutheran Germany, while Kreitzer's study concludes that the symbol of Mary was too polyvalent to fit snugly into this representation: "The image of Mary often rests somewhat uncomfortably on sixteenth-century Lutheran preachers, for it is more complex and occasionally more subversive than they are willing to admit."[73] Fault lines clearly emerge when the complex image of the Virgin is represented exclusively in one of its many guises, and it is an awareness of this polyvalence that underpins my own analysis. Protestant English preachers, as the next chapter will show, embraced the conceptualization of a passive obedient Virgin with enthusiasm, but their efforts to polarize the Virgin's image often had a destabilizing effect.

A Protestant reduction of the Virgin's role led in many ways to a Catholic retrenchment, one described by Miri Rubin as the "subsequent Catholic defence of Mary and all she stood for."[74] The Council of Trent (1545–63) affirmed the centrality of veneration of the Virgin, although it did not take Mariology as a key focus for debate. Instead, it was Counter-Reformation writers such as Peter Canisius who subsequently brought Marian piety to the forefront, sparking, to use Trevor Johnson's words, "Marian fervour throughout Catholic Europe, at both elite and popular levels."[75] Keith Luria describes the cult of Mary as "the most successful of the Catholic Reformation."[76] In Counter-Reformation Europe the Virgin's image was frequently military and was often realized as the empowered Queen of Heaven.[77] A view of the "Catholic"

Mary purely as Queen of Heaven is reductive, however. From the language of early modern sermons, Donna Spivey Ellington has found convincing evidence of a quiet, passive, and contemplative Virgin who emerged in post-Tridentine Europe and formed a model for a devout Christian life.[78] This more restrained Marian piety presented the Virgin as a passive recipient of God's grace: the "Catholic" Virgin Mary here stands uncannily close to the godly "Protestant" model. That the polarization of humble Protestant handmaid and militaristic Catholic queen is not always stable is a driving force behind my own study. It could be argued that instead of coexisting with the humble handmaid, the image of the Queen of Heaven was being forced to exist in opposition. My own study concerns itself with the English experience, finding that further complexities emerge if one translates Counter-Reformation orthodoxies onto English soil, where belief systems were not always clearly demarcated. Did Counter-Reformation representatives in England follow the zealous course of their Continental counterparts when it came to the militaristic role of the Queen of Heaven, or did they adapt the image to fit their own surroundings? How did recusant worshippers, and those whose faith swerved or was secret, reveal or conceal their devotion to the Virgin? It is questions such as this which my book seeks to answer.

The fate of the Feast of the Assumption itself is revealed in the rhythm of the liturgical year. The Prayer Books of 1549 and 1552 greatly simplified the calendar and eradicated many Marian feasts, Thomas Cranmer retaining only the Feasts of the Annunciation and the Purification. In 1561, however, the Conception of the Blessed Virgin, the Nativity, and the Visitation were all reinstated. As Paul Williams observes: "The one, conspicuous, continuing omission was the Assumption, which disappeared from Anglican worship in 1549."[79] The three pageants from the York cycle about the Virgin's assumption and coronation were withdrawn in 1548; briefly reinstated during Queen Mary's reign, they were abolished totally in 1561.[80] How successfully did these measures erase the memory of the Virgin's assumption from the collective consciousness? A glance forward to the year 1592 finds the clergyman controversialist Andrew Willet stating his vehement opposition to the Feast of the Assumption in the celebrated work *Synopsis Papismi*:

We doe not celebrate any festivall daies in the honour of creatures, neither of the Virgine Mary, nor any other Saint, but only to the honor of God: and therefore the feasts of the Annunciation, and Purification, may much better be received, because they belong and are referred unto Christ, then the other festivities, of the assumption and conception of Mary, the institution whereof was most superstitious: the one for the fayned assumption of her bodie, which your owne writers are uncertaine of: the other to maintaine the heresie of the Franciscanes, that she was conceived and borne without sinne.[81]

Synopsis Papismi is a weighty piece of polemic that aims to dismantle Catholic doctrine with Protestant words by presenting a mock dialogue between a "Papist" and a "Protestant." Willet's claims about the Feast of the Assumption come in a section that takes as its theme the errors of "The Honor and worship of the Virgin Marie"; prior to this is a section entirely devoted to debunking the assumption, which Willet describes as "a very counterfeit story, and worthy of no credit."[82] Willet's mistrust of the Virgin's assumption, particularly her bodily assumption, is clearly expressed, but its reference within this text also reveals that this long-eradicated feast is still a matter for debate.

A decade later, the Puritan theologian William Perkins was to describe the Feast of the Assumption as "counterfeit," punning that "there is no certaintie in historie to prove this assumption."[83] Forty years after the Elizabethan authorities had taken concerted steps to eradicate any traces of the Virgin's assumption from the liturgy, a prolific Puritan writer felt the need to express his concern. This telling little detail stands as a salutary reminder that imagery of the Virgin's assumption had not completely vanished. There is a shift in tone—it has become a topic of polemic rather than devotion—but the image remains, still in currency, still capable of arousing a response. The next chapter will turn to confrontational standpoints of figures like William Perkins, as I move to an exploration of polemical representations of the Queen of Heaven.

My brief exploration of the history of the assumption and coronation of the Virgin has encompassed a range of personalities and narratives, presenting the Queen of Heaven as a glorious paradox of humility and power. Within this *bricolage*, two patterns have emerged. The first is that iconography of the Virgin's assumption and coronation was woven into the fabric of cultural consciousness by the Reformation. My history, scant as it is, has given a clear indication of just how beloved and treasured the figure of the Queen of Heaven was. The second is that the image of the Queen of Heaven was frequently a source of debate and was deployed as an expression of religio-political as well as personal confessional concerns. These patterns have a huge bearing on how iconography of the assumption of the Virgin and her role as Queen of Heaven are perceived in the following chapters. The potent mix of devotion and debate established in the Middle Ages made England a fertile soil for a Reformation conflict that frequently centered on the image of the Queen of Heaven as a site of controversy.

PART I

"Some Out of Vanity Will Call Her the Queene of Heaven"

CHAPTER 2

The Queen of Heaven in
Protestant Religious Discourse

I beseech you, marke the fourme and fashion of their prayers.
—John Jewel

She was an overbearing figure who emasculated and infantilized Christ
and who encouraged disruptive and disorderly female conduct. Long
after the figure of the Queen of Heaven was eradicated from the liturgy,
such characterizations ensured that she remained a frequent, powerful
presence in the pulpit and within printed religious tracts. This chapter
takes as its theme this often vitriolic debate. It has at its core the printed
versions of sermons that were delivered in high-profile pulpits throughout the country. The many different, often disparate, characters that
will air their views are an indication of the widespread continued cultural significance of the Queen of Heaven in Elizabethan and Jacobean
England. Their words reveal how the image of the Virgin functioned
within the ideological framework both of early modern secular anxieties about queenship and authority and of a demonizing of the Catholic
Church that frequently used gendered language. I will first explore how
the use of the phrase "Queen of Heaven" as part of a string of titles in

medieval litanies was subverted by Protestant polemicists who repeated these lists in mocking form. I will then examine invective against the Queen of Heaven as an authoritative figure, showing how this often translated to assertions about the papistical image of the Virgin as a mother who many Protestant commentators deduced was overbearing toward her son. From the Queen of Heaven as a mother I turn to the Queen of Heaven as a woman and an exploration of an Old Testament prophetic reference that polemicists often deployed to support their cause. This is the book of Jeremiah's story of the disobedient women of Pathros, whose idolatrous worship of a pagan queen of heaven brought about God's wrath. In spite of the directness of tone of this polemic, pejorative representations of the Virgin as heaven's queen are often complex and nuanced, as commentators take pains, sometimes unsuccessfully, to disentangle appropriate levels of respect and veneration for the Virgin as a humble handmaid from their vitriol and loathing of her elevated form. The balance struck is frequently an uneasy one.

The Reformation's privileging of both the Word and the individual faith of a believer led, inevitably, to a transformation of the role of the preacher and an increased emphasis on the significance of the sermon.[1] To a certain extent, the initial drive for this was in fact the growth of humanism; pre-Reformation humanist scholars such as Desiderius Erasmus and Bishop John Fisher expanded the preacher's role, highlighting the importance of preaching in emulation of Christ's ministry. During the Reformation, this aspect of humanism was retained, and the priest— whose principal role had formerly been one of celebrator of Mass and hearer of confessions—became preacher and interpreter of the Word. An Elizabethan or Jacobean sermon was often a big event: at St. Paul's Cross in the heart of London, an outdoor sermon was delivered every Sunday, attended by thousands of people and lasting between two and three hours.[2] Patrick Collinson has described St. Paul's Cross as "the nearest thing that the age offered to broadcasting."[3] Visiting London in 1599, the Swiss humanist Thomas Platter recalled how "the congregation is so vast that the aforesaid big church will not hold it, so that the sermon is delivered before the church."[4] John Donne, who frequently preached at St. Paul's Cross, observed that the place buzzed with noise and that a sermon could be met with "periodicall murmurings and noises," describing these as "impertinent Interjections" that "swallow up one quarter of his houre."[5]

In spite of the undisputed significance of early modern sermons, they have as a genre been traditionally regarded as a worthy but rather dull area of study, with many earlier monographs wanting to discourage the enthusiast from further investigation.[6] The work of Arnold Hunt, Lori Anne Ferrell, and Peter McCullough has thankfully served to disabuse us of this notion, making a concerted effort to free sermon literature from what Ferrell and McCullough describe as "an indulgent, even condescending, neglect."[7] My own investigations have come about largely as a result of this re-energized academic approach. The historical context of a sermon's delivery and reception is integral to its cultural significance. The topics of an early modern sermon were often interwoven with key events: sermons, for example, were used as a reiteration of national strength after the Armada and the Gunpowder Plot. As Ferrell and McCullough have commented, sermons were not just words on a page "but instruments of policy, documents of religious change, and expressions of public life."[8] Ferrell's aptly entitled monograph *Government by Polemic* is a convincing demonstration of how James I recognized "the remarkable power of the word," highlighting that the sermon was a mouthpiece for the king's policies.[9] The sermon also had an important role to play within what Tony Claydon has termed the "public sphere," where preaching and the dissemination of news and public thought were viewed as intertwined.[10] The views expressed in sermons were frequently echoed in pamphlet literature.[11] *The Antichrist's Lewd Hat*, Peter Lake and Michael Questier's lively review of sermon campaigns against the theater, has explored the overlap between pamphlet and pulpit culture, revealing how the lowbrow writers of Grub Street (the literary underground of London) were often promulgating ideologies similar to those of the preacher in the pulpit.[12]

There is something of an irony about any academic study that has the printed words of a sermon at its core. A sermon was a performance that often packed a hefty rhetorical punch. Bryan Crockett's 1995 study, *The Play of Paradox*, emphasizes the theatricality of the seventeenth-century sermon, observing that the orators of stage and pulpit often used similar rhetorical techniques.[13] Arnold Hunt has described a sermon as "specific to the moment of spoken delivery," and because of this many preachers were actually reluctant to see their work appear in print.[14] Ultimately, however, the thirst for the printed word won out; as James Rigney has observed, the sermon has an important place in the history of the printed book and became "a public space for the inscription and exchange of views."[15] The move from oral delivery into print, however problematic, indicates the long afterlife of a sermon, one that is accentuated by the structured way in which a sermon was heard, from regulated note taking by schoolboys during its delivery to fragments appearing in commonplace books and spiritual autobiographies.[16] The topography of the area around the pulpit at St. Paul's Cross itself is compelling evidence of the printed sermon's popularity, as in close proximity to this preaching venue were a number of booksellers offering prints and reprints of sermons. The same booksellers also sold a variety of other religious books, an indication that sermons were just one of an extensive genre of religious publications that included tracts, biblical commentaries, and devotional books.[17] Researching this chapter has been rather like stepping into one of these booksellers' shops and sampling their wares: my analysis of representations of the Queen of Heaven comes in the main from sermon literature, but I also draw examples from this wider genre of printed religious discourse.

FROM LITANIES OF PRAISE TO EPITHETS OF DISDAIN

A study of the representation of the Queen of Heaven in sermons and other printed religious discourse yields many significant patterns and repetitions. An example is the listing of epithets to the Virgin in a disdainful tone. In the fifth century, the influential Constantinople preacher Proclus gave a sermon in which he delivered a string of titles in the Virgin's praise.[18] This practice of addressing the Virgin using a list of titles became widespread: by the Middle Ages, titles such as "Queen of Heaven," "Gate of Paradise," and "Star of the Sea" were commonplace in primers. Marian litanies, popular from the twelfth century onward, took the form of petitions to the Virgin Mary that were repeated in chant form; perhaps the most popular of these was the Litany of Loreto, sung at this famous Marian shrine, which was printed in 1558.

The listing of multiple, often contradictory titles for the Virgin came under intense fire in Protestant discourse. As is so often the case in the story of the Reformation, the seeds of this mistrust were sown in the writings of Erasmus, who in his *Colloquies* satirized the insincerity of these appellations by mocking sailors who called on the Virgin in distress: "The Mariners, they were singing their *Salve Regina*, imploring the Virgin Mother, calling her the Star of the Sea, the Queen of Heaven, the Lady of the World, the Haven of Health, and many other flattering Titles, which the sacred Scriptures never attributed to her."[19] Reformation writers followed Erasmus's lead and often listed epithets to the Virgin as an amplification of their disgust. The argument was that such appellations of praise were idolatrous; excessive verbal embellishments therefore became analogous to overdecorated visual manifestations. An example of a Protestant writer who expressed disgust is the prominent reformer John Jewel. Exiled during the reign of Queen Mary, Jewel became bishop of Salisbury under Elizabeth and published widely on reformist issues. He was vehemently opposed to veneration of the Virgin as Queen of Heaven, and his views had a lasting impact, as many of his works were printed and reprinted after his death in 1571.[20] In a collection of sermons entitled *Certaine Sermons Preached Before the Queenes Majestie, and at Paule's Crosse*, Jewel observed: "I beseech you, marke the fourme and fashion of their prayers. To the blessed virgin, they sayd, *Ave Maria, salus, et consolatrix vivorum et mortuorum*, Haile Marie, the saviour & comforter, both of quicke and dead. . . . They cal her, *Regina Coeli, domina mundi, unica spes miserorum*. Queene of heaven, Lady of the world, the only hope of them that be in miserie. It were tedious, and unpleasant to recite the like their blasphemies. Howe did these men accompt of the crosse and passion of Christ?"[21] Jewel's "marke the fourme and fashion of their prayers" is certainly an exhortation to ridicule, but it can also be seen as a way of committing these lost liturgies to memory, of repetition rather than eradication. The epithets themselves were vivid descriptions that were presented as a catalog, making them easy to remember and easy to repeat. This further amplified their influence: as Patrick Collinson has observed, repetition was an extremely important element of the afterlife of the sermon, as godly Elizabethan neighbors met to engage in the repetition of a sermon that had been heard in public.[22]

Many polemicists adopted a similar device, loading attributes and titles on the Virgin Mary in a mock encomium. In 1573, the bishop of Oxford and Queen's Chaplain John Bridges made the following comments on the language of the primers: "Dyd ye never say this prayer in your Primer: O moste noble, moste excellent, and ever glorious Virgin, &c. O Lady my Queene, and Lady of all creatures, whiche forsakest none, dyspysest none, nore leavest anye desolate. . . . Ye have in the Primer, a notable prayer to the blessed virgin *Ave domina sancta Maria* &c. Haile Lady S. Marie, mother of God, Queene of heaven, port of Paradise, Ladie of the world, eternall light."[23] Bridges's invective is here directed at the pardons and indulgences associated with Catholic prayer. After exploring the language of prayer used in the primers, he goes on to dismiss it as "horrible stuffe. . . . Yea it were infinite and to tedious, to rake out those most blasphemous prayers, that all your other bookes have" (411). Just as Jewel observes that it would be "tedious and unpleasant" to recite Marian litanies, Bridges professes weariness at the multitude of Catholic prayers. Yet his exposition of the primers is lengthy, allowing time for the residual power and poetry of the language of these devotional prayers to remain. Prayers such as "Haile queene of mercie, our life, our sweetnes, our hope" (408) are repeated.

Both Jewel and Bridges complain that to repeat praise to the Virgin is an act of tedium that borders on disgust, yet, paradoxically, they repeat the prayers of the old faith at length. This paradox is more emotively suggested by the Puritan cleric William Charke, who, in his 1583 text *An Answeare for the Time*, declares: "It were too tedious, and would require an whole volume by it selfe, to set downe al their horrible prayers . . . that they make to the Virgin and other Sayntes."[24] The use of "horrible prayers" shows a profound sense of emotional engagement, and certainly William Charke was a man who was no stranger to controversy. He disputed with incarcerated Catholic priests, including Edmund Campion, whom he failed to convert in the Tower in 1581.[25] Charke's *An Answeare for the Time* is part of a furious pamphlet war with the Jesuit priest Robert Parsons concerning Campion's arrest and execution. It seethes with anti-Jesuit and anti-Marian sentiment and includes a mocking list of Mary's traditional attributes and titles: "A Virgin before her byrth, *and* in her birth, & a virgin after her birth: the fountayne of mercie, the fountaine of salvation and grace, the fountaine of pietie and gladnes, the fountain of consolation and forgivenes &c. The like is *Ave Rosa sine spinis*. All haile rose without thornes, written forsooth with letters of gold in her breast" (sig. H1r). At times, Charke's sarcasm is so sustained that mock encomium stands in danger of becoming an encomium itself. The attributes and titles of the Virgin Mary are listed in order to lampoon worship of her—but they are listed nonetheless. Charke frequently professes that he is tired of the subject. At one point he describes himself as "wearie in stirring this filthie Quakemyre of their cursed abomination" (sig. H1v). He is reluctant, as he puts it, to "blotte paper" with the subject (sig. H2r), but in reality his invective is poured liberally across the page.

Charke uses rhetorical lists to amplify his view that to elevate the Virgin to Queen of Heaven is a gross error, but these lists also reveal his own anxiety. Implicit here is a fear of the residual power that the Virgin could perhaps exercise over English men and women—a fear that was, in Charke's view, being inflamed by Catholic writings and teachings: "But is not this trimme stuffe, that you translate *Te Deum laudamus*, into *Te matrem laudamus*? where you call her the wife of the eternall Father, whom all the earth doeth woorshippe [*sic*]: Whom all the glorious companie all Confessours, doe call the Temple of the whole trinitie: whome the whole Courte of Heaven doeth honour, as the Queene of Heaven. Thou arte the Ladye of Angelles, the gate of Paradise, the Lader of the heavenlie kingdome" (sig. H2r). Charke's denunciation begins here with a sharply observed blow against the perceived aggrandizement of the Virgin to Queen of Heaven, that "Te Deum laudamus" (we praise you, God) is being interpreted as "Te matrem laudamus" (We praise you, Mother). But this descends into a list of epithets that in spite of its sarcastic tone is structured in the same way as a genuine litany. It is possible that Charke, like John Jewel and John Bridges, was keeping titles such as the Queen of Heaven alive in the public consciousness by the very act of repeatedly denigrating them. Rather than eradicating the Queen of Heaven, these polemical representations ironically acknowledge the power of the symbol.

THE QUEEN OF HEAVEN AS AN OVERBEARING MOTHER

This use of a mocking repetition of epithets to the Virgin creates a disqui-
eting effect, expressing an anxiety that to venerate the Virgin as Queen of
Heaven was to overinflate her role. The title "Queen of Heaven" bestowed power on the mother that should be the Father and Son's alone.
For a number of writers, the anxiety that "Te Deum laudamus" was
being changed to "Te matrem laudamus" became entangled with a very
domestic complaint: the authoritative figure of the Queen of Heaven
was constructed as an overbearing mother who was trying to control
her son. In the early stages of the Reformation, Bishop Hugh Latimer
made the dramatic assertion that Mary, far from being free from sin,
was a proud and arrogant mother. He based this on a scriptural reference, observing that she had interrupted Christ's sermon in the Temple
so that she could be recognized by all as his mother (Luke 2:48): "She
was pricked a little with vain-glory; she would have been known to be
his mother, else she would not have been so hasty to speak with him.
And here you may perceive that we gave her too much, thinking her to
be without any sparkle of sin."[26] Latimer's claim here was that according to scriptural text the Virgin was a proud woman who wanted to
bask in her son's glory.

Another biblical reference to the relationship between mother and
son comes in the miracle of the Wedding at Cana in the Gospel of John.
At the point at which the wedding guests have run out of wine, Mary
urges her son to intervene, thus prompting his first miracle. But before
he does so, Christ utters some apparently brusque words to his mother:
"Jesus said unto her, Woman, what have I to do with thee? mine houre
is not yet come" (John 2:4). The text has through time lain itself open
to a patriarchal reading of the Virgin as a domineering mother who fails
to understand the significance of her son's ministry.[27] In 1610, the popular Kentish preacher John Boys offered the following interpretation of
Christ's words: "Christ answered roughly, lest we should account his
mother our mediatrix and advocate. For he foresaw the superstition of
popery, making Mary the Queene of heaven, and assigning greater dig-
nitie to the mother, then to the Sonne. For whereas Gods kingdome
consists of his justice and mercy, the Papists attribute the greatest part,
which is mercy, to Mary, making her high Chanceller, and Christ, as

it were, chiefe Justice: so that a poore Client may well appeale from the tribunall of God, to the court of our Lady."[28] Boys reads Christ's attitude to his mother as direct evidence that he foresaw that the Catholic faith would overinflate Mary's role, elevating her to the position of Queen of Heaven. His scriptural exegesis of the roughness of Christ's tone conflates the Virgin as mother with the Virgin as Queen of Heaven. The sermon functions as a warning to worshippers, but there is a distinct impression that the preacher is also putting Mary herself firmly back in her rightful place. The words of John Boys would have carried considerable weight. His comments on Mary as Queen of Heaven were part of a series of printed sermons that examined the liturgy of the English church throughout the year, ultimately earning him the position of dean of Canterbury. It is a testament to his popularity that his books were reissued at least twelve times.[29]

Many other writers of the period linked the Virgin as overbearing mother with the Virgin as Queen of Heaven. The prominent Calvinist theologian and prolific writer William Perkins had plenty to say on this subject. In many of his works he expresses a fear that the physical and emotional superiority and control of Mary as mother and Queen of Heaven constitutes an enfeeblement of the son.[30] His work, *A Golden Chaine*, develops these ideas in some detail, exhorting readers to consider that to award the Virgin the title "Queen of Heaven" belittles Christ: "For Christ must either be our alone and whole Saviour or no Saviour. Now they make him but halfe a Saviour, and they joyne others with him as partners in the worke of salvation . . . when they adde to Christs intercession the intercession and patronage of Saints, especially of the Virgin Marie, whome they call the Queene of heaven, the mother of mercie, withall requesting her, that by the authoritie of a mother she would commaund her sonne."[31] The Queen of Heaven becomes a rather bossy, domineering mother here.

Later in the text, Perkins returns to the same image, as he explores the error of juxtaposing "mother" and "God":

Againe, the Church of Rome maketh Marie the mother of Jesus to bee as God. In the Breviary reformed and published at the commandement of Pius the V shee is called a Goddesse, in expresse words: and she is further tearmed the Queene of heaven, the Queene of the world, the gate of heaven, the mother of grace and mercy: Yea shee is farre exalted above Christ, and he in regard of her is made but a poore underling in heaven: for papists in their service unto her pray on this manner, saying: Shew thy selfe to be a mother: and cause thy sonne to receive our praiers: set free the captives and give light to the blind.[32]

The erosion of Christ's power through the elevation of the Virgin is seen as a threat to Protestantism's Christocentric vision. Christ the infant, sitting on his mother's knee, becomes Christ the enfeebled servant to the Queen of Heaven, made "a poore underling in heaven." In a later work, the *The Combat Betweene Christ and the Divell Displayed* (1606), Perkins observed: "They call the *Virgin Mary*, the *Queene of Heaven*, and pray to her, that by the authority of a mother, she would command her sonne to heare their praiers; which is to make Christ a punie and underling unto her."[33] In the emotive descriptions of an enfeebled Christ is a misogynistic anxiety about the emasculation of a man by a threateningly dominant woman.

A similar fusion of Queen of Heaven with controlling mother can be found in the works of George Downame, a popular and forceful London theologian. In addition to publishing devotional and moral works, Downame became involved in some of the great controversies in this period, producing a number of anti-Catholic texts. He gained the favor of King James and became bishop of Derry in 1616.[34] In 1603, he produced a passionately anti-Catholic work entitled *A Treatise Concerning Antichrist*; following a commonplace of the time, the "Antichrist" of the title is the pope. Downame's contention is that the Catholic faith denies Christ as God, and to back up his argument he delivers the familiar reproach that the Virgin of Catholicism is an overbearing mother: "In heaven they set above him his mother whom they cal the Queene of heaven, desiring her to commaund him, & to shew her selfe to be a mother (as though Christ were as they paint him a baby under his mothers government)."[35] Here, again, is an anxiety about the emasculation of Christ, who in the presence of the Virgin as Queen of Heaven is literally infantilized, becoming as powerless as a baby under his mother's care. The pejorative tone of "they paint him a baby" expresses a fear of the visual image, of the dangerous and misleading influence of paintings of the crowned Virgin with the baby Christ in her arms. Domestic detail becomes doctrinal unease about the Virgin's role of mediatrix: "The blessed virgin *Mary* . . . hath beene worshipped among them as much or rather more then God. Her they call their Lady and goddesse, and queene of heaven. In her they repose their trust and assiance [sic], to her they flie in their necessitie, of her they crave all good things, and from her they expect remission of sins and eternall salvation, in honour of her they have devised and used diverse services, as offices, letanies, rosaryes, psalters &c. full of blasphemous idolatries."[36] Downame's work, produced in the year of King James's accession in 1603, has the political subtext of cautioning the new monarch that it is dangerous to promise religious toleration.[37] Perhaps it is also sounding a warning note against the role of the queen consort: James's wife, Anna of Denmark, had converted to Catholicism in the 1590s, and his mother was Mary Queen of Scots, who through her execution had become a Catholic martyr.[38] An interesting anomaly about the Virgin's position as Queen of Heaven is that it encompasses the role of queen consort as well as that of queen regnant. The image of Christ the infant, sitting on his mother's knee, shows how Christ the King of Heaven is still bound by the memory of the infant son's dependence on his mother, but the Virgin is iconographically represented as Christ's bride as well as his mother.[39] Chapter 1 discussed the way in which queens consort were often compared to the Virgin in the Middle Ages because of their intercessory role. This figure of an influential woman could also engender vitriol and fear: Margaret of Anjou, for example, was vilified on the Shakespearean stage as the "she wolf of France," framed, to use Kavita Mudan's words, as a "cautionary [tale] for exercising political power."[40] In France, Catherine de Medici came to be known as "The Black Queen" for her influence over her sons, Francis II and Charles IX, and her perceived role in the St. Bartholomew's Day Massacre of 1572.[41]

If a queen consort was a figure who could inspire mistrust, then a queen regnant was much, much worse. In his infamous 1558 polemic, *The Monstruous Regiment of Women*, the Scottish reformer John Knox warned of dangerous consequences if a woman was set above a man in authority: "But as for woman, it is no more possible, that she being set aloft in authoritie above man, shall resist the motions of pride, then it is able to the weake reed, or to the turning wethercocke, not to bowe or turne at the vehemencie of the unconstant wind."[42] Knox's treatise is a damning indictment of the misrule of three Catholic Marys—Mary of Guise, Mary Tudor, and Mary Stuart—and perhaps one should add Mary the Queen of Heaven to this "Monstruous Regiment" of "mischevous Maryes."[43] Knox's words were not directly aimed at Elizabeth, but his pamphlet was published just months before she became queen, and it is a powerful example of gendered polemic about the problems of female rule. Many of the sources analyzed in this chapter were written when Elizabeth was on the throne. Anxiety about the conjunction of authority with the feminine, so prevalent in vilifications of the Queen of Heaven, was also a pervasive aspect of iconography relating to the queen of England. Louis Montrose has foregrounded the way in which representations of Queen Elizabeth were intrinsically bound to her gender; furthermore, negative discourse about Elizabeth expressed a recurring fear about the idea of a woman as queen regnant in an age when women were viewed as unstable versions of men.[44] Elizabeth was also repeatedly fashioned as a mother to the nation as well as its queen, a potent symbolic expression of maternal agency and power. Countering John Knox's treatise in 1559, John Aylmer, who was ultimately to become bishop of London, represented the queen as "a loving Quene and mother to raigne over us."[45] This conflation of queen and mother was often the seat of a profound psychological disturbance for many of Elizabeth's subjects.[46] It is a fruitful exercise to set gendered polemic against the Queen of Heaven in the context of an ongoing debate about the emasculating and debilitating effects of feminine rule, one that often deployed language relating to maternal authority. As Katherine Eggert's research has shown, "ongoing reformulations of female authority" in Elizabethan literature provoked widespread authorial anxiety, although they also led to inventive responses of experimentation with new literary genres.[47]

THE SINS OF THE CITY: JEREMIAH 44 AND THE DISOBEDIENT WOMEN OF PATHROS

The representation of the Queen of Heaven as an overbearing mother thus mapped onto the image a dangerous amount of power and can be set in the context of early modern secular anxieties about women and authority. This association of the Queen of Heaven with disobedient but authoritative women is perhaps best exemplified in the widespread polemical use of one particular reference to a queen of heaven who is idolatrously worshipped by Israelites in the book of Jeremiah. There are two references to this figure within Jeremiah. The first, from Jeremiah 7, describes how the prophet is enraged by the actions of the Israelites: "The children gather wood, and the fathers kindle the fyre, and the women knede the dough to make cakes to the Queen of heaven & to powre out drinke offrings unto other gods, that thei maie provoke me unto anger" (Jer. 7:18). Later in the book of Jeremiah, the idolatrous worship of this queen of heaven is given more weight. Jeremiah 44 tells the story of the people of Pathros, a community of Israelites living in Egypt in the late sixth and early seventh centuries BC. The people of Pathros are described as a disorderly crowd, who have abandoned worshipping Yahweh and instead have devoted themselves to a queen of heaven, their devotion taking the form of burning incense and offering cakes and drink. The women of the community have taken the lead in this rebellion. Their actions are in defiance of the prophet Jeremiah, and their husbands are portrayed as weak and complicit in their wives' spiritual adultery: "All the men . . . knewe that their wives had burnt incense unto other gods" (Jer. 44:15). Jeremiah rails against the people of Pathros, but they refuse to change their ways. Worshipping the queen of heaven has led, they believe, to health and prosperity; the moment they stopped, their luck ran out.

> But we wil do whatsoever thing goeth out of our owne mouth, as to burne incense unto the Quene of heaven, & to powre out drinke offrings unto her, as we have done, bothe we and our fathers, our Kings and our princes in the citie of Judah, and in the stretes of Jerusalem: for then had we plentie of vitailes and were wel and felt none evil.
> But since we left of to burne incense to the Qnene [sic] of heaven, and to powre out drinke offrings unto her, we have had scarcenes of all things, and have bene consumed by the sworde and by the famine. (Jer. 44:17–18)

The queen of heaven in this Old Testament reference is not of course the Virgin Mary, in either literal or typological form. The Israelites are here worshipping either a syncretistic pagan deity, an ancient Semitic goddess, or the planets and the stars of heaven in its entirety.[48] But the use of the phrase "queen of heaven" in translations of the Bible available to early modern commentators gave Protestant preachers and polemicists a very contemporary-sounding exemplum of human weakness for idolatrous worship.[49] It would appear that the compilers of the Protestant Geneva Bible realized just how convenient this reference was to prove. To the people of Pathros's comment that "had we plentie of vitailes and were wel and felt none evil" when they prayed to the queen of heaven, the Geneva Bible adds the gloss, "This is stil the argument of idolaters" (Jer. 44:17, note k).

Many commentators of the early modern period were, like the editors of the Geneva Bible, attuned to the rich relevance of Jeremiah 44. This tale of disobedience and idolatry was told and retold, embellished and expostulated upon in the sermons and polemic of the period. The people of Pathros, worshipping the pagan queen of heaven, became the papists of England, worshipping the Virgin as Queen of Heaven. The widespread deployment of Jeremiah 44 is an example of what Arnold Hunt has called a "common stock of classical and biblical allusions, rhetorical figures and moral observations that passed freely from one text to another, often with little alteration."[50] It also follows the common polemical method of comparing present-day practices with those of Old Testament idolaters. The "Jeremiads" is a name given to a group of St. Paul's Cross sermons in which the sins of contemporary Londoners were seen as mirroring the sins of the Israelites of the Old Testament.[51] Michael McGiffert terms this comparison of England with Israel, and London with Jerusalem, the "Israelite paradigm," upon which preachers "built the towering scaffold of moral nationalism." Patrick Collinson has observed that Jerusalem was such a familiar paradigm for London that "every biblical type and figure of God's people was now applied to England, *ad nauseam.*"[52] This is a useful observation to apply to the deployment of Jeremiah 44. The people of Pathros in Jeremiah 44 are represented as a dangerously anarchic force, and the repeated conflation of the pagan queen of heaven whom they worship with the Catholic Queen of Heaven shows the extent to which the Virgin's image was part of a web of prophetic writings linking Catholic practices with disobedience and a threat to national security. Jeremiah 44 is unequivocal about the fate that awaits idolatrous worshippers: a vengeful God tells them they "shal be consumed by the sworde, and by the famine, until thei be utterly destroyed" (Jer. 44:27). It is fire and brimstone stuff, and in an early modern context, descriptions of the fate that awaits idolatrous Israelites became a barely encoded warning of the fate that faced anyone who was tempted to stray from the nationalistic norm of Protestant worship into Catholic veneration of the Queen of Heaven. To use the words of Millar MacLure: "Moved by the breath of the Judgment trumpet, by national pride, by moral fervour, and indeed by simple custom, the preacher declared himself the voice of the Lord, the prophet calling the sinful city to repentance."[53]

The fusion of Jeremiah's queen of heaven with the Virgin Mary indicates the fine and often controversial line between translation and interpretation. In 1582, a version of the New Testament translated by the Catholic priest Gregory Martin appeared in Rheims. Its very appearance eroded the validity of a core Protestant criticism of Catholicism: that priests denied the laity access to the Word. Lines of attack were thus redrawn, as Protestant theologians instead criticized Gregory Martin for his inadequate powers of translation.[54] In one prominent print war with William Fulke, the Puritan master of Pembroke College, Cambridge, Martin questioned the use of the phrase "queen of heaven" in Jeremiah and its subsequent deployment as an exemplum for the Virgin. He observed that this was a rather convenient misreading, as the Hebrew word in Jeremiah is not translated as "queen" anywhere else in the scriptures. Protestant Bible commentators, "controllers . . . of the Latine texte by the Hebrewe," were, he continued, "content to dissemble the Hebrue worde" when it suited them. When Jeremiah inveighs against those offering sacrifice to the queen of heaven:

This they thinke is very well, because it may sounde in the peoples eares against the use of the Catholike Churche, which calleth our Lady, Queene of heaven. But they know very well that the Hebrue worde doth not signifie Queene in any other place of the Scripture,

and that the Rabbines and later Hebricians (whom they gladly follow) deduce it otherwise, to signifie rather the whole corps and
frame of heaven, consisting of all the beautiful starres and planets. . . .
But the Protestants (against their custome of scanning the Hebrue
and the Greeke) translate here, Queene of heaven, for no other
cause in the world, but to make it sound against her, whom Catho-
likes truly call and worthily honour as Queene of heaven.[55]

William Fulke's reply was that in using the phrase "Queene of Heaven"
he and other Protestants were merely following the lead of the translation of the Hebrew into Latin Vulgate Bible by Jerome. The intention
was not to open up a war of words about the Virgin's role: "But if wee
bee accused of hereticall translation, when we joigne with your vul-
gar Latine, with Hierom, with the Septuaginta, it is very strange, that
they should not beare the blame with us. Certaine it is, no Protestant
did ever teache, that the Jewes did worshippe the virgine Marie for the
Queene of heaven. But the Sunne, the Moone, or some great starre as
Pagnine saith."[56] It is an erudite and elegant answer, but it evades a crucial point: the "Queen of Heaven" translation was an extremely convenient one in terms of providing an exemplum of dangerous religious
practices in the polemic and sermonizing of the period. Worthy of note
is that the Rheims -Douai Bible, Gregory Martin's translation of the Old
Testament, published in 1609–10, retains the phrase "queen of heaven"
in Jeremiah 44, as does the King James Bible.

Most commentators ignored these quibbles of translation and instead directly yoked the worship of the pagan queen of heaven to the
Catholic Queen of Heaven. I am going to discuss four examples of the
use of the Jeremiah reference, the writers of which range from mainstream to marginal.[57] My first example is in the writings of James Bisse,
a fellow of Magdelen College, Oxford. In a sermon delivered in 1580 at
Christ Church, London, he claimed that, like the Jews in Jeremiah's
time, Catholics "follow their own inventions":

Alas, are not yet the people as they were in the time of Jeremy?
they sayde to him, the word thou hast spoken to us, in the name of
the Lord, we wil not heare it of thee: but we wil doe whatsoever

thing goeth out of our mouth, as to burne incense to the Queene of heaven, and to purge out drink offrings unto her, as we have don, both we, and our fathers, our kings and our princes, for then had we plenty of victuall, and were well, and felt no evil. Are not these the sayings of the romanists, and Papists? first to graunt, that we have the word of God: secondly, to say, we will not so much as heare it: thirdly, to follow their own inventions. Againe, are not these their arguments? first of custome wee have done so, and our fathers: secondly of a generalitie: not we onely, but our fathers, our Princes, and al have done so? thirdly of their belly, then we had plentie of victuall, and felt no evill? and to whome would they offer their sacrifice? not to God, but as the Papistes doe, to the Queene of heaven. Aske the Papistes, how they proove their religion to be the trueth, and they will drawe their argumentes from antiquitie, from custome, from universalitie, and from the belly, as did the Jewes in the dayes of Jeremy.[58]

Bisse's "we wil not heare it of thee" underlines the appeal of this Old Testament reference to reformers. The Reformation brought with it the construction of a belief system that privileged the ear over the eye, and this is particularly apposite to an exposition of Jeremiah 44. At its core, it is about the sin of closing up one's ears, of not listening. When James Bisse took to the pulpit and delivered the tale of Jeremiah, he became the star player in his own allegory. Just as the people of Pathros did not listen to Jeremiah, so papists were not listening to the preacher, whose voice thus became that of a contemporary Jeremiah, railing against the corruption he saw around him.

My second example comes from the work of the separatist Henry Barrow, who, writing from his prison cell in 1590, denounced the "wanton feasts" of the Catholic Church, which he saw as opportunities for gluttony, idleness, and superstition. Today's sinners, he observed, found in the Old Testament a precedent for their actions: "This is the fruite of their idolatrie & idlenes: this they learned of their forefathers in the wilderness."[59] Barrow's attack rails against what he sees as a surfeit of sinful feasts, and he is particularly vehement about feasts relating to the Virgin Mary. He treats the feast of the Purification of the Virgin Mary or Candlemass, which was retained by Cranmer, with a sense of mock disbelief. What, he asks, is being worshipped here? If it is the Purification that is being celebrated, then this is strange, as this is only a "legal ceremonie, and not now to be brought into the Church of Christ." If, however, it is the person of Mary that is being worshipped here, then this is a dangerous practice: "How then wil they escape the breach of the first commandement; unlesse peradventure they hope through her mediation to be dispensed withal, & that she wil speak a good word unto her Sonne for them; & therfore they powre out unto her their drinke offringes, and burne incense to the Queene of heaven."[60] Barrow's railings have shifted from the Purification of the Virgin here to idolatrous worship of her as the Catholic Queen of Heaven, and the image of pouring drink offerings and burning incense is clearly an allusion to Jeremiah 44. Henry Barrow stood outside the mainstream of Elizabethan religious views; he was ultimately executed for his extreme religious beliefs.[61] However, in his conflation of Old Testament idolatry with contemporary Catholic practice, and in the allusion to Jeremiah 44 in particular, his writing is exemplary early modern Protestant polemic.

My third example comes from a 1609 sermon by the clergyman Henry Greenwood and is a particularly impassioned juxtaposition of Old Testament and contemporary practices. In it, Greenwood warns his flock of the perils of earthly temptations and exhorts them to follow a sinless way to heaven. The sermon is full of emotive examples of sin and its dangers, as England is described as "a sinke of sinne, a pit of pollution, and a place of abhomination." Greenwood uses Jeremiah 44 as a focus for the sin of Marian idolatry:

Yea these last dayes of the world are like to the dayes of Israels provocation of the Lord in the wildernesse: wherein we preferre the slavery of Egypt above the sweete Manna of heavenly blisse.

Yea that saying of the Prophet is verified of the most part of mankind: That the children gather stickes, the fathers made the fire, and the women bake cakes for the queene of heaven: That is, they offered sacrifice to the Sunne and Moone and planets, which they called the Queene of heaven. So the Beast of Rome with his Antichristian crue, doth sacrifice to Mary, making her an Idol, and calling her (as in their *Salve regina*: and *Regina coeli laetare*: doth appeare) the Queene of heaven. They make ignorance the mother of their devotion: Sir John Lacklatine and Sir Anthony Ignorance are their chiefest clarkes, and best Massemongers.[62]

Greenwood's punning use of the proverbial "ignorance is the mother of devotion" is unmissable; instead of Mary as a mother figure, he presents his listeners with "ignorance."[63] He is careful to direct his satire in the direction of Catholic worshippers, lampooned as "Sir John Lacklatine and Sir Anthony Ignorance," rather than at the Virgin herself. But in describing ignorance as a mother he perhaps implicitly criticizes perceptions of the Virgin, particularly in the light of repeated polemic about her role as an overbearing mother.

For my final example, I return to the writings of John Jewel, who took a different approach to the connection between the women of Pathros and early modern worship. Jewel's deployment of the reference in a 1567 tract drew on a historical precedent for this particular spiritual exegesis. Jewel compares his line of thinking to that of one of the church fathers, Epiphanius of Salamis, who had also used the pagan idolatry of the women of Pathros in the book of Jeremiah to illustrate idolatrous veneration of the Virgin. Epiphanius made the comparison in his fourth-century book on heresies, *Panarion*, in an attack on an early Christian heretical movement of women called the Collyridians. The Collyridians, who originated in Syria, allowed women to be priests and practiced a cult of worshipping the Virgin.[64] We cannot be entirely certain whether this cult existed; what is certain is that there are uncanny similarities between this sect and the women of Pathros, in both the freedom and independence granted to women and the ritualized and touchingly domestic offering of baked goods. Epiphanius capitalized on this by linking the heretical Collyridians with the heretical women of Pathros. Over a thousand years later, Jewel does exactly the same thing. He uses Epiphanius's descriptions of the Collyridians as a way of justifying the comparison of Old Testament idolatry with contemporary Catholic modes of worship: "And therefore the Anciente Father Epiphanius applieth the like woordes of the same Prophete Jeremie, unto the Blessed Virgin Marie, beinge then idolatrousely abused by the Heretiques called Collyridiani, even as the same Blessed Virgin, & other Sainctes are by you abused nowe."[65] Jewel's commentary thus exploits the similarities between the women of Pathros, the Collyridians, and contemporaneous Catholics as he collapses three time scales and three idolatrous forms of worship into each other:

> Although Marie be beautiful, and Holy, and Honourable, yet is she not to be Adoured. But these Women, worshippinge S. Marie . . . prepare a Table for the Divel, and not for God. As it is written in the Scriptures. They are fedde with the Meate of Wickednesse. And againe, Theire Women boulte flower: and theire Children gather stickes, to make fine Cakes in the Honoure of the Queene of Heaven. Therefore let sutche Women be rebuked by the Prophete Jeremie: and let them no more trouble the worlde. . . . Here wee see, the woordes, that were spoken of the Heathenishe Idolles, are applied by Epiphanius unto the Mother of Christe: not to deface that Blessed Virgin, but to declare the fonde errours of those Heretiques.[66]

Jewel's reference to the Collyridians works on a number of levels. First, it adds weight to an exegesis that the worship of the pagan queen of heaven in Jeremiah was congruent with worship of the Virgin Mary: Jewel's claim is that he is simply following the lead of Epiphanius before him. It also gives a more gendered slant to the idolatrous and disruptive actions of early modern Catholics through the use of language such as "these Women" and "sutche Women." There is a sense here of rebellious women worshippers through history, a time line that stretches from the women of Pathros through to the Collyridians and finally to women of early modern England.

These four very different religious commentators have all used the same reference from Jeremiah 44 to promulgate the same anti-Catholic message, one that shows how the image of the Virgin became associated with the general vilification of a feminized Catholic Church. Early modern commentary on Jeremiah 44 illuminated a gendered danger, conflating Catholic worship, and by implication the figure of the Queen of Heaven, with the trope of the disobedient woman. The implication was that women were more susceptible to idolatry. Frances Dolan has shown how early modern polemic often represented its targets as feminine, creating the stock figure of the dangerous and disorderly Catholic woman, portrayed as a troubling Other to emergent English Protestant nationalism. The insubordinate women of Pathros from Jeremiah 44 can be seen as an example of this trope, and by association the Queen of Heaven becomes a dangerously active and authoritative figure, a metonym for the Catholic faith as a disruptive female force.[67]

THE HUMBLE AND OBEDIENT VIRGIN PRAISED

In spite of the misogyny that linked the Queen of Heaven to attacks against mother figures and rebellious women, the writings of Protestant polemicists and homilists often trod a fine line between vilification of the Queen of Heaven and praise of the Virgin herself. Returning to John Jewel's descriptions of the idolatrous practices of Jeremiah, we find positive words used to describe Mary as "beautiful, and Holy, and Honourable." His intention, like that of Epiphanius before him, is "not to deface that Blessed Virgin, but to declare the fonde errours of those Heretiques."[68] An acknowledgment of Mary's holiness and purity is a frequent motif in Protestant polemic. The danger, it is argued, comes not from the figure of the Virgin but from how she is interpreted and perceived. The fundamental dichotomy that drives this distinction is the one between the "Protestant" humble Virgin Mary, a paradigm of faith and prayer that is to be emulated and reverenced, and the "Catholic" Queen of Heaven, an abomination that is to be abhorred.

A number of texts offered an alternative way of perceiving the Virgin as a model of humility. In *Synopsis Papismi*, a popular mock dialogue between "Papist" and "Protestant" by controversialist Andrew Willet, one of the topics for debate was the elevation of the Virgin using names such as "Regina mundi, scala coeli, thronus dei" (Queen of the World, Ladder of Heaven, Throne of God). The Protestant response to this was that the Virgin should be praised, but only as a "holy vessel," and that the awarding of such titles wrongly makes her an active agent of redemption: "We doe allow all praise given unto the Virgine, without

the dishonour of God and her Sonne and Saviour Christ: we doe acknowledge the honour that God vouchsafed her, not to be a meritorious
or principall efficient cause of our redemption, but onely an holy ves-
sell, and instrumentall cause of the conception and birth of Christ. . . .
And therefore, those are blasphemous titles which are given unto her,
to call her the ladder of Heaven, and gate of Paradise, and such like: and
so in a manner to make her our redeemer."[69] Willet is emphatic that the
Virgin is not above the saints in power: she is in heaven because of the
strength of her faith. There is, he asserts, nothing exceptional about
the fact that she bore Christ:

> As for that superioritie & higher kind of honour which she hath
> above al the Saints beside, we finde no warrant out of scripture.
> She is respected now in heaven, not as she bare the flesh of Christ,
> but as she lived by faith in Christ: she also rejoyced in God her
> Saviour. The scripture therefore maketh one condition and estate
> of all that shall be saved: and sayth generally of all, of others as well
> as the Virgine Christs mother, That they shall be as the angels in
> heaven. . . . By the which we learne, that other the faithfull servants
> of God may by their faith in Christ, be as well accepted of God, as
> if they had borne Christ in the flesh. Where then is that high digni-
> tie, which she hath, as the mother of Christ, above all Saints? Au-
> gustine saith: *Tu concinis sine fine choris coniuncta, Angelis & Arch-
> angelis sociata*: Thou (O Virgine) doest rejoyce being joyned unto
> the heavenly quire, being associated to Angels and Archangels. He
> maketh her not Ladie or Queene of heaven, but onely a fellow
> companion of the Saints and Angels.[70]

Thus a delicate balance is revealed between praising the Virgin and re-
ducing her position from Queen of Heaven to one of the elect.

A similar balance was struck by the clergyman Thomas Tuke in a
passage that contains the title of part I of this study. Tuke held a number of positions in London churches throughout his life and published
widely.[71] His views here are poised between veneration of the Virgin
and Christological fervor: "Hee made her, that was made of her: Shee
that gave Him Flesh, received both Flesh and Faith from Him; and

though shee brought Him into the world, yet Hee redeemed her out of the world. Some out of vanity will call her the Queene of heaven, shee is in truth a Saint in heaven, shining in heavenly glory. . . . It is the pleasure of some to call her our Lady, a Title which shee knowes belongs not to her, though perhaps endowed with greater grace and glory, then any other Saint besides."[72] *Faith* is a key word here, as it is the Virgin's faith, and not her elevated position as Christ's mother, that earns her a place in heaven in Tuke's Christocentric and egalitarian Protestant vision. Tuke uses words of great beauty to describe the Virgin, but he is emphatic that she is not heaven's queen. The Virgin here has been elevated by man's vanity alone. Her exemplary faith means that she can serve as a model for the faithful to imitate, rather than as an elevated heavenly figure.

The balance between polemic against worship of the Virgin and respect for the Virgin herself was not always successfully struck, however. This manifests itself dramatically in the writings of Thomas Bell. Bell is an interesting figure: a Catholic priest turned Protestant polemicist, whose work displays all the zeal—and uneasiness—of the reformed convert.[73] His 1605 publication *The Woefull Crie of Rome* is an antipapist tract that devotes its final chapter to "Popish adoration, and invocation of Saints."[74] Here, we find a recognizable anxiety about Mary's role as a dominant woman and as Queen of Heaven. After detailing and translating a number of examples of Catholic prayers to the Virgin, Bell observes: "Loe gentle Reader, these prayers (if they be well marked) doe containe every jote of power, right, majestie, glorie, and soveraingtie, whatsoever is or ought to be yeelded unto our Lord Jesus Christ; yea, the two last prayers make the Virgin *Mary*, not onely equall with Christ, but farre above him" (74). Bell talks in tones of disgust about "superstition and grosse idolatrie," but in describing Catholic worship of the Queen of Heaven he uses emotive and sensuous language: "But wee must sacrifice our bodies in mortifying our fleshly desires, unto (the blessed Virgin) the Queene of heaven" (75). The initial voice is not Bell's: he is Englishing the following words of Jacobus de Voragine, author of *The Golden Legend*, on the Virgin's intercessory role: "Nos autem debemus reginae caeli sacrificare corpora nostra, per mortificationem vitiorum: sequitur, unde legitur in vita." What is interesting is the way that Bell does this with such relish, the imagery of "sacrific[ing] our bodies" and "mortifying our fleshly desires" striking a strangely sensuous note. "Fleshly desires" is a particularly vibrant translation of *vitiorum*, one that Bell repeats twice in his text.

In the midst of this, however, comes a muted declaration of respect for the Virgin, which is modestly placed in parentheses:

> Behold here, the daily practise of the Romish church. For first, we see the merits of Saints joyned as a fellow-commissioner, too and with the holy passion of our Lord *Jesus.* Then, we see remission of sinnes and eternall glory, ascribed not onely to the merites of the blessed virgin *Mary*, (whom I honour and reverence in mine heart, as the dearest childe of God, and most blessed Saint in heaven) but also to the merits of all Saints. Yet not onely the blessed virgin, but God himselfe is by this means, most highly dishonoured, his holy name blasphemed, and his proper glory given to his creatures. . . . Alas, alas, how hath the Romish church seduced and bewitched us? (77)

The final words of this quotation are the final words of the text itself, a diatribe against the papacy in a tone that is as ominous as it is animated, one that represents the Catholic Church as a sinful temptress. Bell's qualification about his devotion to the Virgin, and in particular the use of parentheses, feels like something of an afterthought. Ultimately, a balance is not struck in this text between a passionate tone—seen in both Bell's sensuous rhetoric about Catholic veneration of the Virgin Mary and his diatribe against her position as Queen of Heaven—and the simplicity of his professed reverence of the "dearest childe of God." The passionate language wins out and shows perhaps how easy it is to be "seduced and bewitched."

A psychobiographical reading of the imbalance within Bell's text returns us to the writer's own Douai training and his role, prior to his conversion, as a daring and active force in the world of underground Catholicism. These fascinating confessional oscillations aside, Thomas Bell's *Woefull Crie of Rome* reflects a mind-set that is central to polemic against the position of the Queen of Heaven. It reiterates that the Virgin herself is a blameless figure; the tirade of the polemicist is reserved for man, who in error has raised her up, and her elevated position as Queen of Heaven is in mimesis of man's own vanity and folly. But the uneasy ambivalence within Bell's writing reveals in miniature that the balance between devotion to the humble Virgin and excoriation of her queenly image was often a difficult one to strike. The pure image of the Virgin has thus become tainted.

Bell's ambivalent text attempts to wrest the image of humble handmaid away from Queen of Heaven, but this is an unstable bifurcation. To illustrate this further, my final source in this chapter is the teaching of one of the Reformation's most influential thinkers, John Calvin. In 1584, E. P.'s translation of Calvin's 1555 *A Harmonie Upon the Three Evangelists, Matthew Mark and Luke* was published in London. Within this commentary is an imaginative reconstruction of Mary's humility, which embellishes the scanty evidence of the synoptic Gospels with a powerful representation of self-abnegation. Calvin's exegesis of St. Luke's Magnificat is illustrative of the paradigms that had been created of the "Protestant" *ancilla Domini* and the "Catholic" *Regina Coeli*. He emphasizes the Virgin's description of her own "lowliness": "She sheweth the cause why she had the joy of her heart grounded upon God, even because that he of his favour and love looked upon her for in that she calleth her selfe poore, she resigneth all worthinesse from her selfe, and ascribeth the whole cause of her joy, to the free grace and goodnesse of God."[75] When Mary cast herself down, she exalted God, meaning, the text asserts, that it is inappropriate to heap titles such as "Queen of Heaven" upon her:

Whereby we perceive how much the papists differ from her, for what good things soever she had of God, they made small accompt of and unadvisedly they set her foorth wyth their owne vaine inventions: They aboundantly heape up together for her magnifical & more then proud titles, as that she shuld be the Quene of heaven, the starre of salvation, the gate of life, the life, the swetenes, the hope and the health: yea sathan also carried them so farre into impudencie and madnesse, that they gave her power over Christ, for this is their song: Aske the father, commaund thy sonne. (35)

Calvin's influence on the writers cited in this chapter is perhaps here felt in several familiar tropes: the Virgin's titles are listed, and her perceived power over her son is criticized. The characterization of Mary herself is an interesting one. Titles and power, Calvin comments, are not appropriate for a humble woman whose joy comes from God's grace alone: "The papists differ from her." This repositioning of the Virgin, however, presents its own paradoxes. E. P.'s translation of Calvin's work embellishes Mary's biblical persona by ascribing emotions to the Virgin: we are told that she views being represented by titles such as the Queen of Heaven with disdain: "Furthermore, there is nothing more reproche-full to her, then to have her sonne spoiled of that, which was due to him, and that shee her selfe shoulde bee clothed with those sacrilegious spoiles" (35). The claim here is that the elevation of a humble and godly woman to the Queen of Heaven is not only scripturally and morally wrong but also beyond the Virgin's own expectations and desires. The text rails against the Catholic Church for inventing the Virgin Mary as Queen of Heaven, but it falls rather foul of its own criticisms. It too can be viewed as imagining Mary, using her as a mouthpiece for Protestantism's abhorrence of the titles that Catholicism gives her. It is as if one mirage—that of the Queen of Heaven—is being replaced with another, of the faithful, submissive Virgin who is unhappy with the aggrandizement of her image.

The use of the word *clothed* in the description of the Queen of Heaven as "clothed with those sacrilegious spoiles" is loaded with a sense of artifice and places a striking stress on the visual and material. It gives us a glimpse of Mary as a bedecked idol and is also used to illustrate the transgression of investing the Queen of Heaven with the power and veneration that should be due to the son. Later on in the same text, a similar metaphor is used in an exegesis of the Wedding of Cana, which also takes the view that Christ's rough words to his mother could be seen as a warning about the role of the Queen of Heaven. It is an interpretation I have explored earlier in this chapter via the words of John Boys, who was perhaps adapting these words of Calvin: "Therfore Christ speaketh unto his mother on this wise, that he might deliver unto all ages a perpetuall & common doctrine, least the immoderate honour of his mother should darken his divine glory. Furthermore, it is well knowne howe necessarie this admonition was, by those grosse & filthy superstitions which followed afterward. For Marie was made the queene of heaven, the hope, the life, and health of the world. Furthermore, their mad fury went thus far, that they decked her with the things which they tooke from Christe, whom they left naked" (43). The metaphor of clothing the Virgin in titles is continued at this point: the Virgin is bedecked, but this leaves Christ himself naked. This clothing metaphor, associated here with words, is an apt one for the belief that a false representation of the Virgin is being constructed by the titles that are imposed upon her. As with the text's earlier use of the metaphor, there are also strong associations with physical appearance—for in the "decked" Virgin, "clothed" with her titles, is an image of the wealth and adornment of the bedecked statue. Where is the Virgin located at this point: is she humble handmaid or artificial idol? It is as if the image has splintered into two entirely separate Virgins: the dangerously powerful Queen of Heaven and the humble and obedient Protestant model who is shocked by the title that the Catholic faith is bestowing upon her. This bifurcation—and some of the more extreme reactions to it—will be discussed in my next chapter.

Many different early modern voices have spoken in this chapter, giving an indication of the Queen of Heaven's continuing presence and relevance in Elizabethan and Jacobean culture and of the many ways in which the image was deployed. These frequent references may be transparently derogatory, but they also reveal that the contentious image of the Queen of Heaven was still being discussed and debated. In the vehement excoriations of the Virgin's role as Queen of Heaven is evidence of a profound anxiety, which, set in a secular context, becomes anxiety about female queens. Most prevalent, however, have been the sectarian associations of this image. Attacks on the Queen of Heaven link her with domineering Catholic female presences, and this manifestation of the Virgin was frequently perceived as dangerous. It thus became part of the polemicist's armory in the construction of a powerful sense of otherness with regard to Catholic methods of devotion. The constant repetition of "they" in many of the texts explored in this chapter reinforces this sense of difference. The figure of the Queen of Heaven therefore has a significant part to play in adding to early modern discourses that contributed toward an emerging sense of Protestant nationalism. Invective against the Queen of Heaven was also integral to the Protestant redefinition of the Virgin as a humble and obedient handmaid. She was the "Catholic" rival to the humble "Protestant" model: two opposing forces were constructed within the same symbol. This polarization was not always entirely successful and can be viewed as leading to an unstable representation of the Virgin's pure image.

CHAPTER 3

Sham Queens of Heaven

Iconoclasm and the Virgin Mary

*To pray to a statue is to take the dead for the living, the image
for the substance, the estuary for the source, the false for the true—
and thus the devil for God. These images do have their potency!*

—Hugh Latimer

In 1538, the bishop of Worcester, Hugh Latimer, ordered that a popular
statue of Our Lady of Worcester should be stripped bare of its jewels
and clothing. The statue was taken to London, along with the statues of
Our Lady of Walsingham and Our Lady of Ipswich, and ritually burnt.[1]
On the surface, this seems like a shocking and violent act, the destruction of a beloved material object that had for many years been imbued
with great spiritual value. The symbolic resonances of this example of
Reformation iconoclasm are more subtle than this, however. Hugh Latimer was one of the Reformation's most prolific advocates of iconoclasm. His comment that in praying to images man takes the "devil for
God" is scaremongering stuff.[2] The idol may be alluring—Latimer admits that "images do have their potency," but the devil can of course
adopt an attractive guise. One way of justifying such iconoclastic violence was to state that it was not a representation of the Virgin that

was being destroyed but a devilish figure that had assumed her form. Writing to Thomas Cromwell, Latimer described the statue of Our Lady of Worcester as a "great sibyl." He observed that along with "her older sister of Walsingham, her younger sister of Ipswich," she would "make a jolly muster at Smithfield," a description that holds a chilling prophecy of his own execution at the stake in 1555.[3] Latimer's choice of the word *sibyl* here is an interesting one. Although the first reported association of the word with witchcraft was not until 1589, it is likely, considering the tone of Latimer's observations, that this was his intended meaning.[4] But the word *sibyl* also means prophetess: it describes a woman, often disorderly and maddened, who possesses supernatural powers. The medieval sibylline tradition gave the female seer a powerful role as prophetess of Christ's passion, while *The Golden Legend* told of how the Tiburtine Sibyl had shown to Augustus a vision of the Virgin herself in heaven.[5] Latimer's words to Cromwell ironically animate these popular statues of the Virgin; the iconoclastic and misogynistic zeal of his tone is clear, but he is also representing the Virgin Mary as a dangerously powerful woman who needs to be destroyed.

In the previous chapter, my focus was on words, both written and spoken. The popularity of sermons in late sixteenth- and early seventeenth-century culture is an indication of the logocentricity of early Protestantism, privileging word rather than image. This chapter will explore iconoclastic reactions to the image of the Queen of Heaven. Although it thus appears to be a shift from words to the visual image, my study is still at its core a logocentric one: my focus is on how words can be used to destroy images that are created in the mind. In her magisterial *England's Iconoclasts*, Margaret Aston argued that the breaking of images was the destruction of a mind-set as well as of material objects.[6] The most beloved and most contentious of all female religious images was that of the Queen of Heaven. The iconoclastic story of the statues of Our Lady of Worcester, Walsingham, and Ipswich shows how a concrete image of the Virgin could be stripped of its finery and physically destroyed—but shifting mind-sets was a more subtle process. Taking the view that iconoclasm can occur within texts as well as to material objects, I will show in this chapter how writers attempted to destroy the thread of devotion that clearly still existed between worshipper and the treasured image of the Queen of Heaven by demonizing and mocking the image itself. I have discussed how the representation of the Virgin as Queen of Heaven was frequently the subject of bitter, often misogynistic attacks in printed religious discourse. The radical bifurcation of "Protestant" Mary as *ancilla Domini* and "Catholic" Mary as *Regina Coeli* led to a destabilizing of iconography of the Virgin, as Protestant writers sought to wrest the image away from perceptions of queenly grandeur and power. The passage from Calvin that ended the previous chapter expressed a deep-seated unease that the image of Mary as Queen of Heaven turned her into something she was not. The next step was to decide that if the Queen of Heaven was not Mary, she must be someone else. The most extreme manifestation of this came in the construction of what I will term in this chapter a "sham Queen of Heaven," a dissembling impostor of dubious morality who was masquerading as the Virgin but who was in fact an entirely different figure. This, I will argue, represents a particularly potent iconoclastic literary paradigm.

In the first section of the chapter, I will detail some of the vehement early modern written attacks against man's attraction to the idol. I will then explore examples of literary iconoclasm in two texts. The first, *Pasquine in a Traunce*, is a Protestant satire by the Italian reformer Celio Secondo Curione, which was translated into English in the mid-sixteenth century. In it, the marked distinction between humble Protestant handmaid and Catholic Queen of Heaven is foregrounded by the creation of two different sham Virgin Marys: a statue of the Queen of Heaven, who is peevish, vain, and morally suspect, and the queen of the false Catholic heaven, a shadowy figure empowered only by the artifice of man. My second text is book 1 of Spenser's Protestant allegory *The Faerie Queene*, a work that was possibly influenced by Curione. An analysis of Spenser's work will show how the paradigm of the sham Queen of Heaven can influence readings of oblique Marian imagery in imaginative writing. One of the many layers of allusion within the character of Lucifera is to a false Queen of Heaven. Meanwhile, the sorceress Duessa represents not only loathing for the Catholic Church but also anxiety about the alluring appearance of the idol. Duessa too can be viewed as a sham Queen of Heaven, artificially beautiful but spiritually filthy. Finally, the chapter will foreground some of the paradoxes and problems that come from splintering the image of the Virgin in this way, particularly when the figure of a sham Queen of Heaven is conflated with the loathed anti-Catholic symbol of the Whore of Babylon from the book of Revelation.

Fundamental to this exploration is an awareness of the Protestant reading of female archetypes in Revelation. John Bale's 1547 publication *The Image of Both Churches* offered two diametrically opposed paradigms that soon became commonplace in Reformation thinking, the Woman Clothed with the Sun as the true church, and the Whore of Babylon as the corrupt, popish church.[7] In the book of Revelation, Saint John the Divine is carried into the wilderness, where he encounters the following figure:

> I sawe a woman sit upon a skarlat coloured beast, full of names of blasphemie, which had seven heads, & ten hornes.
>
> The woman was arrayed in purple and skarlat, and guilded with golde, and precious stones, and pearles, and had a cup of golde in her hand, ful of abominations, and filthiness of her fornication. (Rev. 17:3–4)

The figure of the Whore of Babylon is glossed in the Geneva Bible thus: "This woman is the Anti-christ, that is, the Pope with the whole bodie of his filthie creatures" (Rev. 17:3, note f). The Whore of Babylon was frequently evoked by anti-Catholic polemic as a symbol of both a feminized papacy and a disorderly Catholic woman. As Alison Shell has observed, the Whore of Babylon's presence was ubiquitous in early modern literature as "the most powerful anti-Catholic icon of all."[8]

In binary opposition to this is the Revelation figure of the Woman Clothed with the Sun, who has a crown of twelve stars and the moon under her feet. In chapter 1, I discussed how this image was traditionally associated with the assumption and coronation of the Virgin, but it was redefined by Protestant thinkers such as Bale to represent Christ's church. In the words of the Geneva Bible: "The Church which is compassed about with Jesus Christ the Sonne of righteousness, is persecuted of Antichrist" (Rev. 12:1, note a). The image of the Woman Clothed with the Sun was also used in relation to godly Protestant women such as Anne Askew, Lady Jane Grey, and Elizabeth I herself.[9] My exploration of literary iconoclasm in this chapter will indicate the extent to which reformist writing led to a discursive shift in the Virgin's representation in relation to these two Revelation paradigms. The Virgin's associations with the Woman Clothed with the Sun were mocked and discredited, but in pejorative descriptions of the Queen of Heaven she was often represented in a way that was uncannily analogous to the Whore of Babylon.

This is a study about literary iconoclasm: how words can be used as a force for destruction. One of the most influential and evocative studies of the physical iconoclasm of the Reformation is Eamon Duffy's *The Stripping of the Altars*.[10] On another level, however, Duffy's prose also indicates just how destructive words themselves can be. *The Stripping of the Altars* gives a beautifully written reconstruction of the faith of the late medieval everyman, in which the link between the visual image and personal faith is consistently presented as powerful. Duffy's prose is so persuasive in its descriptions of late medieval piety that when it sets about the Reformation's work of destroying this vibrant world one feels almost emotionally engaged. The chapters describing Edward VI's reign are where the real stripping of the altars occurs, and it is here that some of Duffy's most emotive and personal vocabulary is unleashed in analysis that at times shows an almost self-reflexive awareness of the iconoclastic power of words. Amid the linguistic violence of the stripping of the altars, for example, comes a glimmer of late medieval piety, a luxuriantly sibilant description of medieval celebrations at St Paul's Cathedral at Whitsun, when it was the custom for "a great censer, emitting clouds of sweet smoke and sparks, to be swung from the roof . . . and for doves to be released." This beautiful description is followed by the blunt "Such gestures had no place in the world of reformers," and it is hard not to feel a sense of loss.[11]

Duffy's use of imagery shows us how iconoclasm can occur within a text itself: he sets up a beautiful image, only to destroy it before our inner eye. The power of words to evoke pictures in the mind brings with it a number of iconoclastic ambiguities. Sir Philip Sidney's description of poetry as "a speaking picture" in *The Defence of Poesy* is an evocative interpretation of *ut pictura poesis* that shows just how hard it is to disentangle word from image.[12] Sidney's is a positive analogy, but the tension between word and image has underpinned a number of studies exploring the relationship between iconoclasm and literary culture.[13] James Siemon's *Shakespearean Iconoclasm* builds a persuasive case, both historically and theoretically, for adding *iconoclasm* to the arsenal of critical vocabulary used to analyze Shakespeare's language.[14] In *Iconoclasm and Poetry*, Ernest Gilman is similarly convincing about the presence of literary iconoclasm, arguing that in Protestant writing one frequently finds a "creative confusion," the result of a "battlefield" in which the inward imaging of the mind was called into question as well as the outer iconoclasm of picture and statue.[15]

EARLY MODERN ATTACKS ON ICONOCLASM

The worshipper's fraught and emotive relationship with devotional images is one of the touchstones of the Reformation, but by this time, fear of religious images had already engendered a story that had been played and replayed at several junctures in the history of Christianity.[16] England's own iconoclastic history mirrors what Aston has termed "the zigzag course of the Reformation" and is marked by many inconsistencies and reversals.[17] The first big, sanctioned wave of iconoclasm in England in the 1530s included the burning of statues of the Virgin in 1538, but it did not signal an outright removal of all images.[18] Although by Elizabeth's time the laity had become accustomed to worshipping in churches that were stripped of images, this was not a story with a conclusive ending. The anxiety about the image as idol that is displayed in late Tudor writing provides further indication of the inchoate nature of England's Reformation at this time.[19]

The Elizabethan *Homily Against Peril of Idolatry* is an example of this: it is an impassioned, pulpit-thumping piece that aimed to inscribe idolatry on the English conscience as a deadly sin. Probably the work of John Jewel, it is a fine testament both to state-sanctioned attitudes toward images in the late sixteenth century and to the anxiety that the ecclesiastical image still continued to evoke.[20] The dissemination of ideas from the *Book of Homilies* was widespread. The majority of parish priests were required to read from it, and such a uniform delivery of exegesis can be viewed as a way of controlling parish clergy, as well as an attempt to regulate the hearts and minds of their congregations.[21] The *Homily Against Peril of Idolatry* rehearses a number of concepts that are fundamental to iconoclastic polemic of the time. Its recurring message is that image and idol are one and the same in the scriptures. Images used in worship should therefore be removed. "Scriptures use the said two words, *idols* and *images*, indifferently for one thing anyway," the homilist tells us, and those who bedeck images, and the interior of churches, "greatly hurt the simple and unwise, occasioning them thereby to commit most horrible idolatry" (168).

Particularly interesting about the *Homily Against Peril of Idolatry* is the way it gives us an indication of the continuing appeal of the idol to the worshipper. The homilist makes it patently clear that the preacher of the Word has a battle to fight. He uses the imagery of "poison" for the idol and "remedy" for preaching, but it is clear that the poison is an appealing one that is "continually and deeply drunk of many," while "the remedy [is] seldom and faintly tasted of a few" (243). The *Homily* also frequently uses shocking, sexualized language, both following and reinforcing a trope of the period that linked idolatry with spiritual whoredom. This found its roots in Jeremiah 3:9, where Israel, by ignoring the Lord and worshipping Baal, is described as a harlot who "hathe even defiled the land: for she hathe committed fornicacion with stones and stockes." The phrase "stones and stockes" for the deadness of the idol was a repeated motif in Reformist polemic, and the concept of committing fornication with these inanimate objects was both terrifying and scurrilous. Early modern iconoclastic literature frequently dwells on the imagery of this Jeremiah reference, turning idol into whore and worshipper into lecher.

The *Homily* powerfully utilizes this metaphor of spiritual whoredom; it is permeated with the language of lust and sexual attraction. Man, the homilist argues, is sexually weak; if he sees a "wanton harlot" (247), he will be unable to resist her, and the worshipper before an idol is prone to the same weakness. The homilist also likens the Catholic Church, bedecked in finery, to a harlot, demonizing the Catholic Church through gendered language:

For she, being indeed not only an harlot (as the Scriptures calleth her) but also a foul, filthy, old withered harlot . . . doth (after the custom of such harlots) paint herself, and deck and tire herself with gold, pearl, stone, and all kind of precious jewels; that she, shining with the outward beauty and glory of them, may please the foolish fantasy of fond lovers, and so entice them to spiritual fornication with her: who, if they saw her, I will not say naked, but in simple apparel, would abhor her as the foulest and filthiest harlot that was ever seen; according as appeareth by the description of the garnishing of the great strumpet of all strumpets, the mother of whoredom, set forth by St. John in his Revelation. (261)

The extended metaphor is of the idolatrous Catholic Church as a vain and immoral harlot adorning herself in gold and jewels, with the idolatrous worshipper as the lecher. Spiritual filth here is physically animated, as the outward beauty of the idol masks a foul and filthy reality. If men saw the true nature of the idol, they would abhor her, the homilist concludes, in the way that they loathe the Whore of Babylon. The influence of the *Homily Against Peril of Idolatry*, with its vicious invective against spiritual whoredom and fornication, was far-reaching, and its presence (it is by far the longest of the homilies) is an indication of the anxiety that the religious image still continued to evoke. The language of the *Homily* shows how Reformation writing consciously set out to break devotional threads between worshipper and beloved—particularly female—spiritual images. This in itself presents the religious image as a site of discursive power.

The sexualized, gendered language of the *Homily* indicates that a reading of iconoclasm in terms of a misogynistic discourse is a fruitful one. In *Whores of Babylon*, Frances Dolan shows how gender issues were inseparable from religion in early modern discourse, and the prevalence of the use of the term *Whore of Babylon* itself in Protestant polemic perfectly encapsulates how Catholic corruption and otherness were frequently aligned with the female form. Arthur Marotti similarly has observed how Catholic women were often portrayed as seductresses, who were a danger to the souls of Protestant men: "Protestant iconoclasm and misogyny shared a basic set of assumptions about . . . the seductive dangers of the feminine. Woman and Catholicism were both feared as intrinsically idolatrous, superstitious, and carnal, if not also physically disgusting."[22] This discourse can be read into imaginative writing. In *Staging Reform, Reforming the Stage*, Huston Diehl identifies a pattern of "bewhored images," in which the sacred image of a beautiful woman came to be likened by reformers to the sexualized woman, thus turning the devotional gaze into the erotic gaze.[23] Diehl comments that of all idols the Virgin Mary was the subject of the most vitriol: "Iconoclastic discourse transforms the most sacred images of the Roman Catholic Church—and most especially the revered and adored images of the Virgin Mary—into harlots whose betrayal is inevitable and whose allure is fatal."[24] I would like in this chapter to make a further distinction: the iconoclast sometimes was bewhoring an image not of the Virgin but of the Queen of Heaven. This was not the true Virgin but another figure entirely.

One way to eradicate traces of devotion to the "revered and adored" image of the Queen of Heaven was to expose her as a seductive but vain and morally dubious sham. An example of this can be found in the work of Marnix van St. Aldegonde, a Dutch Protestant and prolific author who studied under both Théodore de Bèze and John Calvin. His 1579 anti-Catholic polemic, *The Bee Hive of the Romish Church*, a commentary on the teachings of the Catholic theologian Gentian Hervetus, was translated into English by George Gylpen and was reprinted many times.[25] The text observes that there is another Mary—a Catholic Mary—who seeks the glory that the title of the Queen of Heaven bestows upon her:

> This Ladie is greatly desirous of glorie and honour, and coveteth to bee accepted and worshipped for the Queene of Heaven, and also to have the preeminence before all the Saintes of Paradise: For shee is of an other disposition than the holy Virgin Marie (the mother of Jesus Christ) was, who did acknowledge her selfe to bee a poore handmaide of God, and did direct those which needed any thing unto her sonne Jesus Christ. But this standes bedeckt and garnished with Golde and Silver like a Queene, and willes that we should reverence and adore her clothes and jewels, her Churches and Chappels, her gilded cofers and other her furniture, utensils, and implementes, like unto the everlasting and living God. To conclude, the holie Church hath made her Queene.[26]

Here is another Virgin Mary, one created by the Catholic Church, a proud and vain woman who wants to be worshipped for her finery. She is completely different from the real Virgin, who is "a poore handmaide of God," submissively directing worshippers toward Christ rather than exerting any power herself. Significantly, her appearance is described as being "like a Queene": this alternative figure is not a queen in her own right but has usurped a place that is not rightly hers.

It could be argued that, conceptually speaking, the medieval pilgrimage tradition laid the foundations for this strand of polemic. Michael Carroll has noted that the presence of statues at Marian shrines led to a tendency to "splinter the image of Mary into a range of personalities, each of which [became] the object of an extensive cult."[27] Carroll terms these "madonnine images," observing that different qualities and powers were attributed to each one. This splintering can be seen in the English pilgrimage tradition, where "Our Lady of Walsingham" was perceived as a subtly different entity in the worshipper's mind from "Our Lady of Ipswich" or "Our Lady of Willesden."[28] A statue of the Queen of Heaven thus became a specific, topographical embodiment, a material object that the worshipper had seen and touched, and the implication was of not one but many Marys in different places, with whom the believer might have different relationships. Integral to this was the temptation to animate the inanimate: a statue of Our Lady was frequently both anthropomorphized and imbued with thaumaturgic power. The Reformation's destruction of the Virgin's image represents a rupture from medieval traditions—particularly the pilgrimage tradition, which often had a statue of the Virgin as its heart—but there was also an unnerving continuity at play. The many different statues of the pilgrimage tradition served to splinter the image of the Virgin; Reformation dichotomies of humble handmaid and Queen of Heaven continued to conceptualize the Virgin's image as splintered, albeit in a polemical, rather than devotional, way.

TWO QUEENS OF HEAVEN IN THE PROTESTANT
VISIONS OF CURIONE'S *PASQUINE*

Pasquino in Estasi (1545), by the Italian reformer Celio Secondo Curione, gives a sustained representation of a splintered image of the Virgin Mary. Curione was a leading voice among Italian Protestants living in exile in Switzerland, and he enjoyed considerable fame as a scholar.[29] He was based in exile in Basle but was part of a group of Italian reformers who enjoyed a close intellectual relationship with many English humanists and reformers, including Anthony Cooke and John Ponet. The royal tutor and renowned teacher John Cheke met Curione in 1554, and the two men kept up a regular correspondence. *Pasquino in Estasi* is one of a series of pasquinades in which Curione employs a genre of satire that gives voice to a statue, Pasquine, or Pasquil.[30] It details Pasquine's visions of heaven, hell, and purgatory and his encounters with false representations of the Virgin as Queen of Heaven. The genre Curione uses, the pasquinade, originated in the third century BC, from the popular custom of affixing satirical epigrams to a battered Hellenistic statue in the Campidoglio in Rome. The statue was disinterred in the early sixteenth century, and the custom of attaching satirical writings to its mutilated form was revived.[31] The pasquinade soon found its way from postings in public spaces into print. During the Reformation, Pasquine's voice was often used to lampoon points of doctrine, and a mock literary salon was established, as other statues were introduced to debate with him.[32] Perhaps the most prominent use of the genre in England came from the pen of Thomas Nashe, who used the pseudonym "Pasquil of England" in his anti-Puritan pamphlets written in the Marprelate Controversy.[33]

In 1565–66 and later in 1584, two English editions of Curione's *Pasquino in Estasi* entitled *Pasquine in a Traunce* were published in London, translated by W. P.[34] These editions of Curione's text form part of a revival of interest in translations of theology from Continental reformers. Anne Overell describes "a flood of Italian reform literature appearing on the ever-expanding book market in the 'long seventies,' from 1569 until about 1584"; this revival tapped into anti-Catholic and anti-Spanish war fever and was part of a body of writing that pitted "Italians-against-the-pope."[35] The fact that Curione's text was published by such high-profile Protestant printers is also worthy of note. The initial edition was printed by William Seres, one of the most prominent printers and booksellers of the English Reformation, who enjoyed the protection of William Cecil, while the second edition was printed by the London printer Thomas Este, who was known for producing anti-Catholic books.[36]

Pasquine in a Traunce takes the form of a satirical dialogue between Pasquine and another statue, Marforius.[37] This was a particularly popular form of the satire in which the ignorant but pliable Marforius asked the questions and the knowing Pasquine provided the answers. Pasquine here represents a Protestant reformer while Marforius stands for the old faith, but his is an old faith that is desperate for education from the new. "For this Religion wherein I have so long time lived," he declaims at one point, "hath in such sorte blinded me" (sig. B1r). To educate Marforius, who is something of a proxy for the reader, Pasquine describes his visions, in which he visits a true heaven and a false heaven, and uses this as a way of correcting Marforius's traditionalist Catholic viewpoint. Throughout all of this there runs a rather delicious irony: two animated statues speak out against iconoclasm, in a witty mimicry of the Catholic statue's perceived thaumaturgic powers. The use of the dialogue form gives Curione's waspish satire full rein, as he can criticize the Catholic faith using the voice of others; in Pasquine's seemingly innocent descriptions of his visions, the worst excesses of the papacy are presented as literal embodiments, brought to life in exaggerated form.

Pasquine seeks to reeducate Marforius about the appropriate way to venerate the Virgin, and the result is an intriguingly protean representation of Mary in which several versions of her image exist in conflict with one another. There are a number of pejorative references to the Queen of Heaven within this dialogue. At the beginning of the work, the two statues muse on man's historical tendency toward idolatry. Pasquine describes how the Jews became trapped in a vicious cycle of worshipping Baal. His descriptions include another example of the Jeremiah 44 reference I have discussed in the previous chapter, further evidence of just how embedded a cultural commonplace it was: "For feare and for the Religion of miracles, the Jewes could not rid themselves of the worshipping of Baal, nay, they said sometime, that bicause they had left of worshipping of him, that was cause of all their miseryes, as may be sene in Jeremy, where he sayth: Since we lefte of to do sacrifice to the Queene of heaven, we have had scarsitie of all thinges" (sig. B2r). However, the main Queen of Heaven whom the statues discuss is the Virgin Mary herself. The gulf between Catholic representations of the Virgin as *Beata Virgo* (a bedecked statue of the Queen of Heaven) and the real Virgin Mary is so wide, Pasquine decides, that there must be two Virgin

Marys—the Mary who lived and the Mary who has subsequently been "set upon the Aultars":[38] "Take thou which thou wilt, among all the Saintes, yea if thou wouldest take the Virgin Marye, who hath the chiefest place, and then consider well, after what sorte she was in tymes past, while she lived, and in what sorte she is nowe, after she became to be Deified: And thou shalt finde, that I doubt not without cause, whether she that is set upon the Aultars, be the selfe same that was mother of the Lord" (sig. A4v).

Marforius's description of Mary during her earthly life is a textbook Protestant representation of a modest, humble Virgin. According to the scriptures, he says, "She was Virgin moste chaste, moste modest in behaviour, moste holy, most humble above all other creatures" (sig. A4v). Pasquine develops this image further, adding that she was "full of charity towarde the poore, without anye jote of covetousnesse, without desire of gayne, or ryches, not devouring the price of the Dogge, not esteeming Beades nor costly garments" (sig. A4v).[39] The reference to the true Virgin Mary's dismissal of "Beades" shows the antirosary sentiments of the Protestant reformer, something I shall return to in chapter 6 of this book. How, Pasquine asks, can this bear any resemblance to a grandiose statue of the Virgin? "Thou seest therfore, what she was once, now tel me what thou thinkst by this, that with so much wax, with so much golde & silver, with so many chaynes & brouches, & with so many perfumes, the world doth at this day honor" (sig. B1r). Marforius is frightened to say anything against this *Beata Virgo*, as he fears her vengeful streak: "Beside that I doubt, that if I should say any thing against hir, she would forthwith be revenged upon me" (sig. B1r). He is similarly frightened of the vindictive nature of the saints, for "they have done straunge and cruell miracles" (sig. B1v). Surely, Pasquine says, a saint who has been meek and godly on earth cannot be vengeful and violent in his or her venerated form. If they had been alive, would they have behaved in this cruel way? Marforius capitulates, admitting that they would not, because they showed goodness and patience in their lives.

A similar argument is applied to the differences between the *Beata Virgo*, venerated on earth, and the "true" Virgin Mary in heaven. Curione uses Pasquine's voice to express contempt for the earthly construction of a decorated statue of the Queen of Heaven: "For me thought it a thing unlikelye, that this Saint Mary here belowe, that hath the painting

on hir face, that hath crownes full of Jewels on hir heade, that hath
Chaynes aboute hir necke, that hath Ringes on her fingers, that hath
so costly and so many sortes of garmentes upon hir, like one of those
yong Girles of olde time, me thought it not I say, that this was al one,
with that most humble mother of the Lorde, and so much the more
I confirmed my selfe in this opinion" (sig. C1r). Pasquine's criticism
goes beyond appearances. He also invents patterns of behavior for this
painted sham Queen of Heaven. This Virgin, he confirms to himself,
cannot be the mother of God, not only because of the way she looks
but also because of the way she acts: "I sawe this Lady to be most
covetous, moste desirous to heape uppe treasure, and most nigardly
in spending it, and if she let any thing of hir owne goe out of hir handes, shee delt it most wickedly, so that I sayd often to my self, if this be
the Lords mother, why hath she not compassion upon her sonne,
whom she seeth every day in the church where she is, goe aboute asking almes" (sig. C1r). In a playful literary mimesis, Pasquine, himself
an animated statue, here animates a statue of the Virgin Mary. There is
more than a whiff of the indecorous about Pasquine's *Beata Virgo*. The
descriptions of the bejeweled Virgin with a painted face gesture toward harlotry, an analogy that intensifies when Pasquine describes this
sham Virgin Mary's encouragement of lewd behavior. She is, he says, a
woman who is mean-spirited toward the poor, yet generous with her
bounty to a holy father who goes on pilgrimages to Loreto, offering
him all that she has to spend on "whores, dogges, horses and Gani-
medes" (sigs. C1r–C1v). This embodiment of the Virgin Mary, Pasquine concludes, is very far from "that true and most pure Virgin the
Lord's mother, the which above all other things hated this filthy kind
of men" (sig. C1v).

Some indication of the enduring influence of Curione's text can be
found in the clergyman Thomas Mason's 1615 reworking of extracts
from *Foxe's Book of Martyrs*, which features a lengthy description of
Pasquine in a Traunce. Curione is described as "a zealous, godly,
learned man," in whose writing "the whole packe of the Popes pedlary
wares is laid open, that we may see what stuffe it is."[40] Thomas Mason's
work repeats Pasquine's descriptions of the *Beata Virgo* at length: "The
Virgin Mary was not honored with so many chaines, bracelets, per-

fumes, gold, silver, and wax, as she is now upon the Altar, with paint-ings on her face, and on her head crownes full of Jewels. She is attired with costly and many sorts of garments like a yong gyrle, they make her most covetous and niggardly, and to give nothing to the poore, but to bestow all that is given her, (which is aboundance) upon Cardinals and Hipocrites, to be bestowed upon Whores, Dogs, and Horses."[41] Representations of the Queen of Heaven here intersect with a particu-larly vivid strain of anti-Catholic discourse that portrayed the Catholic Church as a whorish woman whose beauty was merely cosmetic.[42] In Curione's text, retold by Thomas Mason, it is the Virgin Mary in her guise as bedecked queenly statue that is presented as the embodiment of this trope.

Pasquine's Vision of a Papal Heaven

Because Pasquine is perturbed by this duality—between false earthly representations of the Virgin and the saints and the heavenly reality—he decides to take a trip to heaven: "I sawe these Saintes to be so farre different from that they were sometime, I would nedes goe to heaven purposely to see, whether they have there above the selfe same nature" (sig. C1r). *Pasquine in a Traunce* describes Pasquine's visions in detail. Once he has succeeded in reaching a state of trance, Pasquine is visited by an angel of true and sacred visions, who becomes his guide. The angel tells him that there are in fact two heavens, the true heaven that Christ ascended to and a false heaven, which was "builded by the handes of Popes and mortall men, who had small skill in building" (sig. D1v). Pasquine is first led by an angel, not to the true heaven, but to the false "Pope's heaven," which is situated some way from the sun (sig. D1v). He finds himself in a great walled city, a pseudo-Rome with a maze of towers and many gates by which spirits enter laden with rosa-ries, oil, incense, and precious stones. This false heaven is a place of greed and materialism. It has the appearance of a great city, but, Pas-quine wryly observes, "I thinke surelye that it will shortly come to naught, bycause it hath the foundations of it very weake, and made with little skill for so great a building" (sig. D4r).

After debating the representation of the saints and the Virgin on earth, Marforius is understandably anxious to know whether the saints are to be found in this papal heaven. Pasquine answers that the saints are there in name "but by their looke and by their maners, they be very unlyke Saintes" (sig. E1r). Instead, they are "divelles, in forme of Saintes, that under this coverture deceive the world" (sig. E1r). This chapter began with Bishop Latimer's assertion that, in praying to an image, man is taking "the devil for God"; just like Latimer, Curione here warns that, in praying to images of the saints, man is being trapped into consorting with the devil. These devil-saints are at home in a place of materialism: the whole heaven, Pasquine observes, "seemed rather to be a Market, or a Court, than a heaven" (sig. E1r). The climax of Pasquine's vision comes when he reaches a palace, which stands in the middle and at the highest part of this popish parody of the heavenly city. This palace has clearly been built at great cost but is as yet unfinished. It is completely covered over and is lit only by candles and the glare from tables that are laden with gold and silver, for "the Saints of this heaven can abide no light" (sig. R2r).

It is here that Pasquine encounters the text's second sham Queen of Heaven: "In the heart of the Pallace in a highe seate sate a Queene, of a duskishe colour, which had at her backe the Sonne and at her feete the Moone" (sig. R2v) The queen of this materialistic, false heaven is a shadowy and exotic figure, who is "of a duskishe colour." This is perhaps a conflation of two forms of otherness, Catholic and Islamic, in a text that elsewhere states that "Mahomet and the Pope are brothers" (sig. S2v), an alliance of two loathed enemies that can be frequently found in the polemic of the period.[43] Although this strange and exotic queen has the sun at her back and the moon at her feet, she does not emit the radiance and light that one might expect. The sun that clothes her "hath not his beames at libertie," says Pasquine, as its light has been obscured: "This Sonne is compassed about with a payre of Beads, the which, Saint Dominicks Friers have put rounde about it, so that it can not spread forth his light: & for this cause the place remaineth darke, and needeth candels and lampes" (sigs. R2v–R3r). Curione's sham Queen of Heaven is also a sham Woman Clothed with the Sun in a satirical mockery that destabilizes traditional Catholic associations of the Virgin with this figure from Revelation. Curione's false queen is clothed not in true light but in the artificial light of candles and lamps. The sun itself has become stifled, in imagery that speaks of popish darkness obscuring the light of truth. The "payre of Beads" that obscures the sun is "That, which they call our Lady Psalter, that which the hoggish herde of Friers, do also cal the Rosarie, that with the which the Paternosters, or rather the Avemaries, are given by tale to God, nay rather to the Devill, that which every foolishe woman caryeth in her hande, when she goeth out of her dores in the morning, that which is sayde more with the hands then with the heart" (sig. R3r). Pasquine's description of "every foolishe woman" carrying the rosary is a further savaging of this Catholic prayer, as well as an indication of how frequently pejorative descriptions of Catholic worship became gendered.

There is a deeper level of deception and artifice to the image of the queen of the popish heaven. Marforius wonders how the sun, with all its magnificence and power, can be captured and contained in such a space. Pasquine replies that the sun and moon that surround this queen are not as they seem: "Thou must understande, that there is a great difference betweene that Sonne and the Moone, which we see in this world, and them that clothe this Queene" (sig. R3r). Our perceptions of what is real and what is artificial constantly collapse in these descriptions. Pasquine's shadowy, sinister queen of his popish heaven sits surrounded by artificial light. At first we think this is because the symbols of light that clothe her are signifiers of obfuscating Catholic practices—the candles and lamps around her seem to be from the interior of a Catholic church—but the sources of natural light in this false heaven are themselves revealed to be false.

Within this heaven is a Council of Saints and Angels. It is a parodic Council of Trent, which prefigures the Stygian Council in Milton's Pandemonium. This complicated and hierarchical body is driven by a desire to maintain the pope's tyrannical authority and to break "the bonds of peace and love, and the yoke of our Maister and Savior Christ" (sig. R4v). Marforius wonders about Christ's role in this council: "Thou haste told me nothing of Christ," he observes, "sawest thou him there in the councel among those Saintes?" (sig. T1v). Pasquine's reply shows the extent to which this false heaven breaks the bonds of Christ's authority:

"I sawe him not, but as I came out afterward, I sawe before the Pallace a little childe that played with certaine other children there, of whome, when I had asked, it was tolde me that it was Christ, who fell to playing and therefore came not to the Councell, for his mother had the whole charge of all things" (sigs. T1v–T2r). "Is Christ alwayes a childe in this heaven?" asks Marforius; Pasquine's reply is an unequivocal "Yea always" (sig. T2r). Anxieties about the role of the Virgin as Queen of Heaven and overbearing mother, so prevalent in the printed religious discourse discussed in the previous chapter, are here imaginatively brought to life in a witty vision of Mary as a manipulative queen-mother-regnant figure. Christ is kept as a child who is more interested in playing than theology, and this allows his mother to exercise full control.

PASQUINE'S PROTESTANT HEAVEN

After his visit to this false heaven, Pasquine's trance takes him to an alternative, Protestant heaven. In the false heaven he has encountered dimness, shadows, and artificial light, but here he is dazzled by natural brightness. The true heaven does have a queen; Pasquine initially presumes that she is the Virgin Mary but soon realizes that she is in fact the church: "One I saw clothed in that garment, that the Psalme speaketh of. My hart hath indyted a good matter. Hir espouse was Christ, and I tooke hir to have beene the virgin Mary, but myne Aungel tolde me, that it was the Church" (sig. U2v). Marforius asks whether the Virgin Mary has any ruling role in this heaven; he receives the reply that foregrounds the Virgin's humility: "Shee for hir part, and after hir maner, adourneth & garnisheth the body of the espouse" (sig. U2v). Marforius is still perplexed. Why is this true queen, this spouse of Christ, so little known? Pasquine's reply is that the jealous popes have raised up the Virgin Mary: "Bycause the Popes have advaunced themselves above hir, and have usurped unto themselves hir authority, and made lawes after their owne devises, without having any regarde unto hir. And bycause the things should not be applyed unto them, whiche the holye scripture speaketh of the Church, therefore have they thrust into the place of the Church, the virgin Marye, and have attributed all things unto hir, and have called hir Queene and Empresse of heaven, and our Advocate, so that the name of the true Queene is utterly abolished and lost" (sig. U3r). The sham Queen of Heaven that this text has constructed is a figure who is a reflective representation of man's own vanity, a false monarch who has usurped the place of the true church. The fact that she has been elevated by man also explains the evasiveness of this figure in the popish heaven; Curione's image needs the machinations of man to maintain it.

The statues then fall to discussing the appearance of this alternative queen, the church, which is in stark contrast to the bejeweled earthly representations of the Virgin Mary as Queen of Heaven: "I remember it well, she had the whole shewe of a most chaste Matrone, and albeit they consist of dyvers members, they are notwithstanding with so great proportion joyned to their heade Christ, that nothing can be more agreeable" (sig. U3r). The hierarchy of this Protestant heaven is firmly established. While the Christ in the false heaven is always a baby, unable to exercise his true power, the real Christ in the true heaven reigns supreme. All are of one mind, Pasquine says—including the Virgin Mary—that it is Christ who is the head of this heaven. Marforius then realizes the error of everyone's ways: man has elevated the Virgin beyond both her expectation and her capabilities:

> I se that al the fault procedeth hereof, in that we measure heavenly things according to our owne brayne. And therfore doe we thinke that the Virgin Mary is more mercifull than Christ, whome we imagine to be some cruell Tiraunt and fierce Judge, an error growen of the diversitie in nature betweene man and woman, bicause we see, that Women are more pitiefull than men. But what a divellish madnesse was that, to take away the governement from Christ, and gyve it to hir: as though Christ who is the wisdome of the Father, doted or coulde not tell what he had to doe. (sigs. X1r–X1v)

Pasquine's work is done. Marforius has become, he proudly notes, "a good and playne Gospeller" (sig. X1v).

Pasquine in a Traunce thus presents its readers with conflicting representations of the Queen of Heaven. There is the striking popish earthly version, which takes the form of a bedecked statue, the *Beata Virgo*, anthropomorphized by Pasquine and given unpleasant characteristics of jealousy and small-mindedness. There is also the shadowy and evasive figure of the queen of the false heaven, who is clothed with artificial light. This deceptive embodiment of the Virgin needs all the efforts of man to animate it and is simultaneously a jealous mother who keeps her son in a state of perpetual infancy so she can reign in his place. And finally there is the real Protestant Virgin Mary, the humble handmaid, a marginalized figure who is the least substantially depicted. This Virgin Mary takes her place in heaven not as its queen but as a handmaid of the church.

PASQUINE IN A TRAUNCE AND *THE FAERIE QUEENE*

An awareness of this splintered representation of the Virgin Mary can illuminate readings of other oblique references to her image in early modern writing. To demonstrate this, I am going to read through *Pasquine in a Traunce* into book 1 of *The Faerie Queene*, a text that presents us with particularly powerful realizations of sham Queens of Heaven. There is some evidence to suggest that Spenser was aware of Curione's work. A 1977 article by Timothy Cook builds a persuasive case that Spenser was influenced by *Pasquine in a Traunce*.[44] Cook's evidence for this comprises the following observations made by Spenser's friend and tutor Gabriel Harvey in one of his many letters: "I like your Dreames passingly well: and the rather, because they savour of that singular extraordinarie veine and invention, whiche I ever fancied moste, and in a manner admired onelye in Lucian, Petrarche, Aretine, Pasquill, and all the most delicate, and fine conceited Grecians, & Italians."[45] "Lucian, Petrarche, Aretine and Pasquill" are all, Harvey goes on to comment, associated with an extended vision. With this in mind, Cook's literary detective work focuses on Harvey's use of "Pasquill," concluding that this is a reference not to the genre but to Curione's text. Harvey had a strong intellectual influence upon Spenser and was well versed in his former pupil's reading habits.[46] Although Harvey's observations concern Spenser's lost *Dreames*, Cook persuasively gestures toward a number of similarities between the imagery in Curione's text and book 1 of *The Faerie Queene*, and it is a valuable exercise to set these two texts side by side. Book 1 of *The Faerie Queene*, like Curione's text, holds many echoes of the book of Revelation.[47] Both texts also powerfully evoke sham Queens of Heaven: I will argue that, in Spenser's text, both Lucifera and Duessa can be seen as covert expressions of the sham Queens of Heaven that Curione has constructed with such clarity.

Lucifera is the queen of Spenser's House of Pride, a setting that bears many of the hallmarks of Curione's false heaven. That the House of Pride is a place of danger is signaled to the reader by the way its architecture connotes tropes relating to the Catholic Church: it is cosmetically glorious on the outside but ruined underneath:

And all the hinder parts, that few could spie,
Were ruinous and old, but painted cunningly.
(1.4.5.8–9)

Like Pasquine on his visit to the papal heaven, the reader encounters a sumptuous building that rests on shaky foundations. Lucifera herself is an enchanting and authoritative figure who is associated with sumptuous, excessive wealth. Dripping in precious gold like an adorned idol, she seems literally to glitter:

High above all a cloth of State was spred,
And a rich throne, as bright as sunny day,
On which there sate most brave embellished
With royall robes and gorgeous array,
A mayden Queene, that shone as Titans ray
In glistring gold, and perelesse pretious stone;
Yet her bright blazing beautie did assay
To dim the brightnesse of her glorious throne,
As enuying her selfe, that too exceeding shone.

Exceeding shone, like Phoebus fayrest childe,
That did presume his fathers fyrie wayne,
And flaming mouthes of steeds vnwonted wilde

Through highest heaven with weaker hand to rayne;
Proud of such glory and advancement vayne,
While flashing beames do daze his feeble eyen,
He leaves the welkin way most beaten playne,
And rapt with whirling wheeles, inflames the skyen
With fire not made to burne, but fayrely for to shyne.
                                          (1.4.8–1.4.9)

Lucifera's beauty is swiftly undermined, however, by what Anthea
Hume has described as "Spenser's characteristic accumulation of pregnant words and images."[48] She seems to blaze with light, but this imagery is tainted by associations with envy, pride, and violence. She is
depicted as shining "as Titans ray," an image that evokes not only the
sun's brightness but also the rebellious and power-hungry Titans' wars.
Her brightness is also compared in an extended simile to Phaeton, the
rebellious son who stole Jove's chariot and whose own "feeble eyen"
were dazzled by the true light of the sun. Like the imagery surrounding Curione's queen of his papal heaven, the light that surrounds Lucifera is both worldly and artificial. Her robes shine like the sun but are
not the sun, and her true sources of light are the "glistring gold" and
"pretious stone" of her garments and the mirror into which she gazes,
a signifier of her pride and vanity. Lucifera is a woman clothed not with
the sun but with false light. The negative associations do not end there.
Lucifera's name, a feminine form of Lucifer, is a clear demarcation of
evil. There are echoes of the Whore of Babylon of Revelation in her descriptions, particularly in the dragon under Lucifera's feet, which calls
to mind the beast that the Whore rides, and her glittering, lavish appearance. She jealously and impotently sets up her own beauty in com-
petition with her surroundings, using it to "dim the brightnesse of her
glorious throne." Inherent in her strange belief that her throne envies
her dazzling appearance is a paranoid acknowledgment that she is not a
rightful queen.

      Robin Headlam Wells has noted that this description is rich in the
iconography of Queen Elizabeth, thus creating an undertow of criticism of the queen.[49] Sayre Greenfield similarly describes this as an "ideo-
logically dangerous" moment, as realistic details about Lucifera, such

as the way she greets visitors and presides at a tournament, make her a metonym for how the state of monarchy can corrupt.[50] But as with all Spenser's allegorical figures, a search for one sole meaning is reductive. Harry Berger has memorably described the relationship between an image in Spenser's poem and its related idea as "one of similarity rather than identity."[51] Here the correspondence between the image of Lucifera and the idea of England's queen is not intact; it is a refraction rather than a reflection. Through the character of Lucifera, Spenser associates a figure of female authority with pride and vanity, but the imagery surrounding her character gestures away from Elizabeth I by connecting her to the Protestant invention of a peevish and materialistic Queen of Heaven that is so powerfully evoked in Curione's text. Spenser frequently reiterates that Lucifera is an unlawful queen: she has no kingdom and no right to reign:

And proud Lucifera men did her call,
That made her selfe a Queene, and crownd to be,
Yet rightfull kingdome she had none at all,
Ne heritage of native soveraintie,
But did usurpe with wrong and tyrannie
Upon the scepter, which she now did hold.
                                    (1.4.12.1–6)

If Lucifera is read as a parody of the Queen of Heaven, the concept of the Virgin's unlawful queenship and authority, so frequently evoked in Protestant polemic, is echoed in this evocation of a seductive but false female ruler whose authority is falsely given but jealously guarded. This false rule is ultimately rejected within Spenser's text. That Lucifera is a sham monarch and not a real one also distances her from Gloriana, the rightful anointed monarch: Spenser's allegory could in fact be seen as deflecting criticisms of Elizabeth.

Lucifera can thus be viewed as a sham Queen of Heaven, in a section of Spenser's narrative that bears many similarities to Curione's account of a false papal heaven. Spenser deploys imagery of a sham Queen of Heaven in a different way in one of his most memorable characters, the sorceress Duessa, whose dazzling external appearance bewitches the weak eyes of the book's hero, the Redcrosse knight. Redcrosse's susceptibility to Duessa's appearance is a metonymic expression of man's susceptibility before the beautified and painted idol, something that Spenser expresses through patterns of imagery relating to Redcrosse's weak eyes and insight. A preoccupation with the frailty of man's vision hovers over much of book 1 of *The Faerie Queene*, one that is informed by the shift from visual to logocentric modes of religious devotion. Redcrosse, Spenser tells us in his "Letter to Raleigh," is a character "in whom I express Holynes," but he is, of course, a far more multilayered representation than this (716). At the end of book 1, slaying the dragon of sin, he becomes Saint George, symbol of the English nation and defender of the Protestant faith. Before he reaches this point, however, he makes terrible errors of judgment that signal that he is a representation of the spiritual weakness of England's idolatrous Catholic past as well as the hope and strength of its Protestant future. His eyes constantly deceive him.

Tricked into believing that he has seen his beloved, Una, with another man, Redcrosse becomes dazzled by the beautiful and virtuous-seeming lady Fidessa. Fidessa is in fact the sorceress Duessa, who like the House of Pride is cosmetically beautiful on the outside but almost unspeakably loathsome within. Her first appearance in the poem is on the surface an alluring one:

> A goodly Lady clad in scarlot red,
> Purfled with gold and pearle of rich assay,
> And like a Persian mitre on her hed
> Shee wore, with crownes and owches garnished.
>   (1.2.13.2–5)

However, the surface of the narrative is very different from the reality, as Spenser sets up one visual perception only to distort it. With both Duessa and Lucifera, Spenser uses images of Persia to signify excess and exoticism. The House of Pride is a place of "endlesse richesse" and "sumpteous shew" that "Ne Persia selfe, the nourse of pompous pride / Like ever saw" (1.4.7.5–7), while a "Persian mitre" is deployed as a comparison with Duessa's exotic headgear. Jane Grogan has termed this the "dreaded pairing of Catholic and Islamic forces," which was "a deathly combination to the Protestant imagination."[52] It is a trope that Curione's text expresses via the duskish hue of his exotic sham queen of the papal heaven and his observation that the pope and Mohammed are brothers. Spenser's descriptions of Duessa, it has often been observed, are also freighted with allusions to the Whore of Babylon, connecting Duessa not only with papal corruption but also with the figure of the dangerous Catholic woman.[53]

The reader may have been alerted to the disturbing symbolism of Duessa-Fidessa's appearance, but Redcrosse is so bedazzled by her artificial beauty that his ears become too dull to listen properly to her tale of woe:

> He in great passion al this while did dwell,
> More busying his *quicke eies*, her face to view,
> Then his *dull eares*, to heare what shee did tell.
>   (1.2.26.5–7, italics mine)

A pervasive fear in iconoclastic writing, that the eyes are more powerful than the ears, is here keenly felt.[54] David Miller has observed that the "many-ways ironic 'quicke' is a nice touch, partly because it plays into the contrast between life and death that organises all these motifs: lively as well as hasty in adoring the body of death, these eyes blind the knight to the life-preserving risen body he is supposed to adore."[55] The frailty of man's eyes was the subject of a number of iconoclastic discourses in Spenser's time that frequently associated vision with uncertainty and unreliability. In 1590, Anthony Munday described the eyes as a dangerous source of evil: "There cometh much evil in at the eares, but more at the eies, by these two open windowes death breaketh into the soule. Nothing entereth in more effectualie into the memorie, than that which commeth by seeing."[56] Munday's 1590 antitheatrical polemic encapsulates a sense of anxiety about the extent to which a man can trust his eyes, and Redcrosse's actions at this point start to mimic those of the fallen, idolatrous worshipper, attracted to the outward beauty of the idol. Duessa in her finery is therefore not just the Whore of Babylon but also Curione's *Beata Virgo*, the richly bedecked statue of the Virgin as Queen of Heaven.

The richness of the imagery that surrounds Duessa, of color and precious stone, only serves to heighten the tension between how she appears and how she is. Her true nature is revealed first to the reader when Fradubio tells his story:

A filthy foule old woman I did vew
That ever to have toucht her I did deadly rew.
Her neather partes misshapen, monstruous,
Were hidd in water, that I could not see,
But they did seeme more foule and hideous,
Then woman's shape man would beleeve to bee.
(1.2.40.8–1.2.41.4)

Fradubio's voice resonates with animosity; like Redcrosse, he was initially lured by Duessa's artificially seductive appearance. His initial attraction has shifted to misogynistic loathing. Duessa's fate in book 1 is to be stripped, like the idol, of her dazzling clothing and jewels:

Ne spared they to strip her naked all.
Then when they had despoyld her tire and call,
Such as she was, their eies might her behold,
That her misshaped parts did them appall,
A loathly, wrinckled hag, ill favoured, old,
Whose secret filth good manners biddeth not be told.
(1.8.46.4–9)

The reader has earlier been exposed to her true nature via Fradubio's descriptions and so is aware that what will be revealed underneath is one of Spenser's monsters. The imagery Spenser employs to describe the stripping of Duessa makes uncomfortable reading, expressing a mix of iconoclastic and misogynistic anxiety about the female form.

This episode works on a number of levels. It mimics the stripping of the Whore of Babylon that is prophesied in Revelation 17, a biblical reference that in the Reformation came to represent the stripping of the trappings of the Catholic Church. It also mimics the iconoclastic destruction of statues of the Virgin. A different level of meaning thus comes into play, one that is illuminated when one considers an intertextuality that exists between Spenser's descriptions of the foulness of the stripped Duessa and the *Homily Against Peril of Idolatry*, when the homilist likens the Catholic Church, bedecked in finery, to a harlot and an idolatrous worshipper to a lecher. Redcrosse's locus in the action of the stripping of Duessa is significant here. He is placed as spectator, and the reader, coming to the text with all of fallen man's idolatrous tendencies, is forced to watch with him in an episode that David Miller has described as one of "Western literature's grimmest mornings after."[57] When Fradubio earlier described Duessa's sexual organs they were obscured by water: Spenser is not so circumspect here. His muse may claim reticence when it comes to Duessa's filthy appearance, but this is merely lip service. He lingers over his foul descriptions, laying before the reader images of her bald head, foul teeth, and shrivelled breasts:

Her dried dugs, lyke bladders lacking wind,
Hong downe, and filthy matter from them weld;
Her wrizled skin as rough, as maple rind,
So scabby was, that would have loathd all womankind.
(1.8.47.6–9)

Theresa Krier notes that compared with Fradubio's glimpse of Duessa's true nature, which was an accidental encounter, here Duessa is "intentionally exposed and degraded."[58] Because it is deliberate rather than accidental, the stripping of Duessa further mimics the controlled vandalistic ritual of the iconoclastic act. A woman once adored as beautiful is exposed as a horrific sham, and Redcrosse—and the reader—must see the full depths of her evil before he can be fully redeemed. Here is an imaginative representation of Bishop Latimer's affirmation that in praying to the idol a man is mistaking the devil for God—a representation that illuminates the full horror and disgust of this notion.

Gary Waller has observed that Duessa "stands for both the Church of Rome and what, as a loyal Protestant, Spenser saw as papist exaggeration of the role of the Virgin Mary."[59] This interesting reading deserves more detailed attention: "exaggeration" is perhaps too careful a word. In the iconoclastic stripping of Duessa, and the sheer unpleasantness of the imagery used, Spenser is forcing the reader, like Redcrosse, to face up to the filth that resides in the impure soul of the idolater. But just as the vitriol in the *Homily* is directed at the idol rather than the worshipper, so Spenser's vitriol is reserved for Duessa rather than Redcrosse. On a figurative level, Spenser, like Curione, is creating an alternative Queen of Heaven: an impostor who functions both as a metonym for fallen man's sinful tendencies toward idolatry and as a vessel into which misogynistic hatred and scorn can be poured with integrity. She is a tyrannical queenly figure who is brutally and viscerally unqueened.[60] Spenser's Duessa thus becomes the site of an unsettling collapse of the image of the Queen of Heaven into the image of the Whore of Babylon. She is overtly identified with the Whore of Babylon, the focus of man's spiritual adultery, but she is also the Queen of Heaven in the form of a crowned and bejeweled statue that bedazzles feeble-eyed man and therefore needs to be destroyed. Men such as Redcrosse and Fradubio are seduced by her appearance, but when they know the reality behind the artifice they come to loathe her. A pattern can thus be observed that mimics the shift from entranced worshipper in front of a beautiful statue to iconoclastic loathing and destruction. Through the character of Duessa, the image of the Queen of Heaven is violently wrested away from associations of goodness and purity. The loathing and vitriol of the iconoclast are both amplified and justified, as they are directed toward this representation as a symbol of Catholic excess and hypocrisy that is exposed as rotten to the core.

Spenser's iconoclastic narrative presents two different visions of the Queen of Heaven in Lucifera and Duessa, and each associates the image with unpleasant qualities. The motif of the frailty of the eyes and the initial allure of both characters remind us that what is spiritually corrupt is also alluring. Redcrosse is, for a while, seduced by Duessa's appearance, and he willingly enters Lucifera's realm of the House of Pride. But after a number of trials in which he learns true faith, it is ultimately to Una that he turns. The Virgin Mary in her Protestant representation as humble handmaid is not perceived as a strong enough opponent for these powerful sham Queens of Heaven. Instead, Spenser, like Curione, follows John Bale's paradigms of setting the true church in opposition to false Catholic figures. Curione gives us a godly matron who is the queen of his true heaven, and the homilist presents the chaste matron of the church as a "contrary part" to its idolatrous harlot (262). Spenser's ideal of perfection is Una, his true Protestant Church.

Una's links to the true church are most powerfully revealed by her association with imagery connected with the Woman Clothed with the Sun. Mapped onto Una's narrative are similar details to Revelation 12; she too has been persecuted by a dragon and has fled into the wilderness. When she removes her veil, the imagery that Spenser uses is rich in allusion to this biblical figure:

> Her angels face
> As the great eye of heaven shyned bright,
> And made a sunshine in the shady place.
> (1.3.4.5–8)

Una's angelic appearance has the power to emit the clear, unpainted light of truth. Her association with the image of the Woman Clothed with the Sun marks her out as different from both Lucifera and Duessa, as she is able to reveal the difference between real light and false light.

Like *Pasquine in a Traunce*, *The Faerie Queene* flickers with imagery of true and false light. Artificial light surrounds Lucifera, and Una's description of the stripping of Duessa shows us man's propensity to be dazzled by the false light of the idol. Una describes Duessa's beauty with language that resonates with this tension:

> Such then (said Una) as she seemeth here,
> Such is the face of falshood, such the sight
> Of fowle Duessa, when her borrowed light
> Is laid away, and counterfesaunce knowne.
> (1.8.49.3–6)

When Duessa no longer has her artifice of "borrowed light" to cloak her, all that is left is "counterfesaunce": at her core, she is deceit. The light that has surrounded this false idol is in fact artificial, but our vision is frequently too frail to comprehend this. In a text that constantly causes us to doubt our judgment about what we have seen, this is a warning to be on our guard against artificial light. Lucifera and Duessa are both representations of a false Woman Clothed with the Sun, surrounded by "borrowed light." There are marked similarities between this description and Pasquine's descriptions of the false light around the shadowy queen of the papal heaven—the artificial light of candles and lamps and the glare of tables of gold and silver.

PARADOXES AND PROBLEMS

The Faerie Queene and *Pasquine in a Traunce* present splintered representations of the Virgin Mary by constructing alternative Queens of Heaven that are associated with falsehood and sin. Both texts can be viewed as iconoclastic in that within them a formerly beloved devotional image is destroyed. Curione's and Spenser's impostors are presented as covetous, materialistic metonyms for spiritual whoredom that must be cast out of man's hearts and minds, to be replaced, not by the Virgin as humble handmaid, but by heaven's true queen, the church. The Virgin herself in her Protestant guise as humble handmaid is virtually excluded from the scene. The sham Queen of Heaven, and all the opportunities she offers for vivid description and emotive language, clearly exerts such a fascination that representations of the "real" Virgin Mary as humble handmaid are marginalized. This bifurcation of the Virgin's image brings with it a number of paradoxes and problems. On one level, the need to imbue the Queen of Heaven with such unpleasant traits can also be seen as an indication of how attractive the image was to the worshipper. There is, perhaps, an element here of protesting too much, almost in the way one reminds oneself of a lover's faults to justify the end of an affair. Margaret Miles has observed how this residual affection can often be a driving force behind iconoclasm, as iconoclasts "destroyed images not because they loved them too little or were indifferent to them but because they loved them too much and found themselves too attached to them."[61]

Spenser's repeated motif of the eyes and their frailty teaches that we should not always trust appearances, a literary reminder of the alluring and attractive nature of the idol that man must destroy. This leads to another fundamental paradox: we have seen a nuanced attempt to bifurcate the images of Queen of Heaven and humble handmaid, but is fallen man capable of grasping this? The fact that Redcrosse is attracted to Duessa-Fidessa as well as to Una pinpoints a blurring rather than a bifurcation of the two figures that many have found disturbing. Claire McEachern, for example, has observed that Spenser's text reveals "the precariousness of the binary structure of the difference between women."[62] This blurring reveals itself in a different way in *Pasquine in a Traunce*, which, by lampooning perceptions of the Virgin Mary, presents conflicting referents of the same signifier. Curione's polemical versions of the Virgin, the bedecked earthly *Beata Virgo* and the shadowy, artificial Queen of Heaven, are parody figures designed to satirize the perceived excesses of the Catholic faith. Yet all versions of the Virgin in Curione's text coexist within the same image, and this serves to destabilize and corrupt positive perceptions of the Virgin Mary, particularly when one considers the marginalization of the humble handmaid figure in Curione's Protestant heaven. Reformers such as Curione may assert their pious respect for the Virgin, but in seeking to save the "true" Virgin from misrepresentation they often end up barely representing her at all.

A final problem comes with the extreme nature of the idea, implicit in both Curione's and Spenser's writing, that the sham figure of the Queen of Heaven is on some level also the Whore of Babylon. An extraordinarily explicit example of this conflation can be found in a 1582 translation by Thomas Rogers of *Of the Ende of This World, and Seconde Coming of Christ*, a study by the Emden lawyer Sheltco à Geveren. This was a popular work that ran into several reprints.[63] In it, the trope of the church as Christ's true spouse is presented, and with this imagery the Whore of Babylon becomes a love rival, a dangerous, powerful, and seductive figure who has both slandered the true church and usurped its place. The work bewails the misfortunes that the church has suffered: "And yet most of all it greeves thee to see the shamelesse boldnes of that abhominable strumpet the whore of Babilon, which blusheth not to call her selfe the onely spouse of thy Christ: and to call thee an harlot. . . . Hence it is, that before the world, which is the Sonne of this naughtie houswife, thou art contemned, hated, and afflicted: and she as the Queene of heaven is adored, loved, and advaunced: with her have all nations committed fornication, and the Kings of the earth have be-come frantike with Idolatrous wyne of her poysoned doctrine."[64]

Of the Ende of This World goes beyond the creation of an alterna-tive Queen of Heaven by explicitly stating that corrupt man has been venerating the Whore of Babylon as Queen of Heaven, that by "Kings of the earth" she has been "reverenced as the Queene of heaven" (sig. B6v). The true church, however, is to take heart, for Christ, her hus-band, is exposing her true nature: "She which was so loved is now hated, and was glorious for her externall fairnes, is nowe become odious to many, for her spiritual filthines. Have pacience therefore but a little whyle, and thou shalt see her, to be of none accompt: for thy lover in whom thou delightest, shall bring her to such shame, as she shall not be able to showe her head out of hell, when thou shalt be in glorye with thy beloved."[65] The structure of this is a mirror of the end of book 1 of *The Faerie Queene*, as the whorish and false Duessa is stripped of her finery and cast out into the wilderness, and the trope of spiritual whore-dom and filth is frequently repeated.

The sustained use of allegory makes this text unstable. The lexis of marriage and family dominates, with Christ as the husband and the church as his spouse. There is an echo here of the language of the Book of Common Prayer that marriage signifies the mystical union between Christ and his church, and this perhaps reflects Protestantism's increased emphasis on godly marriage.[66] The Whore of Babylon, in counterfeited show as Queen of Heaven, is a seductive but morally polluted mistress. The language of marriage and infidelity, of the true church usurped as God's spouse by the Whore of Babylon, is deployed to criticize the Catholic elevation of the Virgin Mary to Queen of Heaven and Christ's spouse. What strikes one forcibly about this piece of polemic, however, is that the analogies are so violently and explicitly drawn that fault lines emerge. By turning the Catholic Queen of Heaven and bride of Christ into the Whore of Babylon, the text comes dangerously close to the blasphemous implication that Christ, as the true church's spouse, has become an adulterer. So mired is this reformist text in the language of spiritual filth, whoredom, and adultery, so vitriolic is the language that constructs the Queen of Heaven as the Whore of Babylon, that the writing slips from invective to blasphemy.

Through the creation of an alternative version of the Queen of Heaven, the collapse of the image into that of the Whore of Babylon is rationalized and justified. The tensions in *Of the Ende of This World* reveal that the concept is an extreme one, as it yokes two diametrically opposed forces together. For all the careful positioning of the sham Queen of Heaven as something entirely different from the Virgin Mary herself, this particular strain of literary iconoclasm was, ultimately, problematic and paradoxical. It also reinforced, rather than remedied, one of the fundamental paradoxes surrounding iconoclastic controversies— that the iconoclast can be seen as animating the idol, imbuing it with a potency, however negatively portrayed. Elizabeth Mazzola has pertinently observed how "iconoclasm's loathing of sacred images imagines their power more forcefully."[67] We have seen in the previous chapter how the repeated polemical use of the Queen of Heaven served to keep the phrase alive. The construction of sham Queens of Heaven is a further indication of how the attempt to destroy an image stood in danger of becoming exactly the reverse: the imaginative evocation of an alternative and animated version of a stock and stone.

PART II

Voices from the Shadows

CHAPTER 4

The Virgin Mary and
the Godly Protestant Woman

But in the other's silence do I see
Maid's mild behaviour and sobriety.
　　　　　　　　—The Taming of the Shrew, 1.1.69–70

The previous chapters have outlined how reformist writers attempted to set the true "Protestant" humble handmaid and the false "Catholic" Queen of Heaven in binary opposition. Inherent within this has been a debate on the position of women in early modern England, one that I now bring to the forefront. My intention is to interrogate how the relationship between the two models of *ancilla Domini* and *Regina Coeli* manifested itself in early modern Protestant writing both about women and by women. This is a chapter in three parts. I first explore how the image of the Virgin as humble handmaid was mapped onto the figure of the ideal woman. For the male writers of conduct books, the Virgin herself, in a state of mute acquiescence to the will of God, often became a model of the silent, godly, and obedient Protestant woman. One particularly influential example of this conflation can be found in *De Institutione Feminae Christianae* by Juan Luis Vives, a pre-Reformation text that, with a number of significant emendations, became a template for many of the conduct books of Tudor and Stuart England.

I then turn to two Jacobean female-authored texts that subtly undermine this dichotomy. The first is *The Mother's Blessing* by the Protestant writer Dorothy Leigh, a posthumously published tract in the very popular "mother's legacy" genre that proffered advice on a range of spiritual and domestic issues. Leigh is vitriolic about Catholic worship of the Queen of Heaven, but her descriptions of the Virgin do not conform wholly to the silent and obedient ideal. Instead, they associate Mary with power and authority. References to the Virgin as a universal mother figure invite implicit comparisons with Leigh herself, a woman whose pious but frequently strident and authoritative maternal voice gained a wider platform than the home only. A different, more radical, presentation of the Virgin Mary can be found in the Passion poem *Salve Deus Rex Judaeorum* by Aemilia Lanyer. Lanyer's work constitutes an even more marked disruption of the binaries of humble handmaid and Queen of Heaven by embracing the paradoxes of the Virgin as a woman who obeys but who is simultaneously crowned in glory. That Lanyer is writing from a Protestant standpoint is not in doubt, but her imaginative representation of the Virgin adapts and realigns empowered Catholic elements of Marian spirituality. In very different ways, both Leigh and Lanyer covertly undermine the dominant Protestant discourse of the Virgin as a silent and acquiescent model of female conduct. Their writing thus problematizes the conflict between a powerful queenly Virgin and an obedient humble Virgin and also explores a number of other conflicts: between silence and speaking out, between women as figures of spiritual authority and as passive vessels, and between a sinful Eve and a redeeming Mary.

THE VIRGIN MARY AS A CONDUCT-BOOK WOMAN

In Edward VI's reign, the reformist clergyman Thomas Becon outlined a perceived connection between the Virgin Mary and the ideal silent and obedient woman: "There is nothing that doth so commend, avaunce, set forthe, adourne, deck, trim, and garnish a maid, as silence. And this noble vertue may the virgins learne of that most holy, pure and glorious virgin Mary, which, when she eyther hard or saw any worthy and notable thing, blabbed it not oute straight wais to her gossips, as the manner of women is at thys present day, but being silent, she kept al those sayinges secret and pondered them in her hart."[1] The biblical source for Becon's words is Luke 2:19, which tells of the Virgin's reaction to the wonders of Christ's nativity: "But Mary kept all those sayings and pondered them in her heart." It can be used to construct the character of a thoughtful, restrained woman, one who does not speak out. Axiomatic to early modern thinking on female behavior was the threefold ideal of the "silent, chaste, and obedient" woman.[2] The message promulgated in the pulpit and in printed word by reformed religion was that chastity and silence were virtues to be applauded in a woman and that it was her duty to obey in the home, which was seen as a microcosm of social and religious order.[3] Representations of a humble and acquiescent Virgin fitted comfortably into this discourse. As Elaine Beilin has observed, the image of the ideal woman "is a domesticated version of the Virgin: remaining at home to keep the household goods, a good woman was pious, humble, constant, and patient, as well as obedient, chaste, and silent."[4]

The construction of this silent and obedient ideal was greatly aided by the popularity of the early modern conduct book: screeds of printed matter proffered advice on female behavior. A typical example is *A Godlie Forme of Householde Government for the Ordering of Private Families*, a 1598 treatise on godly family life by Robert Cleaver that gives the following description: "The best meanes therefore that a wife can use to obtaine, and maintaine the love and good liking of her husband, is to bee silent, obedient, peacable, patient, studious to appease his choler, if he bee angrie."[5] It is stock advice from a Protestant conduct book, but it is worthy of close attention: what is interesting about Cleaver's text is that it drew its inspiration from a Catholic source. Many passages in it were copied closely from the treatise *De Institutione Feminae Christianae* (1523), by the Erasmian humanist Juan Luis Vives, a work that outlined a code of conduct for both single and married women.[6] A Spanish Catholic, Vives dedicated his text to his countrywoman Catherine of Aragon; he was tutor to the princess Mary, and much of his advice was written with the young princess in mind. *De Institutione* was originally written in Latin and was translated into English in 1529 by Richard Hyrde, a member of Sir Thomas More's household, appearing under the title *The Instruction of a Christen Woman*. It was reprinted nine times in the sixteenth century, shifting from an advice manual for a Catholic princess to a Protestant conduct book.[7] This in itself is an indication of the porousness of Catholic and Protestant texts: just as Erasmus's ideas were given different emphasis by Reformation thinkers, the humanist concepts developed by Vives were transmitted and reshaped.[8]

Vives's conduct book repeatedly presents Mary as silent and decorous and includes many passages in praise of the Virgin that chime with later Protestant thought. Women, Vives observes, should emulate "the moste excellent and flower of virginite our lady, the mother of Christe, god and man: whose lyfe, nat only maydes have for an example to forme and fashen them selfe after, but also wyves and wydowes: for she hath been all thynge unto all folkes to provoke all and brynge them unto the example of her chastite: unto virgins the moste demure virgin: unto wyves, the most chaste wife: and unto wydowes, the most devout widow" (53). The Virgin is here seen as an example to women at all stages of life: she is both Virgin and mother, and as the bride of Christ mourning her son's death she is perceived as a widow as well. The repetition of "most"—she is "the most chaste," "the most devout"— underlines her position as the ideal.

Other descriptions of the Virgin Mary within Vives's treatise are concurrent with Reformation thinking. Vives discusses at length how a woman's silence, particularly in public, was a desirable state. He observes, for example, that a woman should "holde her tonge demurely. And let few se her, and none at al here her" (23), invoking the Pauline injunction that women should not speak in church (1 Cor. 14:34–35). Again, the model for this is the Virgin Mary, whose silence in Gospel accounts of Christ's nativity is foregrounded:

Tell me howe moche redeste thou in all the historie of the gospel, that our lady ever spake. The angell cometh in unto her: and she fynished the matter with fewe wordes, and those wyse and sad, and also holy: She goth for to se Elisabeth, and speketh to the preyse of god: She bryngeth forth a sonne, whiche is god: She is lauded of the angelles, worshyppedde of the hyrde men, and holdethe her peace, gatherynge and kepynge in her remembraunce all their sayenges. She was honoured of the wyse men of the easte, that came thither a great waye: and what doste thou rede, that she ever spake? Some other paraventure wold have asked of theyr countre, of theyr trea-sure, of theyr lernynge, or of the sterre: but she, as became a yonge mayde, spake never a word. (62)

An evocative image is constructed here of a decorous young woman who knows her place. Vives's focus is on the Virgin's virtually silent presence within the pages of the Bible, including her lack of verbal response to her son's crucifixion: "And at the crosse she was clene dumme: she asked never a whytte of her sonne, neither with whom he wolde leave her, nor what he wold commaunde her to do, whan he dyed: For she had nat lerned to prattle amonge folkes. All maydes, and all women folowe you her: for she was but of fewe wordes: but won-derous wise" (63). The Virgin is here "clene dumme," a virtual mute within the text, and her passivity and silence equate to female wisdom: she is to be emulated by all, as she was "wonderous wise."

With the positive virtues of silence in early modern discourse came negative views of speech, something that can be seen in Vives's pejorative descriptions of women who "prattle amonge folkes." Women's speech was linked with disobedience and disruption; if silence was being trum-peted as a virtue, excessive speech became a sign of sexual transgres-sion. As Gail Kern Paster has shown, Renaissance discourse frequently constructed the woman's body as a leaky vessel. A copious production of fluids—menstrual blood, breast milk, tears—connoted a shameful lack of control. Excessive garrulousness was linked to this, as the prat-tling female gossip was viewed as a figure who copiously leaked words.[9] A woman's speech was frequently elided with wantonness in an age where a man accused of slandering a woman by calling her a "whore" might defend himself by claiming he meant "whore of her tonge" not "whore of her body."[10] Peter Stallybrass comments that in discourses relating to speaking and sexual immorality, "the closed mouth is made a sign of chastity," conceptualizing the link between "the enclosed body, the closed mouth, the locked house."[11] The Virgin's silence can thus be read as a metonym for her chastity, verbal restraint becoming sexual restraint. Vives encapsulates this in his descriptions of Mary enclosed in the home, industriously reading and praying. As a result, she is at first frightened by Gabriel's presence: "And hit is no doubte, but the angell founde Mary doyeng some suche thynge, whiche was a frayde, whan she sawe a mannes face, where she was nat wonte. Therfore she is called in Ebrewe alma that is as ye wold say, a vergin closed in. And this is she that Esaie the prophet speketh of in these words: Beholde a virgin closed up shall conceyve and beare god and man. Therfore shall the mayde let no man in to the house at home, but whom her father by special words commaundeth to be let in" (49). The description of the Virgin "closed in" here encompasses her silence, her chastity, and her containment within the domestic sphere.

The conflating of the Virgin with the ideal of the "silent, chaste, and obedient" wife made *De Institutione* germane to Protestant thinking, as it mirrored the reformist shift from the active empowered Virgin as Queen of Heaven to the domestic, obedient, and passive Mary, an ideal godly Protestant wife. It also shows that the humble and obedient Virgin Mary cannot be viewed as an exclusively Protestant construct. That is not to say that Vives's views were taken verbatim. Protestant writers such as Robert Cleaver may have liberally copied from the views of *The Instruction of a Christen Woman* on female conduct, but their selection of passages reflected their religious stance: Vives's reliance on patristic sources was not to their taste, but biblical examples were.[12] Significant revisions were also made to the words of *The Instruction of a Christen Woman* itself as it was repositioned as a Protestant conduct book. One of the most striking indications of this is found in the 1585 edition, published by the Puritan printer Robert Waldegrave. In the original translation, Mary is described as "quene and lady" (132). This phrase is omitted from the 1585 version, where at the same point in the text, Mary is referred to as simply "the virgin," ensuring that no trace of the Queen of Heaven is left to threaten the humble and obedient ideal. The same edition deleted a description of Mary as "quene of the world" and instead described the Virgin simply as "mother of Christ."[13]

Humble handmaid and Queen of Heaven coexist in Vives's original version; but in the text's incarnation as a Protestant conduct book, the intercessory Queen of Heaven disappears from view, leaving an image of the Virgin as a model of the silent, chaste, and obedient woman only. It would be overly simplistic to view early modern thinking as constituting purely a stranglehold on women. Marriage was privileged as ordained by God, the bond between husband and wife mirroring the union between Christ and his church.[14] Many conduct books talked of the spiritual responsibility given to wives for educating their children, and the state of true companionship between man and wife was frequently exalted.[15] But a good wife tended to be a silent wife, and a wife's obedience to her husband was frequently stressed as a vital component of the ideal state of companionship. The proliferation of conduct books in early modern England acts as a telling indication of the impossibility of maintaining the patriarchal ideal—one only has to look at the amount of diet books on the shelves today to realize that obesity is a problem. The language of some conduct literature makes it tellingly clear that the ideal of the silent, chaste, and obedient woman was strongly resisted. Lurking behind the ideal wife is the specter of the disobedient wife who refuses to hold her tongue, a Katherina untamed by a Petruchio, and Protestant emphasis on the godly marriage added a new spiritual layer of significance to the shrew literature of folklore and stage.[16] In his popular treatise on marriage *A Bride Bush or Wedding Sermon*, the seventeenth-century preacher William Whately opined: "Then it is laudable, commendable, a note of a vertuous woman, a dutifull wife, when shee submits herselfe with quietnesse, cheerfully, even as a well-broken horse turnes at the least turning, stands at the least check of the rider's bridle, readily going and standing as he wishes that sits upon his back."[17] Whately's use of the image of the bridle connotes a containing and stilling action. There is perhaps an allusion here to the scold's bridle, used by communities both to curb the tongue of a shrew and to shame her publicly.[18] The inflammatory language presents the husband as a dominant figure who has broken his wife: a warning, perhaps, to men who were not dominant enough. There was in the period a strong inference that a husband who could not control his wife's speech would be unable to control her sex drive.[19]

A more notorious example of advice on controlling a shrewish wife can be found in the pamphlet *The Arraignment of Lewde, Idle, Froward and Unconstant Women*, in which, among other things, Joseph Swetnam claimed that the husband of a shrew was justified in beating her: "As a sharp bit curbs a froward horse, even so a cursed woman must be roughly used."[20] This staggeringly misogynistic text attracted lively criticism, but embedded in Swetnam's invective are some truisms of the early modern treatise and pulpit on the position of women.[21] Fascinatingly, *The Arraignment of Lewde, Idle, Froward and Unconstant Women* does provide a small glimpse of a perfect marriage, using the Virgin Mary as the model of the ideal wife: "Although some happen on a devillish and unhappy woman yet all men doe not so. . . . Amongst dust there is Pearle found, and in hard rockes Dyamonds of great value, and so amongst many women there are some good, as that gracious and glorious Queene of all women kinde the Virgin Mary the mother of all blisse, what won her honour but an humble minde and her paines and love unto our Saviour Christ."[22] In an interesting word choice, the Virgin is here a "Queene of all women kinde." Is it something of a slip on Swetnam's part to allow into his vitriol even an echo of the Virgin as Queen of Heaven? Certainly, the word *queen* was one that the editors of the 1585 edition of Vives's *Instruction* more fastidiously eradicated. Perhaps the empowered implications of this phrase are quashed by Swetnam's own definition of what the ideal woman actually *is*. In associating "Queene" with "women kinde," Swetnam drains the word of any associations with power and authority. His Virgin Mary exists in opposition to the Queen of Heaven; it is her "humble minde" that she is honored for. Yet the echo of the Virgin's empowered state in Swetnam's use of *Queene* is destabilizing.

MATERNAL AUTHORITY IN *THE MOTHER'S BLESSING*

For all its outrageous assertions, Swetnam's work is an indication of the fissures that existed in the creation of the silent and obedient conduct-book woman. His text presents us with a rather cartoonish figure of a resistant and rebellious shrew. The work of many women writers disrupted the dominant discourse on female conduct.[23] Dorothy Leigh and Aemilia Lanyer are examples of two Jacobean women writers who fashioned themselves as pious Protestant women yet trod a fine line between resistance and conformity. In very different ways, the views they express on the Virgin Mary reflect ideological tensions. Dorothy Leigh was a Protestant wife and mother who toward the end of her life wrote *The Mother's Blessing*, an advice book for her three sons. In a period where women's speech was frequently elided with wantonness, a woman writer whose work was published stood in danger of being viewed as a garrulous, dangerous, and immoral figure.[24] The posthumous publication of Leigh's book in 1616 placed it into the "mother's legacy" genre, a way of evading criticism of work written by a woman. *The Mother's Blessing* was also on the surface a private affair, written for Leigh's sons, George, John, and William, but its transmission in printed form indicates that it was clearly intended for a wider audience than the family alone. As the book's frontispiece reiterates, this book of "the godly Counsaile of a Gentle-woman, not long since deceased," contains "godly admonitions profitable for all Parents." Within *The Mother's Blessing* itself, Leigh shows that she is conscious of the paradox of a godly woman speaking out. To lessen any censure, she clothes her words in humility, stating that she wishes "to encourage women (who, I feare, will blushe at my boldnesse) not to bee ashamed to shew their infirmities, but to give men the first and chiefe place."[25] Yet she does speak out, and boldly so, in a book that offers guidance on a range of domestic matters from managing poverty to the importance of education and reading. Dorothy Leigh states that her reason for writing is "motherly affection" (3), and her little book of counsel consistently employs the role of a mother to discuss female authority.

There are only a few, sketchy details of Dorothy Leigh's life. When she wrote *The Mother's Blessing* she was the widow of Ralph Leigh, a soldier who had served in Spain with Robert Leicester, Earl of Essex, and she was linked to a community of Puritans whose radicalism was to increase at the end of James I's reign.[26] Our main impressions of Leigh come from the memorably strong and often forceful voice that breathes through the words of her book. Leigh's vehemently anti-Catholic stance is clear in the advice she offers on the correct way to pray. There are, she says, "so many wicked prayers in the world, for they that make them, have no faith in Christ" (114). Leigh stridently rejects all forms of Catholic prayer, dismissing it as "vaine babbling" (119). It is while advising on the correct way to pray that she makes her opposition to the figure of the Queen of Heaven palpably clear. She uses a familiar example to illustrate this, equating early modern Catholics with the disobedient women of Pathros in the book of Jeremiah:

> They pray while they live, that they may goe to purgatory; and when they die, they give much goods to others, to pray that they may come out of purgatorie againe: these are most vaine praiers never warranted by the word of God. They pray also to our Ladie to helpe them, much as the Israelites praied to the Queene of heaven: and as the Israelites praiers were accepted, so are theirs. But I pray God, for Christs sake, that you, nor none of yours may make such prayers. And I pray God to blesse his whole Church, that their prayers may bee right and faithfull, for prayer is the key which openeth unto vertue. (115–16)

The fact that Dorothy Leigh equates the women of Pathros with early modern Catholics, a link commonly forged in sermons of the period, means that she was probably repeating a sermon she had heard, a further indication of how widely this reference was disseminated. Women were collectors, readers, and annotators of sermons and often repeated the teachings of sermons in commonplace books, which were then used in the teaching of children. Thus a woman would become a consumer of sermons and religious literature, but in the domestic sphere she could act as a preacher herself.[27] Leigh does indirectly reference herself as a preacher by saying that this is a career path she hopes her sons may follow: "Me thinks if I were a man and a Preacher of Gods Word, as (I hope) some of you shall bee," she comments, adding that if she were a preacher she would "bring many to pray rightly, which now pray unadvisedly, or not at all" (130). Denied the pulpit, Leigh presents her exegesis in advice form.

Leigh's advice against wicked prayers extends to instructing her sons on choosing a wife. Maternal authority seeps through her words here. Sons must choose "a godly wife, that she may be a helpe to you in godlinesse" (49). She uses the example of Solomon, whose wife's influence is said to have led to his downfall, to outline the dangers of an ungodly wife: "The world was drowned, because men married ungodly wives. Salomon, who was not only the wisest man that ever was, but was also mightily indued [*sic*] with the Spirit of God, by marrying idolatrous women, fell for the time to idolatry. Never thinke to stand where Salomon fell. I pray God that neither you, nor any of yours may at any time marry with any of those, which hold such superstitions, as they did, or as some doe now; as namely to pray to Saints, to praye in Latine, to pray to go to Purgatory" (50–51). The influence that the wrong wife—a Catholic wife—could have over a husband is keenly felt. Apostasy brought with it a different slant on views on female obedience in marriage. In his 1591 *Preparative to Marriage*, Henry Smith claimed that as a marriage partner is like Christ's spouse she cannot be "a harlot, heretic or atheist."[28] Within the microcosm of the recusant family, it was often the matriarch who was vilified for wielding a power that was disobedient to the state.[29] The Jesuit priest Henry Garnet's *A Treatise of Christian Renunciation* (1592), which was aimed at a Catholic female readership, stated: "It behoveth to obey God more then men. This same let us understand both of servants to their masters, and of wives to their husbandes."[30]

Although *The Mother's Blessing* follows a recognized Protestant model of perception of the Queen of Heaven as a "Catholic" and idolatrous figure, Leigh's representation of the Virgin is more complex than a reiteration of the silent and acquiescent Protestant ideal. Instead, her depiction of the Virgin, to use Catharine Gray's words, "rescues Mary from anti-Catholic obscurity."[31] Leigh's book of maternal counsel does not dismiss or marginalize the Virgin but instead lauds her as an exemplary mother. "Can a Mother forget the childe of her wombe?" she asks at one point (9), and there is an element here of implicit identification with the Virgin, who is presented throughout her text as a site of maternal power. *The Mother's Blessing* foregrounds the Virgin's importance in a number of ways. In an argument similar to one made by Vives in *The Instruction of a Christen Woman*, Leigh observes that because Mary is both "maid" and "wife" she is seen as a role model of chastity for all women:

Mary was filled with the Holy Ghost, and with all goodnesse, and yet is called the blessed Virgin: as if our God should (as hee doth indeed) in briefe comprehend all other vertues under this one vertue of chastity: wherefore I desire that all women, what name so ever they beare, would learne of this blessed Virgin to be chaste: for though shee were more replenished with grace then any other, and more freely beloved of the Lord, yet the greatest title that she had, was, that she was a blessed and pure Virgin; which is a great cause to move all women, whether they bee Maids or Wives (both which estates shee honoured) to live chastly. (36–37)

Leigh also celebrates the Virgin Mary as a positive contrast to Eve. To set Mary in opposition to Eve is to follow a path well trodden since the Middle Ages, but *The Mother's Blessing* adds its own particularly striking spin on things by foregrounding the culpability of men. It is hypocritical, she says, for men to blame women in the form of a beguiling Eve when it is men, from ancient times to the present day, who have been deceiving women, betraying them with a kiss as Judas betrayed Christ. Leigh is particularly critical of society's double standards that allow a man to destroy a woman's virtue and get off scot-free: "Men sayd once, The woman which thou gavest me, beguiled mee, and I did eate. But wee women may now say, that men lye in waite every where to deceive us. . . . Once Judas betrayed his Master with a kisse, and repented it: but now men, like Judas, betray their Mistresses with a kisse, and repent it not: but laugh and rejoyce, that they have brought sinne and shame to her that trusted in them" (32–33). The Virgin is given an active, almost heroic role. She is described as "a woman virtuous above all other women" (34), as in acquiescing to God's command she brought Jesus into the world, taking away the sin of Eve's disobedience. A woman made a mistake, but the actions of another woman expiated it. Mary is thus praised for rescuing mankind from the Fall—and womankind from guilt and shame:

I presumed, that there was no woman so senselesse, as not to looke what a blessing God has sent to us women, through that gracious Virgin, by whom it pleases God to take away the shame, which

Eve our Grandmother had brought us to: For before, men might say; The woman beguiled mee, and I did eate the poysoned fruit of disobedience, and I dye. But now man may say, if he say truly; The Woman brought mee a Saviour, and I feede of him by Faith and live. Heere is this great and wofull shame taken from women by God, working in a woman: man can claime no part in it. (35)

Mary's active role in taking away the shame attached to Eve is clearly stressed. It is entirely a woman's doing—"Man can claime no part in it." Leigh thus rescues the Virgin Mary from her role as silent subordinate and instead places her as a woman who has actively saved mankind and who is to be emulated.

These descriptions of the Virgin come in a section of Leigh's book that gives advice about giving children "good names." Leigh's argument here is that children should be named "after the names of the Saints of God" (28) so that they can think about the saints' virtues and read about them in the Bible. She practically and rather authoritatively lists a series of saints and virtuous biblical women whose names could be given to her sons' children. She admits that her readers may be wondering why she has not included Mary in this list, particularly as the Virgin has saved mankind from Eve's disgrace. In fact, Mary's presence is paramount, as for suitable girls' names Leigh chooses five virtuous women whose names form an acrostic of "Maria": "Michal, Abigail, Rachel, Iudith [Judith] & Anna" (41). As Leigh explains, "The first letters of [their] names doe make her whole name, to shewe, that shee had all their vertues wholy combined in her" (41). This correct naming of children is seen as a way to use words to educate children about the dangers of the image:

If ye shall thinke me too tedious about the naming your children, I tel you that I have some reason for it; and the first is this, to make them reade in the Bible, the things which are written of those Saints, and learne to imitate their vertues. Secondly because many have made a God of the Virgin Marie, the Scripture warranting no such thing, and have prayed to her, (though there they shal finde that she was a woman, yea, and a comfort to all women: for she hath taken away the reproch which of right belonged unto us, and by the seed of the woma*n* we are al saved) it was therefore fit I should speake largely of that name. Thirdly, seeing many have heretofore, and now doe make Images of Saints, to put them in minde of the Saints . . . I thought it better to have you remember them, by hearing their names, and by reading what they taught us in the Scripture, and how they led their lives, then by looking upon a painted piece of paper, or a carved stone. (43–45)

Images of Mary and biblical saints are thus replaced by the Word—or more specifically, the words of their names. Leigh is not encouraging readers to view the Virgin as Queen of Heaven—she is clear in her criticisms of those who have "made a God of the Virgin Mary." But far from being placed on the margins, the Virgin is an active agent in a Puritan fight against Catholicism. She may not be described as the Queen of Heaven, but the power invested in this role has not melted away into a marginalized acquiescence. The dynamic force behind the words "she hath taken away the reproch which of right belonged unto us" almost turns Mary into a leader, and her maternal agency is made clear—"by the seed of the woma*n* we are al saved."

Dorothy Leigh's godly Protestant wife and mother is a zealous and active figure whose advice rippled through generations. *The Mother's Blessing* was successful in its quest to reach a wider audience: the book went into at least nineteen editions before 1640.[32] For all its qualifying statements of obedience, it is a work that has a highly individual voice. Its publication as a conduct manual by a female writer can be seen as a riposte to male-authored conduct books. One particular edition of the work shows the extent of its influence and how its afterlife became political. In a 1627 edition, *The Mother's Blessing* was bound together with *The Father's Blessing*, a popularized spin-off of King James's *Basilikon Doron*, the treaty on kingship that is also an advice book to princely sons. James's use of patriarchal rhetoric in his theories of kingship creates a series of mirror images between obedient wife and patriarchal husband, subject and king, Christian and God. Catharine Gray has perceptively suggested that the binding of these two texts together suggests that readers could set them in dialogue with each other. The pairing pitted Leigh's words against the patriarchal semantic field adopted by the king himself. Read in this way, Leigh's book becomes a subtle challenge to the paternalist rhetoric of the conduct book that placed a woman as a silent subject within the domestic sphere. Gray observes that Leigh's emphasis on the Virgin Mary is crucial: "Central to this expansion of maternity into a site of public, spiritual authority is a rehabilitation of the Virgin Mary, herself a model for the role of mother-as-redeemer that Leigh takes on."[33] Leigh thus identifies with the Virgin as a figure who embodies the pervasive maternal authority that characterizes her own writing.

AEMILIA LANYER'S CORONATION OF THE VIRGIN

A more radical response to the presentation of the Virgin Mary as silent and acquiescent can be found in the poetry of Aemilia Lanyer. Hers is a far more scandalous life story than Dorothy Leigh's. Her father was a court musician, possibly of Jewish origins, and the young Aemilia received all the benefits of a Protestant, humanist education under the supervision of Susan Bertie, dowager Countess of Kent. At Queen Elizabeth's court, this intelligent, spirited young woman embarked upon an affair with the Lord Chamberlain Henry Carey, who was many years her senior. In 1592, Aemilia married the royal musician Alfonso Lanyer. It is highly probable that this was for propriety's sake: she was pregnant with Carey's baby at the time. Aemilia Lanyer's marriage of convenience was blighted with misfortune. In 1597, she began to visit the astrologer Simon Forman for help with predictions about difficult pregnancies, as after the birth of Carey's child she suffered a series of miscarriages. Forman was a self-confessed lothario whose professional diary reveals titillating, though highly unreliable, details of the sexual turn that their consultations took.[34] Lanyer did give birth to a daughter, Odillya, in 1598, but the baby died the next year. Meanwhile, her husband, Alfonso, who was something of a failed social climber, made several unsuccessful attempts to earn a knighthood. By the early years of the seventeenth century, Aemilia and Alfonso were living apart: Alfonso remained in London whilst Aemilia spent time with

Margaret Clifford, Countess of Cumberland, and her daughter Anne at Cookham, an estate near Windsor. We do not know the precise nature of Aemilia Lanyer's role in this aristocratic household: she was perhaps a gentlewoman servant and tutor of music and languages, or even, as her own verses would have us believe, she was there as a poet, supported by a countess who was patron to the male poets Daniel and Spenser. Aemilia Lanyer's husband, Alfonso, died in 1613, and we have a few hazy details of her life after this. She died in 1645, aged seventy-six, and was listed as a "pensioner" on her burial, a title that indicates that, in spite of the vicissitudes of her life, she was a woman of regular income at its end.

It is Lanyer's volume of poems, *Salve Deus Rex Judaeorum*, that is her true legacy, and not the presumed scandals of her life. Like Dorothy Leigh, she produced a work of Protestant piety that foregrounds the spiritual authority of a woman's voice, and in doing so she succeeded in disrupting the representation of the Virgin as a silent and obedient role model only. *Salve Deus Rex Judaeorum* was first published in 1611, the same year as the King James Bible. In three parts, it comprises dedicatory works to a range of virtuous and influential women, a long meditation on Christ's passion, and a country-house poem about Lanyer's time at Cookham with the Countess of Cumberland and her daughter. The work of scholars including Susanne Woods, Barbara Lewalski, Janet Mueller, and Naomi Miller has earned for Lanyer a place in the canon, and studies of her poetry are now a staple of many university Renaissance courses. Lanyer's volume of poems, printed and not circulated in manuscript form, trumpets her desire to be perceived not as a silent woman but as a professional poet. In it, she constructs a clear identity as a female poet writing for women.[35] The prefatory poems of dedicatory verses are all addressed to women. Some of these addressees—Queen Anna, Princess Elizabeth, and Lady Arbella Stuart—seem optimistically aspirational when one considers that Lanyer's marriage had seriously diminished her association with the court, but there are also poems dedicated to women who directly influenced her life.[36] The subject of one poem is the dowager Countess of Kent, who had helped with her humanist education, and the chief addressee throughout the entire volume is her possible patron the Countess of Cumberland. Aspirational or no, Lanyer's poetic relationship with women sets an important tone through its conscious creation of an imagined community of pious women. *Salve Deus Rex Judaeorum* is ostensibly about the passion of Christ—but it is really concerned with the position of women. While Lanyer conforms to Protestant belief systems, she also interrogates and reshapes them, and her depiction of the Virgin Mary is fundamental to this.

Lanyer's poetry shows an acute awareness that a woman writer resists the "silent, chaste, and obedient" construct of a woman who is subordinate to her father and her husband. Dorothy Leigh's work circumvents this through its posthumous publication and domestic subject matter; Lanyer's solution is to turn directly to God's will in a miscellany of poems that, in Barbara Lewalski's words, fuses "religious devotion and feminism."[37] She admits that her muse flies "above the pitch" of its "appointed straine" (274) and compares it to Icarus, flying dangerously beyond boundaries. As a female poet she too is straying close to danger, but she uses divine inspiration as an excuse for this:

> Therefore I humbly for his Grace will pray,
> That he will give me Power and Strength to Write,
> That what I have begun, so end I may,
> As his great Glory may appeare more bright;
> Yea in these Lines I may no further stray,
> Than his most holy Spirit shall give me Light.[38]

Humility and weakness thus coexist with a "power and strength" that is given and guided by God. Through her own role as a writer of spiritual subject matter, Lanyer thus both adheres to and evades the woman's role as "Weaker . . . in Sexe" (289–90).

Lanyer's story begins *in medias res*, on the night that Christ was betrayed, and takes the reader to a brief glimpse of the moment of his resurrection. It is punctuated throughout with frequent meditations on the views of the women who are traditionally on the margins of the tale. These include the weeping women of Jerusalem and Mary Magdalene, but one of the lengthiest of these digressions comes from Pilate's wife, the subject of a single verse in Matthew's Gospel (Matt. 27:19). In a section of the poem entitled *Eves Apologie in defence of Women*, Pilate's wife urges her husband not to execute Christ, using Eve as a vehicle for a rhetorical argument about the culpability of men who make weak decisions.[39] Lanyer's views on Eve in this section are even stronger than Dorothy Leigh's. Pilate's wife argues that Eve had no idea of the consequences of giving Adam the forbidden fruit to eat but that Adam, as the ostensibly stronger sex, should have known better:

> But surely Adam can not be excusde,
> Her fault though great, yet hee was most too blame;
> What Weaknesse offerd, Strength might have refusde,
> Being Lord of all, the greater was his shame.
>
> (777–80)

Pilate is even more culpable than Adam if he betrays God's son "in malice" (816). Lanyer creates in Pilate's wife a female character who professes obedience to her male husband and Lord, while simultaneously using a woman's position as the seemingly weaker sex as a weapon to chastise him:

> Let not us Women glory in Mens fall,
> Who had power given to over-rule us all.
>
> (759–60)

Through this, women's superiority is established, and thus their subordination is subtly questioned.

This apparently contradictory blending of subordination and empowerment is a constant motif in Lanyer's poem. It is present in her descriptions of a daring and dangerous muse, and it underpins her bold descriptions of the Virgin Mary. For sixteen stanzas, Lanyer's narrative invites the reader to consider "The sorrow of the virgin Marie":

> His woefull Mother wayting on her Sonne,
> All comfortlesse in depth of sorrow drowned;
> Her griefes extreame, although but new begun,
> To see his bleeding body oft shee swouned;

> How could shee choose but thinke her selfe undone,
> He dying, with whose glory shee was crowned?
> (1009–14)

The multilayered depiction of the Virgin in these lines is characteristic of Lanyer's approach. Mary is not a passive victim; instead, she is a woman elevated by her suffering. The grief that she experiences is so intense that "to see his bleeding body oft shee swooned." Gary Kuchar has persuasively argued that the addition of the swoon before Jesus on the cross assigns to Mary a priestly role, as it evokes a medieval iconographical tradition of the Virgin's swoon, where her experience of a physical pain identical to Christ's portended her role as co-redemptrix. The poem's account of the Virgin thus reinstates a late medieval tradition of representing the Virgin as a physically anguished priestly co-redeemer—a role that is considerably at odds with the general Protestant view of her as having no active or direct role in the work of redemption. On one level, this can actually be seen as a particularly gendered Protestant stance: in Kuchar's words, it makes "the Lutheran promise of the priesthood of all believers genuinely meaningful for women, particularly for [Lanyer] as poet-priestess."[40] However, there is also a powerful evocation here of the Virgin's intercessory role as Queen of Heaven. Lanyer's Mary is clearly a *Mater Dolorosa* figure, but she is also "crowned" in the glory of Christ (1014). Theresa DiPasquale has described Mary here as "exposed and vulnerable on the road to Calvary in precisely the way that a secular queen mother would be on the occasion of her son's deposition and execution."[41] DiPasquale's is a particularly apposite reading of this moment of the poem, for although Lanyer's Virgin Mary is an abject figure who is engulfed by her sorrow she seems still to inhabit the glorious role of Queen of Heaven. The plurisignification of the image of the Virgin, taken as given in medieval writing and eradicated by many Protestant writers, is here restored.

Patterned throughout Lanyer's descriptions of the Virgin are allusions to her coronation. An evocative example of this comes in Lanyer's description of Mary's tears, which are described as both healing and powerful, as they literally wash away the blood of Christ:

Her teares did wash away his pretious blood,
That sinners might not tread it under feet
To worship him and that it did her good
Upon her knees, although in open street,
Knowing he was the Jessie floure and bud,
That must be gath'red when it smell'd most sweet:
Her Sonne, her Husband, Father, Saviour, King,
Whose death killd Death, and tooke away his sting.
                                                        (1017–24)

Humility and power coexist in these lines: the Virgin is "upon her knees," but her tears are not signs of feminine weakness. Instead, they perform a potent action. The intimate image of the Virgin's tears mingling with her son's "pretious blood" transforms the violence of the tortured Christ's blood into something beautiful, rescuing it from the degradation of being trampled on by the male agents of his death. This action is an adaptation of Mary's role as intercessor and Queen of Heaven. In washing away Christ's blood, she is saving the sinners who have put Christ to death from committing yet another sin: they may have caused him to shed blood, but they are actively prevented from treading it underfoot. The Virgin is not verbally interceding on a sinner's behalf, but her tears intercede between the sinner and further sinful action. Her actions control the arc of the narrative at this point: she is more than a passive griever, and far more than simply a model of modest female behavior for the godly Protestant woman to emulate. As the weeping Virgin prays to Christ, Lanyer presents a litany of Christ's many roles: to Mary he is "Her Sonne, Her Husband, Father, Saviour, King" (1023). The use of the words *Husband* and *King* alludes to Christ the King's spiritual marriage to Mary the Queen of Heaven.

Lanyer's depiction of the Virgin includes several stanzas in which the speaker apostrophizes Mary, describing the moments of her annunciation and the incarnation of Christ. Throughout these stanzas, Lanyer weaves in references to the Magnificat, Mary's song of praise on visiting her cousin Elizabeth (Luke 1:46–55), which is the most sustained example of the Virgin's voice in the Bible. By the time Lanyer wrote *Salve Deus Rex Judaeorum*, the Magnificat had become integral to the Anglican service of evening prayer, or evensong, a place that it still holds today in the Anglican liturgy. In *The Book of Common Prayer*, the Magnificat begins with the following words from Luke's Gospel:

My soule doeth magnifie the Lorde.
And my spirit hath rejoyced in god my saviour.
For he hath regarded the lowelines of his hand maiden.
For beholde from hencefurth al generacions shall call me blessed.
For he that is mightie hath magnified me: and holy is his name.[42]

Protestant depictions of the Virgin of the Magnificat stressed her lowliness and poverty; these qualities, along with Mary's humility and obedience at the Annunciation, created an *ancilla Domini* figure.[43] Calvin's commentary on the Magnificat, discussed in chapter 2 of this study, presents the Virgin, in a state of utter self-abnegation, attributing "the whole cause of her joy, to the free grace and goodnesse of God."[44] In *The Instruction of a Christen Woman*, Vives brushes over the Magnificat, referring to it simply as she "speketh to the preyse of god" (62); his emphasis instead is on the muteness of the Virgin.

In Lanyer's poem, both the Annunciation and the Magnificat are reimagined, and her descriptions of the Virgin's annunciation actively resist the humble and obedient paradigms of the Protestant model:

For the Almightie magnified thee,
And looked downe upon thy meane estate:
Thy lowly mind, and unstain'd Chastitie
Did pleade for Love at great *Jehovaes* gate,
Who sending swift-wing'd *Gabriel* unto thee,
His holy will and pleasure to relate;
To thee most beauteous Queene of Woman-kind
The Angell did unfold his Makers mind.
                                                          (1033–40)

As in Luke's Magnificat, God magnifies Mary, looking down on her lowly state, but this is also a stanza that depicts the Virgin as an active agent of her own fate. Her "lowly mind" and "unstain'd Chastitie" dynamically plead on behalf of "Love" of mankind, and God responds by sending "swift-wing'd Gabriel" to her. Like Pilate's wife, like Lanyer herself, the Virgin is empowered as well as humble. Gabriel in many Annunciation traditions is portrayed as a symbol of God's masculine authority, but in Lanyer's version the Virgin's feminine authority presents her as his equal.[45] She is the "most beauteous Queene of Womankind." Lanyer uses the same phrase as Joseph Swetnam to describe the Virgin Mary here, but the effect is very different. In the context of Swetnam's misogynistic tract, the phrase seems drained of all associations of power. In Lanyer's hands, the same phrase makes the Virgin Mary the apogee of her imagined group of pious women, able simultaneously to inhabit the roles of humble servant and authoritative queen. Like Lanyer herself in her role as a poet directed by a godly muse, Mary becomes a spiritual guide, a force to be reckoned with, appropriate indeed for a poem that places women, to use Achsah Guibbory's words, "at the heart of the sacred."[46]

Lanyer's choice of language for Gabriel's greeting to Mary, "Haile Mary full of grace" (1041), is also highly charged:

He thus beganne, Haile Mary full of grace
Thou freely art beloved of the Lord.
(1041–42)

To describe Mary as "full of grace" at a moment in time before Christ's sacrifice on the cross jarred against Calvinist belief systems. Inherent in the words is an understanding of the Virgin's immaculate conception, the purity that allowed her to be assumed bodily into heaven. There is also the possibility of interpreting the greeting as indicating that Mary herself is able to bestow grace. The Greek words used for Gabriel's greeting (Luke 1:28) are "Chaire kecharitōmenē," translated by Jerome in the Vulgate version as "Ave gratia plena." The Douai-Rheims translation of this is "Hail full of grace," a greeting used in the rosary prayer Ave Maria. This translation was retained by Wycliffe and Tyndale but was eradicated from the Bishop's Bible, where instead the angel greets Mary with the words "Hayle freelie beloved," while the Geneva Bible renders the words as "Haile thou that art freely beloved." The glossing in the Geneva Bible at this point reminds the reader that the Virgin is beloved "not for her merites: but onely through Gods fre mercie, who loved us, when we were sinners" (Luke 1:28, note s). The King James Bible also omits "full of grace"; its rendering of the Greek is "Hail, thou art highly favoured."[47] Yet Lanyer chooses to revert to "full of grace" at this point, and the result is that her representation of the Virgin is further empowered. Lanyer also alludes to the Magnificat in Gabriel's assertion that praise of Mary "should last so many worlds beyond thy daies" (1048); this, along with the earlier line "Deere Mother of our Lord, whose reverend name / Al people Blessed call, and spread thy fame" (1031–32) recalls the Magnificat's "Al generacions shall call me blessed." Mary's role in bearing Jesus is one that guarantees her place in history, and Lanyer's verse uses this to create a legacy for the Virgin as a powerful spiritual female figure.

In Lanyer's reimagining of the Magnificat and the Annunciation, humility and power constantly coexist. There is no doubt that the Virgin is being praised for her humility and submission to God, as phrases such as "on the knees of thy submissive heart" (1073) indicate, but language such as "humbly didst demand" (1074) juxtaposes this submission with an active—even forceful—petition to God. The image Lanyer uses to describe the moment of the Incarnation itself is here significant:

> When he, to answere this thy chaste desire
> Gives thee more cause to wonder and admire.
> (1079–80)

The phrase "chaste desire" indicates that the Virgin actively and joyously desires to bear Christ. This joy is affirmed at the moment of the Incarnation:

> Yea that the holy Ghost should come on thee
> A maiden Mother, subject to no paine,
> For highest powre should overshadow thee:
> Could thy faire eyes from teares of joy refraine,
> When God look'd downe upon thy poore degree?
> Making thee Servant, Mother, Wife and Nurse
> To Heavens bright King, that freed us from the curse.
> (1082–88)

Lanyer's listing of the Virgin's many roles—itself an echo of a Catholic litany—here consciously resists the passive Virgin created by many Protestant writers. The roles of "mother" and "nurse," marginalized in Protestant writing, are freighted with the controversial significance of the Virgin's control over her baby son. In the prose piece entitled "To the Vertuous Reader" that forms part of the prefatory section of *Salve Deus Rex Judaeorum*, Lanyer exalts the superiority of womankind in general, commenting that Christ was "borne of a woman, nourished of a woman, obedient to a woman" (44–45). Mary's role as a mother commanding obedience is foregrounded here; this flies in the face of the anxieties of the Protestant writing this study has already explored, which frequently linked the Virgin's maternal power over the infant Christ with her perceived overaggrandizement as Queen of Heaven. The intertwining of these states with "wife" is more incendiary still, gesturing as it does toward the Virgin in her queenly state as the spiritual bride of Christ. Lanyer's subsequent descriptions of Christ's incarnation further evoke the coronation of the Virgin, as the act of conceiving Christ is seen as "being crown'd with glory from above / Grace and Perfection resting in thy breast" (1089–90).

Lanyer's meditation on the role of the Virgin ends with the *Mater Dolorosa* viewing her son's battered body "with faire eies" (1131). The vivid physicality and emotion of Lanyer's imagery, particularly of the suffering Christ, creates in her poetry effects that are not dissimilar to those of the Counter-Reformation Baroque.[48] She lingers over descriptions of the body of Christ in a way that mirrors the affective piety of Counter-Reformation writing, showing the reader "his alabaster breast, his bloody side / his members torne" (1162–63). After this, Mary's explicit presence from the poem fades, as instead the Countess of Cumberland is placed directly into the scene, viewing the distorted but beautiful spectacle of the crucified Christ

This with the eie of Faith thou maist behold,
Deere Spouse of Christ, and more than I can write;
And here both Griefe and Joy thou maist unfold,
To view thy Love in this most heavy plight.
(1169–72)

The countess is here the "Spouse of Christ"—as an individual wor- shipper becoming the embodiment of the church, and the embodiment of the soul—but in light of the imagery of the eyes Lanyer has earlier used, she is the Virgin Mary too, the grieving mother standing at the foot of the cross who is also Christ's spiritual bride. The Virgin's con- tinued implied presence in the poem is reinforced by the language that connects her to the countess; just as the Virgin with "faire eies beholds his bodie torne" (1131), the countess "with the eie of Faith thou maist behold."[49] The countess, the Virgin, the reader, and the poet thus stand together at the foot of the cross. The poem's imagined community of women readers, with the Countess of Cumberland at their head, be- comes a community of brides of Christ, exhorted by Lanyer to stand in the place of the Virgin Mary, a woman whose purity made her able to bear Christ into the world and who thus is an active agent in the salva- tion of all. When the countess is described at the end of the poem as the "Great Ladie of my heart" (1836), one feels that Lanyer is addressing the Virgin too as a model of virtue who has been brought out of the shadows, empowered by a female poet's words.

Aemilia Lanyer's representation of the Virgin Mary in *Salve Deus Rex Judaeorum* strains at the leash of the reductive models of a chaste, obedient, and pious woman, while simultaneously adhering to them.[50] But although Lanyer invests the Virgin with a significance that can be viewed as unusual in Protestant writing, this is not to argue that her character of Mary is a "Catholic" construct.[51] As Achsah Guibbory has powerfully suggested, Lanyer's identification with the Virgin Mary is "a Protestant revision of Catholic Mariolatry," in which "the Virgin Mary becomes a pattern for the individual woman's unmediated con- nection with the divine."[52] This valuable reading indicates that for the Virgin Mary to remain a significant figure in Lanyer's verse, she needs to be seen as an active, rather than a passive, agent. Lanyer's repeated al- lusions to Mary's queenly state are fundamental to her creation of a powerful but pious Virgin. When seen in light of the enforced bifurca- tion of the Virgin's image into humble handmaid and glorious queen that this study has already identified, Lanyer's Virgin Mary can be seen as posing a direct resistance to a Protestant paradigm. Allusions to the Queen of Heaven in *Salve Deus Rex Judaeorum* do not directly present

Mary as man's mediatrix, but along with the Virgin's active representation in this poem, they disrupt the discourse of Mary as a submissive
and obedient vessel. Instead, many of the more empowered associations
of the role of Queen of Heaven—a nursing mother of the infant Christ,
a queen mother, and a matriarch who elicits obedience—are added into
the mix, coexisting with the sorrowful woman who has actively yearned
for Christ's love. Ultimately, Lanyer's radical interpretation of the Virgin Mary stands outside both "Protestant" and "Catholic" models. In a
utopia of pious, priestly women, a reductive image of the Virgin is not
enough.

For all its professions of a harmonious godly marriage, conduct literature created a fictional construct of a woman, an aspirational figure
who was contained, mute, within male-authored texts. To inscribe such
a two-dimensional figure onto the elusive, protean image of the Virgin
is equally aspirational. In very different ways, Dorothy Leigh and Aemilia Lanyer indicate this through their privileging of the Virgin's spiritual relevance. The Virgin is for them an ideal woman—but she is an
active rather than a passive, force. Both writers deploy the image of the
Virgin as an authoritative mother figure to mount subtle challenges to
Jacobean religio-political ideologies where the father figure was both
king and spiritual leader; as Naomi J. Miller has observed, both writers
"locate both wisdom and authority in maternal affection."[53] In *The
Mother's Blessing*, Leigh invests the role of a mother with a spiritual authority that overshadows that of the patriarchal father figure. The Virgin, as an exemplary mother, becomes a site of maternal power. More
boldly still, Lanyer uses allusions to the Queen of Heaven as an indication that the Virgin should be perceived as the apogee of a powerful
priesthood of women. More than anything, these female-authored
texts reveal the instability of the Virgin's image in Elizabethan and Jacobean writing, presenting to us an implicit but extremely evocative
disruption of the Queen of Heaven/humble handmaid binary.

CHAPTER 5

The Queen of Heaven
and the Sonnet Mistress

The Sacred and Secular Poems of Henry Constable

Now is he for the numbers that Petrarch flowed in.
—*Romeo and Juliet*, 2.3.36

In the late sixteenth century, the courtier poet Henry Constable wrote a sequence of love sonnets in which he adopted the position of a servile lover seeking favor from a cruel mistress. In many of these poems, the addressee was Queen Elizabeth herself. On the surface, Constable's poems are expressions of an anguished love. But as Arthur Marotti has so succinctly observed, love is not always love in an Elizabethan sonnet, which is frequently encoded with the ambition and social status of its creator. The lover-speaker's anguish thus becomes an analogy for the courtier's pursuit of preferment or patronage, something that becomes particularly acute in poems that took the queen herself as an unattainable, virginal object of desire.[1] Constable's secular work is indicative of this complex semiosis, but his conversion to Catholicism in the early 1590s resulted in a radical change in poetic voice. In seventeen "Spirituall Sonnettes," the focus of Constable's adoration shifted from the mistress of the secular sonneteering tradition to the Virgin Mary. Perhaps because he was so steeped in a poetic tradition that elevated the mistress, and also because a number of his secular sonnets had been written to the queen, he chose to represent the Virgin almost exclusively as the Queen of Heaven. The resulting poetry is encoded in a very different way, as it seeks heavenly, rather than earthly, patronage.

Constable's oppositional representation of the Queen of Heaven is at the core of this chapter. An initial focus on Constable's secular poetry will illustrate how his was the voice of the fashionable Elizabethan gentleman poet, particularly in his use of the Petrarchan language of love and self-abnegation as a coded reference to patronage and service. He was also an exponent of a particularly intriguing poetic fashion of using sacred—particularly Catholic—language to express erotic desire. Hovering over this analysis is the figure of Queen Elizabeth, the idealized addressee of a number of Constable's poems. I will then move to Constable's sacred sonnets to the Queen of Heaven, where I will show how Constable's depiction of the Virgin as an archetype of beauty feels like a conscious rebuff of his earlier use of devotional language to configure erotic desires. Rather obliquely, this analysis contributes to scholarship that connects the Virgin Queen and the Virgin Mary, as it discusses how Constable used the image of the Queen of Heaven as a way of criticizing the Petrarchan cults surrounding Elizabeth. After this, my discussion widens to include other writers in an examination of two different aspects of Elizabethan and Jacobean culture. The first is an analysis of the way in which Constable, like other Catholic writers of his time, placed the Virgin within a clearly defined heavenly hierarchy, showing a Counter-Reformation development of Neoplatonic concepts of beauty and love. In Constable's poetry, love of Mary, as a mirror of perfection, could lead man to God. My final extended area of investigation is into the context of Constable's striking use of the image of the Virgin as both Queen of Heaven and Virgo Lactans. In depicting the Virgin in this way, Constable was entering a discourse freighted with cultural and ideological controversy.

Constable's life story shows how the path of the apostate in Elizabethan England was frequently a checkered one.[2] He was born in 1562 into a distinguished family, and his early history is one of privilege and advantageous social connections. He was educated at Cambridge, and after graduating he spent some time in France, possibly as a spy. He was also a prominent figure at court, a popular gentleman poet who had links to the Sidney-Pembroke coterie and whose social standing was only slightly below that of courtly writers such as Sidney, Dyer, and Fulke Greville.[3] During this time in his life, he carved for himself a reputation not only as a poet but also as a Protestant polemicist.[4] This was soon to change. In 1591, Constable left England for France on an expedition led by the Earl of Essex. He never returned during Elizabeth's reign; at some point after his arrival in France, he publicly announced his conversion to Catholicism. It is thought that this occurred in 1591 and that Constable's father's death, in the same year, may have been related to the shock of his son's decision.[5] Upon leaving England, Constable spent time in Paris and Rome and undertook a mission to Scotland in 1599 in an attempt to convert James to the Catholic faith. He returned to England on James's accession, again with the aim of converting the king to Catholicism. His attempt was thwarted by Robert Cecil, leading to his imprisonment and ultimate exile, again in France. He died in Liège in 1613.

The main body of Constable's extant secular work is a series of sixty-three sonnets whose source is the Dyce, or Todd Manuscript, housed in the Victoria and Albert Museum.[6] Constable's influence as a secular poet has long been recognized. His work was integral to the development of the sonnet form in England, and his influence is felt in the works of many other writers of his age, including the poetry of Shakespeare, Drayton, and Daniel.[7] A sequence of twenty-three secular sonnets was published in a collection entitled *Diana* in 1592, when the English sonneteering craze, sparked by the 1591 publication of *Astrophil and Stella*, was at its height.[8] In the nineteenth century, Constable's secular sonnets were championed by William Hazlitt, who described them as the work of "a mind rich in fancy and invention."[9] The secular sonnets have subsequently enjoyed a place in many anthologies of Elizabethan verse. Circulated in manuscript in Constable's lifetime were seventeen "Spirituall Sonnettes, to the Honour of God and Hys Saintes."[10] Hazlitt observed that they "rarely rise above mediocrity," but more recently these verses have been viewed as a body of culturally and aesthetically significant work and have gained a rightful place in anthologies of Catholic writing.[11] Constable's sacred verses are now read by scholars including Alison Shell, Helen Hackett, and Gary Kuchar in a way that acknowledges their deployment of imagery of Catholic devotion.[12] Although the specific date of composition of these sacred sonnets is not known, their marked difference in tone from Constable's secular work supports a generally accepted theory that they were written after his public conversion.[13] As this chapter will show, they are written from a standpoint that not only is passionately Catholic, but also frequently seems to be set in opposition to the poet's own secular work.

CONSTABLE'S SECULAR SONNETS

Constable's secular sonnets are a series of elegantly crafted and rhetorically adept poems that reveal that their writer is a man of fashion. The addressee is repeatedly represented as an idealized archetype of beauty through language that brims over with Petrarchan motifs. She needs no weapons but her eyes, she is white-skinned, and she has decorously blushing cheeks. Constable's lady is cruel and tyrannical as well as sweet: a series of sonnets project the speaker's anguish as he complains of misfortune in love. When the lady in question is the queen herself, Constable's work exemplifies a tradition in both poetry and pageantry that portrayed Elizabeth as a beautiful but cruel Petrarchan mistress. His sonnets to the queen were written to a woman who was well versed in Petrarchan language, having followed the style herself in a poem written following the departure of her French suitor Alençon.[14] Elizabeth also understood that the language of love was frequently a codified expression of a courtier's thwarted ambitions. It is highly significant that during her reign the word *courtship* took on the meaning of wooing a woman as well as behaving like a courtier, in what Ilona Bell has described as "a telling concatenation of meanings."[15]

A sonnet entitled "To the Queene touching the cruell effects of her perfections" epitomizes this:

Most sacred prince why should I thee thus prayse
Which both of sin and sorrow cause hast beene
Proude hast thow made thy land of such a Queene
Thy neighboures enviouse of thy happie dayes.

Whoe never saw the sunshine of thy rayes
An everlasting night his life doth ween
And he whose eyes thy eyes but once have seene
A thowsand signes of burning thoughts bewrayes
Thus sin thow causd envye I meane and pride
Thus fire and darknesse doe proceed from thee
The very paynes which men in hell abide
Oh no not hell but purgatorie this
Whose sowles some say by Angells punish'd be
For thow art shee from whome this torment is.[16]

Here is all the Petrarchan hyperbole of the rejected lover, as those denied the light of Elizabeth's gaze dwell in "everlasting night." Meanwhile, those on whom the queen's gaze has alighted are plunged into the "fire and darknesse" of tortured love, wracked with envy. This sonnet speaks very strongly, however, of love as a political exchange: in the first quatrain, the speaker uses the gender-neutral term *prince* to describe the queen as a monarch who has made her realm proud. However, in the sonnet's final lines, the speaker's state of jealous torment shows all the self-abnegation of the secular sonneteer, with the queen in the position of a *belle dame sans merci*.[17]

Constable uses a particularly arresting metaphor to describe this sense of rejection—"not hell but purgatorie this." The qualifying "some say" creates a sense of distance between speaker and Catholic beliefs, but when one considers the poet's own personal history of apostasy, this creates in the poem an extraordinary moment of tension. In reality, this is an image that tells us everything and nothing. The Catholic signifier *purgatorie* is one of many examples of sacred language used to configure the erotic in Constable's verse and may exist here simply for aesthetic purposes. Constable was a man of poetic fashion after all, and a fascinating interchange of sacred and erotic imagery, commonplace in medieval courtly love poetry, was popular in the latter years of Elizabeth's reign, when the use of Catholic lexis became particularly fashionable.[18] Constable's lover-speaker often expresses his agony in terms of martyrdom, for example. In one poem, "To his Ladies hand upon occasion of her glove which in her absence he kissed" (131), the beloved's glove is fetishized into a relic, as he places himself in the position of

Christ. Her hand has given him, like Christ, five wounds, and these secular stigmata, he observes, cause him to feel pain at a greater intensity than Saint Francis:

Now (as Saint Francis) if a Saint am I
The bow which shotte these shafts a relique is
I meane the hand which is the reason why
So many for devotion thee would kisse
And I thy glove kisse as a thinge devine
Thy arrowes quiver and thy reliques shrine.

The variegated religious landscape of Reformation England makes the use of language such as this particularly perplexing.[19] In the case of an apostate such as Henry Constable it is tempting to read the poet's own confessional anxiety into his erotic use of images such as *relique*. John Carey's 1981 study of John Donne's poems showed how personal confessional details can influence this interchange, in what Paul Franssen has termed a "Resurrection of the Author." This is certainly a productive methodology to apply to Constable's verse; it is hard not to feel that Constable's apostasy freights his use of imagery such as "purgatorie" and "relique" in his secular verse with a certain significance.[20] But although his words may imply a swerve toward Catholicism, they can simultaneously be read as images used by a courtier poet who was simply following the fashion of the times.

Constable's only secular poem that specifically refers to the Virgin deploys religious language in a different way and is a thought-provoking piece with regard to both the encomiastic use of the Virgin's image and the fluidity of confessional standpoints in the writing of an apostate. Entitled "To the Countesse of Shrewsburye," this elegant and sophistic sonnet is about names, turning on the fact that the countess, Mary Talbot, is herself called Mary. Constable here uses the image of the Virgin as a vehicle for poetic praise. Other women named Mary, Mary Queen of Scots and Mary Tudor, had reigns of "bloud and fire." But although the Countess of Shrewsbury may not have worn a crown on earth, her goodness means she is worthy of a crown in heaven and can thus be likened in praise to the Virgin:

Playnlie I write because I will write true
If ever Marie but the Virgin were
Meete in the realme of heaven a crowne to beare
I as my creed believe that it is yow.
And soe the world this Ile and age shall rue
The bloud and fire was shed and kindled heere
When woemen of youre name the croune did beare.
(145)

A number of factors indicate that this sonnet was written around the time of Constable's conversion. Its title suggests that it was written after November 10, 1590, when Mary succeeded as countess. Constable's public renunciation of Protestantism came just after this, in 1591, after which time he was to rely on the Talbots' protection.[21] However, the actual confessional perspective of this sonnet is an evasive one. Certainly, the Catholic and contentious figure of the Queen of Heaven is an overarching presence, but the overall impression the poem leaves is of a man who is covering his tracks. As Alison Shell comments, the other Marys in the sonnet, excoriated by the speaker, are both Catholic queens.[22] And although the Virgin is described as "meete," or worthy, to wear a crown in heaven, the sonnet stops short of explicitly stating that she actually is doing so. The use of "I as my creed" certainly does suggest an alternative belief system, but the religious beliefs in question are bound up with the flattering tropes of patronage and service. It is an image, therefore, that gestures toward Constable's postconversion fascination with the Virgin as Queen of Heaven, while simultaneously distancing itself from it. This creates in this sonnet a sense of theological instability that pushes beyond the use of sacred language for erotic purposes.

CONSTABLE'S SACRED PARODIES

By contrast, the figure of the Virgin in Constable's sacred sonnets is explicitly—almost ostentatiously—venerated. Constable wrote four sonnets addressed directly "To our blessed Lady," and in all four he represented the Virgin as Queen of Heaven. The image of the Virgin itself forms one of the most evocative *topoi* in the interrelation of sacred and secular; the roots of this are in the medieval tradition of courtly love, which often redeployed imagery of Mary as a way of connoting erotic devotion. This was a two-way exchange, as the Virgin was frequently described in sacred verse using language associated with the mistress of the courtly love tradition.[23] As Julia Kristeva has observed, "Both Mary and the Lady were focal points of men's aspirations and desires."[24] In Elizabethan England, the image of the Virgin Mary was, both explicitly and implicitly, part of the Catholic language that became fashionable in literature written toward the end of the queen's reign. Imagery connected with the Virgin was also used by some courtly poets in more extravagant panegyric to the queen.[25] Constable did not use images connected with Mariology to describe the queen in his secular verse, but his sacred works should be seen as a significant addition to discourses that connect Queen Elizabeth with the Virgin Mary. Written from outside the court, but in full awareness of courtly language and politics, they consciously adopt a standpoint of censure rather than of praise. Constable's representation of the Virgin as both queen and object of affection in his "Spirituall Sonnettes" is analogous to descriptions of Elizabeth in encomiastic poetry, his own included. His sacred poems are an apologia for the Virgin in her Catholic, controversial guise of Queen of Heaven and a criticism not only of Queen Elizabeth herself but also of the extravagant love poetry written about her.

In his secular verse Constable used sacred language to connote the erotic, but in his sacred poetry there is a transformation, as erotic and sensual language now expresses spiritual love. The term *sacred parody* is frequently used to describe sacred poetry that responds directly to trends in secular verse.[26] There are many examples of sacred parody in works of writers of varying religious persuasions. The Jesuit poet Robert Southwell, whose poetry is the subject of chapter 7, presents a perfect model of this in his poem "Dyers Phancy turned to a Sinners Complainte," which turned a secular poem by Sir Robert Dyer about unrequited love into a sacred poem about sin and repentance.[27] The extravagant language in Dyer's poem can be viewed as a coded reference to falling out of favor with the queen. Influenced by Southwell, George Herbert reshaped the secular poems of his predecessors to give them spiritual emphasis, entitling one of his sacred poems "A Parodie."[28] What is particularly interesting about Constable's "sacred parodies," however, is that his sacred verse is situated in a dialogue with his own secular voice, as he redeploys the Petrarchan diction he had himself previously used in his secular verse. The resulting effect is, however, the same: the language of secular love poetry in Constable's sacred works expresses a love that the poet perceives as infinitely superior to profane love. In Constable's case, this is a love for the Queen of Heaven rather than the queen of England.

In the first of Constable's four sonnets entitled "To our blessed Lady," the speaker describes the Virgin as "Queene of queens" and connects this with her immaculate conception, a "byrth" that is "free from guylt":

In that (O Queene of queenes) thy byrth was free
from guylt, which others doth of grace bereave
when in theyr mothers wombe they lyfe receave:
God as his sole-borne daughter loved thee.
To matche thee lyke thy byrthes nobillitye,
he thee hys spyryt for thy spouse dyd leave:
of whome thou dydd'st his onely sonne conceave,
and so was lynk'd to all the trinitye.
Cease then, O Queenes who earthly crownes do weare
to glory in the pompe of worldly thynges:
if men such hyghe respect unto yow beare
Which daughters, wyves, & mothers ar of kynges;
What honour should unto that Queene be donne
Who had your God, for father, spowse, & sonne.

(185)

The phrase "byrthes nobillitye" is significantly placed. It connotes that the Virgin Mary, conceived immaculately, is full of the grace that sinful humankind lose from the moment they receive life in their mother's womb. It also underlines the validity of Mary's lineage, justifying her role as Queen of Heaven by emphasizing that she comes from noble stock as a descendant of David's line.[29] This declaration of Mary's true lineage serves the purpose of elevating the Virgin, but it has political implications too. By representing Mary as the "Queene of queenes," Constable is affirming her rightful place in heaven as man's mediatrix. In a more immediate way this cuts Elizabeth I firmly down to size: the sestet's message to all earthly queens is that they are merely daughters, wives, and mothers of kings, while the Virgin is all three. Elizabeth failed to be either wife or mother of a king—and in Catholic eyes was not even a legitimate daughter of a king. In *Rise and Growth of the Anglican Schism* (1585), the Catholic controversialist Nicholas Sander aimed to discredit Elizabeth by advancing the theory that her lineage was incestuous, as Anne Boleyn was in fact Henry VIII's daughter as well as his wife.[30] Elizabeth's legitimacy was also denied in the propaganda war waged by followers of Mary Queen of Scots.[31] The Virgin rises above such sordid scandals, her power resting on the paradox that God was, to her, both "father, spowse & sonne." There is no shadow of a debate about her fitness for rule here. The genre of this sonnet, an encomiastic poem in praise of the Virgin, means that it also functions as a criticism of secular poets who frequently deployed devotional imagery of a goddess, a saint, and even the Virgin Mary to praise the queen, a "hyghe respect" that is viewed as misplaced.

In the second of Constable's sonnets to the Virgin, this sense of criticism of secular poetry is amplified through an examination of beauty. Like the idealized Petrarchan beloved of his secular sonnets, Constable's Virgin is represented as beautiful, but as this sonnet demonstrates, hers is a beauty that outshines that of the earthly mistress. In this poem is a more personal sense of atonement on Constable's part for the former wrongs of his sonnets written in praise of Queen Elizabeth:

> Sovereigne of Queenes: If vayne Ambition move
> my hart to seeke an earthly prynces grace:
> shewe me thy sonne in his imperiall place,
> whose servants reigne, our kynges & queenes above.
> And if alluryng passions I doe prove,
> by pleasyng sighes: shewe me thy lovely face:
> whose beames the Angells beuty do deface:
> and even inflame the Seraphins with love.

So by Ambition I shall humble bee:
when in the presence of the highest kynge
I serve all his, that he may honour mee.
And love, my hart to chaste desyres shall brynge,
when fayrest Queene lookes on me from her throne
and jealous byddes me love but her alone.

(189)

The opening of this sonnet places it firmly in the lexicon of monarchy, patronage, and power, but this is a speaker who focuses on heavenly, rather than earthly, rewards. The Virgin is viewed as a powerful mediatrix, through whom the speaker can see Christ. She is an archetype of beauty, whose face has the power to emit light and whose beauty is above the angels. In an earlier secular sonnet, "Of the excellencye of his Ladies voice" (124), Constable had similarly compared his mistress to angels in the lines "The basest notes which from thy voyce proceed / The treble of the Angells doe exceed." Here the comparison is used for sacred, rather than erotic, purposes. Constable's poem to the Virgin functions as a sacred parody, its use of the language of the lover, so familiar from Constable's earlier secular sonnets, connoting sacred devotion.

The use of imagery so explicitly connected with the love poems of the secular sonneteer serves as a reminder of the poetic style that the speaker has rescinded. His love for the Virgin ennobles him, turning him away from "alluryng passions" and toward "chaste desyres." There is an echo here of the secular Petrarchan sonneteer, who also claimed to be spiritually elevated by devotion to his unattainable mistress; however, this was often delivered with a knowing sense of hypocrisy, masking sexual desire as well as a political subtext. In Sidney's Sonnet 71, for example, Astrophil's "chaste desyres" for Stella collapse into the carnal, as he cries out for physical pleasure: "But ah, desire still cries: 'Give me some food.'"[32] In Constable's sacred sonnet to the Queen of Heaven, the speaker's earthly ambitions, both for self-aggrandizement and for sexual love, are transcended by the Virgin's radiant presence, perhaps to emphasize that only Mary can inspire truly "chaste desyres."

The duality of Constable's representation of Mary as Queen of Heaven—in both her own right and as a vehicle to criticize Queen

Elizabeth—is seen in the extraordinary shift that occurs in this sonnet's final rhyming couplet. Within Constable's vision of heaven, the
"fayrest Queene" of these lines is the Virgin herself, an awe-inspiring
figure who shows justifiable anger at the speaker for seeking earthly
love. Constable's poem here counters Protestant representations of
Mary as a humble handmaid via descriptions of the Virgin as both active and empowered. But the image also evokes Elizabeth, the "fayrest
Queene" at the fulcrum of a backbiting court, who knowingly used the
language of love to demand loyalty and service from rivaling courtiers.
The final lines of this poem function as a criticism not only of secular
poetry such as Constable's own, which presented Elizabeth as the
beautiful but cruel Petrarchan mistress, but also of the queen herself.

THE HIERARCHY OF HEAVEN

Descriptions of the Virgin's beauty also figure strongly in another of
Constable's four sonnets to the Virgin:

> Sweet Queene: although thy beuty rayse upp mee
> From syght of baser beutyes here belowe:
> Yett lett me not rest there: but higher goe
> to hym, who tooke hys shape from God & thee.
> And if thy forme in hym more fayre I see,
> What pleasure from his diety shall flowe,
> by whose fayre beames his beuty shineth so
> when I shall yt beholde aeternally.
> Then shall my love of pleasure have his fyll,
> when beuty self in whom all pleasure ys,
> shall my enamored sowle embrace and kysse:
> And shall newe loves, & newe delyghtes distyll,
> Which from my sowle shall gushe into my hart
> and through my body flowe to every part.
>   (190)

The reference to "baser beutyes" exists as further criticism of secular
poetry for raising up as its idealized beloved a woman who is unworthy

of such praise. In the figure of Christ, Constable sees Mary's form even more beautifully reflected, but the Virgin's own beauty is not enough. This sonnet presents a Christianized version of the Neoplatonic ladder or staircase of virtue. Just as a follower of Castiglione or a Petrarchan sonneteer would claim that adoration of the beauty of an earthly mistress led him upward to an understanding of divine beauty, so here the speaker's adoration of the Virgin's sacred beauty directs him toward an even higher goal: adoration of the beauty of Christ and spiritual communion with him.[33] The erotic imagery that Constable the courtier poet had used to describe "baser beutyes" is here directed wholly toward the sacred, in a poem that builds to a climax of sensual imagery of a soul in ecstasy. As in Donne's *Holy Sonnets*, most notably Sonnet 17, "Batter my hart, three person'd God," sacred and profane love are delicately poised, with love of God superior to erotic earthly love.[34]

Although Constable embodies the Virgin in triumphalist form as Queen of Heaven in this sonnet, the poem's structure clarifies that the Virgin is not at the pinnacle of heaven. Catholic reformers both before and after the Council of Trent preached of a theocentric heaven that was not unlike the vision of their Protestant counterparts. The fundamental difference was the placing of the Queen of Heaven within the divine center.[35] Other Catholic writers of the time who represented the Virgin as Queen of Heaven also clearly delineated her place within the hierarchy of heaven. An example of this can be found in a poem by the Jesuit poet and martyr Henry Walpole entitled "A Prisoner's Song."[36] In this, Jerusalem represents both heaven and a state of mind as Walpole presents us with the double imprisonment of his own literal incarceration and of the soul imprisoned within the body:

My thirstie soule Desyres her Drought
at heavenlie fountains to refreshe
my prisoned mynd would faine be out
of chaines and fetters of the flesh.

In this visionary poem the feminized soul travels to a sensory heaven. The speaker ascends a clearly delineated hierarchy, moving from the perfectly realized natural world through to the inhabitants of heaven. He is able to feast his eyes on the saints in glory and a choir of angels,

but above both of these we find the Virgin, heaven's queen, who is more
elevated than saints or angels:

> Each Confessor a goulden crowne
> adornd with pearle and precious stone
> Thapostles pearles in renowne
> like princes sit in regall throne
> Queene mother virgine Iminent
> then saintes and Angels more devine
> like sunne amids the firmament
> above the planetes all do shine.
>
> (262)

But the Virgin is not the apogee of Walpole's theocentric vision, as the
speaker moves through this vision to one of Christ:

> O princlie palace royall court
> monarchall seate imperiall throne
> where kinge of kinges and sovraigne lord
> for ever ruleth all alone.
>
> (264)

The poem affirms that Christ is heaven's ruler, but like Constable's it
gives a distinctly Neoplatonic take on the concept of Mary as mediatrix; through contemplation of the Virgin, the speaker is able to contemplate the beauty of Christ.

A similar awareness of the Virgin's place in heaven's hierarchy is
seen in a poem, "Of the Joys of Heaven," by Sir Philip Howard, Earl
of Arundel, the man who was probably the author of "The Walsingham Ballad" that began this study. This poem is also written from the
point of view of incarceration; Howard was imprisoned in the Tower
of London on suspicion of treason, dying there in 1595. It is the last in
a series of four meditations on death, the Day of Judgment, hell, and
heaven. In it, the speaker, who has been consigned to hell, has a vision
of the heaven that he is unable to reach, in a poem that speaks volumes
of the martyr's hope for heavenly release from the "hell" of earthly im-

prisonment. Arundel's vision holds echoes of the book of Revelation, and the reader of the poem is invited on a journey through gates of pearl and streets of gold, in a heaven that is lit by the light from the Lamb. It is a beautiful vision, but the language of the poem speaks of "order and degree," as the reader rises through ranks of patriarchs, prophets, saints, and angels. Higher than all of these is the Queen of Heaven. Three stanzas are devoted to a vision of Mary rich in visual imagery that connects her to the Woman Clothed with the Sun:

> Above them all, the Virgin hath a place,
> Which caused the world with comfort to abound:
> The beams do shine in her unspotted face,
> And with the stars her head is richly crowned:
> In glory she all creatures passeth far:
> The moon her shoes, the sun her garments are.

> O Queen of Heaven! o pure and glorious sight!
> Most blessed thou above all women art!
> This city drunk thou makest with delight,
> And with thy beams rejoicest every heart:
> Our bliss was lost and that thou didst restore,
> The Angels all and men do thee adore.

> Lo! here the look which Angels do admire!
> Lo! here the spring from whom all goodness flows!
> Lo! here the sight that men and saints desire!
> Lo! here the stalks on which our comfort grows!
> Lo this is she whom Heaven and earth embrace,
> Whom God did choose and filled full of grace.

This extended meditation represents the Virgin's beauty using imagery reminiscent of secular love poetry. Beams radiate from her face, and she surpasses all around in beauty, her radiance even making the gazer drunk with delight. However, this hierarchical vision of heaven reaches its pinnacle not with Mary but with a vision of Christ as the Lord of Heaven:

And next to her, but in a higher throne,
Our Saviour in his manhood sitteth here:
From whom proceeds all perfect joy alone,
And in whose face all glory doth appear.[37]

The Queen of Heaven is described with rich evocative wonder in this poem, but she is clearly placed below Christ in the heavenly hierarchy. It is Christ who is on the "higher throne," and he alone is the source of "all perfect joy." The Virgin's place within the hierarchical Christocentric heaven of these poems contrasts to her place in the false papistical heaven of Curione's vision in *Pasquine in a Traunce*, where she rules as an overbearing queen-mother over a perpetually infantilized Christ.

THE QUEEN OF HEAVEN AS *VIRGO LACTANS*

The thirteenth of Constable's "Spirituall Sonnettes" contains a particularly striking description of the Queen of Heaven as *Virgo Lactans*, in a sonnet that illustrates a familiar contempt for earthly queens:

Why should I any love O queene but thee?
if favour past a thankfull love should breede?
thy wombe dyd bear, thy brest my saviour feede;
and thow dyddest never cease to succour me.
If Love doe followe worth and dignitye?
thou all in [thy] perfections doest exceede:
if Love be ledd by hope of future meede?
what pleasure more then thee in heaven to see?
An earthlye syght doth onely please the eye,
and breedes desyre, but doth not satisfye:
thy sight, gyves us possession of all joye,
And with such full delyghtes ech sense shal fyll,
as harte shall wyshe but for to see thee styll,
and ever seyng, ever shall injoye.

(190)

Central to this sonnet is the image of the Virgin as *Virgo Lactans*, breast-feeding the infant Christ. In the opening quatrain she is fecund and full, spiritually nourishing the speaker as she physically nourishes Christ. There is a sacred reappropriation here of the language of the secular sonneteer who seeks patronage, service, and hospitality, as well as an echo of Luke 11:27: "Blessed is the wombe that bare thee, and the pappes which thou haste sucked." The whole tone of the sonnet is one of satisfaction and repletion, seen through its repeated imagery of gestation, suckling, and feeding. In it, the Virgin's power is located in her breasts, which physically nurture Christ and spiritually nurture the speaker. Constable's sonnet culminates in a pejorative description of secular pleasure, tainted by the limits of "earthlye syght," which only "breedes desyre." Here the image of breeding is given unpleasant and spiritually sterile associations of lust. In gazing upon an earthly mistress the speaker is using only one sense, and the paucity of this is underlined by the fact that in gazing upon the Virgin he achieves a state of rapture in which all of his senses are engaged and satisfied. Drawing on Platonic theories of vision, Margaret Miles suggests that in gazing at a painting of the Virgin's nursing breast a late medieval and early modern worshipper both "touched the breast and assimilated its nourishment by the act of looking."[38] Certainly, Constable's poem evokes the physical power of sight, creating a corporeal work in which a fecund Virgin is able to nourish the "thankfull love" of the speaker. This image of the Virgin can be perceived as an implicit criticism of Elizabeth, the Virgin Queen who had failed to provide an heir. It thus directly counters iconography surrounding the queen, which, taking its source from Isaiah 66, evoked the image of the feeding mother. Descriptions of Elizabeth as the nursing mother of both the Protestant Church and her subjects amounted almost to a secular reappropriation of the *Virgo Lactans* image.[39]

Constable's descriptions of the *Virgo Lactans* are particularly confrontational, as the image of the Virgin suckling Christ was at this time a discursive site of complex and often conflicting meanings. Initially adapted from pagan images of suckling goddesses, in particular the Egyptian goddess Isis nursing Horus, the *Virgo Lactans* was a part of Marian iconography from the fourth century. Conceptually, there are strong links between the Virgin's roles of nurturer of Christ and intercessory Queen of Heaven. A number of medieval representations of the *Virgo Lactans* show her enthroned and crowned. An example of this is a thirteenth-century wall painting in a church in Great Canfield in Essex that shows the Virgin with the infant Christ on her knee. Her breast is bared, as if she is about to suckle Christ.[40] The image of the Virgin's milk nourishing souls in torment in purgatory was common in the Middle Ages, while representations of the Virgin at the Last Judgment often showed her baring her breast to Christ, as if to remind him of his infant dependency upon her.[41] There were even elements of a power struggle in some late medieval iconography, which showed the Virgin suckling Christ to appease his anger, so that he might show mercy on humanity in the Last Judgment.[42]

The links between the *Virgo Lactans*, *Regina Coeli*, and Mary's role as mediatrix are exemplified in a belief in the powerful spiritual properties of the Virgin's milk. As belief in Mary's corporeal assumption led to the absence of bodily relics, the Virgin's milk itself became a powerful relic. A vial of Mary's milk, for example, supposedly brought from the Holy Land, was the most important relic at the English shrine in Walsingham.[43] The proliferation of similar relics was to come under attack in the Reformation, with Calvin's sarcastic observation that "had the breasts of the most Holy Virgin yielded a more copious supply than is given by a cow, or had she continued to nurse during her whole lifetime, she scarcely could have furnished the quantity which is exhibited."[44] The Virgin's milk was linked with the blood from the wound in Christ's side, both liquids having the power to nurture and heal. Blood, milk, and Eucharistic wine thus become interchangeable: as Susan Signe Morrison has observed, the conflation of the Virgin's milk with Christ's blood "enhances the Virgin's role as co-redemptrix, the mother of the Eucharist and salvation."[45] Associations between milk and blood were further enhanced by the belief, common in both the Middle Ages and Elizabethan England, that breast milk was a purified form of menstrual blood.[46] The physician Thomas Raynalde's manual, *The Birth of Mankind*, reprinted several times during Elizabeth's and James's reigns, observed that "the milk which cometh to the breasts is engendered of the terms."[47]

Commonplace in medieval and early modern discourses was the belief that breast milk carried with it a sense of psychological and moral as well as physical nourishment. One result of this was widespread concern about wet-nursing and the mental and moral characteristics of the nurse, particularly among Puritan writers, although wet-nursing remained the popular choice for most women of higher social status.[48] What if, via suckling the child, the mother or the nurse was passing on negative and immoral personality traits? The image of the nursing mother leaking milk can also be perceived as one of female incontinence and embarrassment.[49] Embedded conceptual links between breast milk, moral rigor, and the instability of the female form led to the breast becoming a site of theological as well as psychological instability in reformist discourse.[50] Feeding and theology fused. It is not surprising, therefore, that breastfeeding came to be associated with a cluster of negative images that were driven by an often misogynistic anxiety. Breast milk also represents the passage from one generation to the next, and in a world where parents were often raised on a different system of beliefs from their children, it came to be associated with dangerous religious beliefs. In Tyndale's *The Obedience of a Christian Man,* the image of the breast is equated with the Catholic faith of the mother, in a warning against following the example of the church's history and using violence: "In as moch (I saye) as we have sucked in soch bloudy imaginacions in to the botome of oure hertes even with oure mothers milke."[51] A similar figurative use of the image can be found in the Elizabethan *Homily Against Peril of Idolatry,* which described the "rabblement of the popish church" as having "drunk in idolatry almost with their mothers milk."[52]

Perhaps because breast milk was so powerfully linked to blood, both physiologically and iconographically, it was often conflated in early modern writing with violent images. In a pamphlet decrying the lack of support given by the Jesuits to Henri IV of France, the persuasive orator Antoine Arnauld made the following observation:

Whence is it, that wee have so often seene the son directly opposite in opinion to his Father, but that the auncient sort did never sucke this milke of Jesuitisme?

But will your Majestie beleeve, that they can be so audacious, as to glory and vaunt, how great, and ghastly a wound they have made in the harts of your subjects, which they enlarge, teare wider, and make bigger from day to day?[53]

Arnauld's subverted use of the image of suckling encompasses the belief in the relationship between breast milk and moral instruction in his
image of the young turning against the old, polluted by the "milke of
Jesuitisme." The nurturing image of breastfeeding here collapses into
the violent image of a body ripped apart, as milk metamorphoses into
the blood of a ghastly, tearing wound.

Literary representations of the suckling breast could also be negative
and violent. Encoded within the proverbial phrase "pap with a hatchet,"
used most famously by Lyly in his contribution to the Marprelate Controversy, is the idea of the nipple being a force for ill rather than good.
In *The Faerie Queene*, Spenser creates the figure of Error, an image of a
nursing mother that is redolent with anxiety about the relationship between breastfeeding and moral and religious instruction. When Redcrosse encounters this monster in book 1 of *The Faerie Queene*, she is
described as suckling her children, all of whom represent monstrous
births:

> Of her there bred
> A thousand yong ones, which she dayly fed,
> Sucking upon her poisnous dugs, eachone
> Of sundrie shapes, yet all ill favored:
> Soone as that uncouth light upon them shone,
> Into her mouth they crept, and suddain all were gone.
>   (1.1.15.4–9)

The image of Error's "poisnous dugs" locates a frightening power
within the breast. It is also significant that Error's monstrous offspring,
unlike those of Milton's Sin, creep back into their mother's mouth and
not her womb. For it is from her mouth that Error, under attack from
Redcrosse, vomits "a floud of poison horrible and blacke" that "full of
bookes and papers was" (1.1.20.6). It is as if her young, nurtured by
their mother's milk, have become the physical embodiment of anxiety
about religious instruction and can therefore continue to propagate
their mother's false creed. The description of Error's vomit as "poison"
links it directly to Spenser's earlier description of her suckling breast.
Mouth, womb, and breast are, in this creation, interchangeable orifices,
all leaking dangerous and terrible propaganda.

Spenser's *Error* is a particularly vivid embodiment of how the suckling breast was perceived in both literature and polemic as a highly complex site of sectarian resistance. In the light of this, the image of the *Virgo Lactans* becomes fraught with a sense of conflict. Regardless of the religious changes to come, the *Virgo Lactans* was already being perceived as a contentious devotional image toward the end of the Middle Ages.[54] One reason for this was a reduced emphasis on Mary's maternal characteristics.[55] Christine Peters notes a gradual diminishing of the view of the figure of Mary baring her breasts in the fifteenth century, which she sees as "part of a general trend in devotion in late medieval England that emphasised the adult Christ at the expense of the infant."[56] Another reason can be found in a cultural shift in the way in which the breast was perceived, moving from a sacred to an erotic, secularized image, one that led to increasingly negative associations of the naked, suckling breast.[57] But as the Reformation gathered pace, sectarian and iconoclastic zeal sealed the fate of the *Virgo Lactans* in Protestant countries. Although the image of breastfeeding can be seen as connoting the Virgin's humility, it is also one in which an infantilized Christ seems powerless before his mother, needing her milk for nourishment and survival.[58] As Sarah Jane Boss has identified, the coexistence of heavenly queen and nursing mother is a paradox, one that "elevated the qualities of lowliness and poverty to the status of virtues of the highest order."[59] Reformation debates about the Virgin tended to construct the suckling mother as a powerful figure, in both a positive and a negative way.

Frances Dolan comments that one way to combat this disturbing dependency on the Virgin was to destroy statues of the Virgin and thus to "unmother Mary through iconoclasm, wrenching the infant from her arms."[60] Another way to "unmother" the Virgin was with words. A particularly compelling example of this is *The Jesuites Gospell* (1610), by William Crashaw, the Protestant polemicist and father of Catholic poet Richard.[61] William Crashaw's text was written as a riposte to a Latin poem by the Antwerp Jesuit Carolus Scribianus, "The Virgin of Halle."[62] In the Middle Ages, Halle in Holland was a popular pilgrimage site whose thirteenth-century statue of the Virgin depicted her as enthroned and crowned, offering her breast to the infant Christ. The statue was said to have performed many miracles, including healing the sick and saving the residents of Halle from attack. Crashaw's text reprints Scribianus's poem in full, with an English translation, thus contributing to the paradox created by many reformist writers, whose polemical attacks on the Queen of Heaven on some level preserved the potency of the image.

In "The Virgin of Halle," the Virgin's milk is conceptually linked with the blood in Christ's side, both having the power to assuage spiritual thirst. The speaker longs, like the infant Christ, to suckle at the Virgin's breast but contents himself with asking for only a drop of blood from Christ's wounds:

> Yongling that in thy mothers armes art playing,
> Sucking her brest sometimes & sometimes staying,
> Why dost thou view me with that look of scorne
> Tis forcelesse envie that gainst thee is borne.
> Oft hast thou said, being angry at my sinne,
> Darest though desire the teats my foode lies in.
> I will not, oh I dare not (noble childe)
> Dutie from me is no so far exiled:
> But one, even one poore drop I doe implore,
> From thy right hand, or side I aske no more.[63]

Crashaw's commentary on the poem revisits the Protestant complaint that to make Christ a dependent infant diminishes his power, turning his mother into an idolatrously all-powerful figure. The conflation of *Virgo Lactans* with the Queen of Heaven is clear:

> Speaking unto Christ, God coaequall with the father, and whose very humanity raigneth now in glory at Gods right hand, as to a seely infant in his mothers armes: and to him whose very humanity is fedde with the glorious presence and contemplation of the deity, as to a poore childe sucking his Mothers brests: such conceits are common, and such words and writings rife with them, of our blessed Saviour, who never speake of the Virgin Mary, but with the Title of Queene of heaven, Lady of angels, the gate of Paradise, the fountaine of mercy, or some such other titles, fitting none but him that is God, or at least she is always a comaunding Mother, and he an infant governed and an obedient childe. (sig. 13r)

Crashaw argues that in daring to desire a drop of Christ's blood and not the Virgin's milk, Scribianus is demonstrating a blasphemous privileging of the Virgin over Christ: "You are content to have Christs blood, but as for the virgin Maries milke thou darest not desire it: what, is her milk more precious, more dainty, more sacred then the blood of the Mediator?" (sig. L2r). A perceived overinflation of the value of Mary's milk here speaks metonymically for the idolatrously overinflated value of the Virgin herself.

Crashaw's vilification of the *Virgo Lactans* comes in response to a triumphalist construction of the image from a Counter-Reformation European writer. Several English Catholic writers, like Constable, used the image of the *Virgo Lactans* as a way of expressing a devotion to the Virgin that can be deemed confrontational. In "The Song of Mary the Mother of Christ," Henry Walpole ventriloquizes the Virgin's voice and portrays the infant Christ as vulnerable as he suckles at his mother's breast:

O how my crosse was ever mixt with sweet!
My paine with joy, mine earth with heavenly blisse!
Who alwaies might adore my Saviours feete,
Imbrace my God, my loving infant kisse.
And give him sucke, who gives the Angels foode,
And turne my milke, into my Saviours bloud.[64]

Walpole uses the image of the breastfeeding Virgin as a way of fore-shadowing the Crucifixion, as milk intermingles with blood. In suckling Christ, the Virgin is nurturing a child and turning him into a man, but the image of her feeding is here seen as a vital part of the sorrow that she experiences at his death.

Christ's vulnerability in Walpole's poem is presented as coexisting with his overall power. The poem creates a paradoxical chain of nurturing where the infant Christ, nurtured by his mother, becomes himself the nurturer and "gives the Angels foode." The prolific Catholic writer Richard Verstegan presents a similar paradox. "Our Lady's Lullaby," also written from the Virgin's point of view, commences with the following striking image:

Upon my lap my soveraigne sits,
And sucks upon my brest,
Meanewhyle his love sustaines my lyf,
And gives my body rest.[65]

The image of the suckling Christ is strikingly direct and physical, but nourishment and nurture in this poem are inverted. Instead of the Virgin nurturing the infant Christ, Jesus is represented as the "soveraigne" whose love has the power to sustain all, including his mother. The juxtaposition of the helpless and dependent "upon my lap" with "soveraigne" encapsulates the paradox of Christ the King of Heaven assuming the fragile form of a baby, a paradox mirrored in the coexistence of humble handmaid and Queen of Heaven. That the infant Christ is suckled by the Virgin is indicative of his vulnerability, but Christ is a mother figure too here, as he has the ability to nurture his mother spiritually.

Constable's use of the image of the *Virgo Lactans* is more controversial than that of both Walpole and Verstegan, as a return to the first four lines of his sonnet shows:

Why should I any love O queene but thee?
if favour past a thankfull love should breede?
thy wombe dyd bear, thy brest my saviour feede;
and thow dyddest never cease to succour me.

The Virgin's power to nurture both Christ and the speaker is here foregrounded, and she is also simultaneously represented as Queen of Heaven. The poem is Constable's defiant reiteration of an empowered Virgin, and his depiction of Mary as both Queen of Heaven and suckling mother is highly engaging. Throughout his "Spirituall Sonnettes," Constable's repeated representation of the Virgin as Queen of Heaven can be seen as a way of counteracting Protestant depictions of the Virgin as a humble handmaid. Perhaps the most controversial of all Constable's representations of the Queen of Heaven, however, is the image of her as the *Virgo Lactans*. It is an image that is worthy of note for more than its medieval resonances; when read in the context of Reformation discourses on the religious significance of breastfeeding, it becomes as confrontational as it is arresting. It can also be viewed as a subtle but potent criticism of the iconography that surrounded Elizabeth I as both queen and nursing mother to her subjects. In the light of Constable's deployment of the image of the Queen of Heaven throughout his sacred verse, it epitomizes a representation of the Virgin that is as polemical as it is triumphant.

Henry Constable's conversion to Catholicism meant that a life that began in the center of Queen Elizabeth's court ended in the shadows of exile. As a secular sonneteer, he was steeped in a tradition that viewed a poem as a political construct, deploying its expressions of love as a tool to gain patronage and service. His sacred poems can also be viewed as politicized constructs—though in a very different way. They are not only devotional writing to the Virgin but also poems that forcefully reclaim and reaffirm the iconography of the Queen of Heaven that Protestantism sought to eradicate. Constable's sacred sonnets simultaneously function as a criticism of secular love poetry and of Queen Elizabeth. The representation of the Queen of Heaven by a man who was both apostate and well trained in the pursuits of courtly verse shows extraordinary tension and power. Constable's deployment of the image of the Queen of Heaven expresses this most polyvalent of images in a way that is acutely oppositional but also articulates a very personal devotion.

CHAPTER 6

A Garland of Aves

The Queen of Heaven and the Rosary

But in this troublous time what's to be done?
Shall we go throw away our coats of steel,
And wrap our bodies in black mourning gowns,
Numb'ring our Ave-Maries with our beads?

—*3 Henry VI*, 2.1.159–62

Imprisoned in the Tower of London in 1594, his hands destroyed by torture, the Jesuit priest John Gerard used a highly inventive and unusual means of communication.[1] He created rosaries out of orange peel and sent them to fellow prisoners wrapped in paper that concealed notes, written in orange juice.[2] Gerard's act of defiance blurred the lines between rebellion and devotion, and his improvised rosaries are a testament to a continued—even revitalized—Marian piety among England's Catholics. His story encapsulates in microcosm both the importance of the rosary in early modern England and its increasing association with secrecy. The fact that Gerard was able to find a way to craft a material object that was clearly identifiable as rosary beads shows how portable and adaptable the rosary was in a world where Catholic rituals had been driven underground and where the prison was frequently reimagined as a spiritual space. A driving force behind the rosary's popularity in early modern England was the many rosary books that were smuggled into the country from the Continent and distributed among the country's recusant community. The portrayal of the Virgin Mary in these books is the subject of the first part of this chapter. Within the pages of early modern rosary books, the Virgin is much more than the humble pious figure of Protestant writing: she is above all else a triumphant, often militant, Queen of Heaven, who is able to intercede for man to God and who provides succor to a beleaguered Catholic community.

After a brief history of the rosary, I will show how frequent pejorative references to it in Protestant English writing indicate not only its continuing cultural vitality but also its growing associations with secrecy. My study of the recusant rosary books themselves begins with *The Societie of the Rosary* (1593 or 1594) by the Jesuit superior Henry Garnet. Garnet was at the forefront of a concerted effort by the Jesuit movement to reposition the rosary so that it was not a medieval prayer to be repeated nostalgically but a valuable and pragmatic method of disseminating Tridentine Catholic values. *The Societie of the Rosary* directly references the difficulties faced by England's recusants, and it depicts the Virgin as a figure who can provide mercy and deliverance in the absence of a priest. Garnet does not present the Queen of Heaven and the humble handmaid as binary opposites; instead, many different aspects of Marian iconography all comfortably coexist in his writing. A similar plurisignification of the Virgin's image can be seen in rosary books written by John Bucke, I. M., Sabine Chambers, and Thomas Worthington.[3] A particularly powerful representation of Mary here is as a model of suffering in adversity whom female readers could emulate. Arguably the most important aspect of the Virgin's image within all recusant rosary books studied, however, is that of intercessory Queen of Heaven, and the use of both visual images and Loyolan meditative methods powerfully evokes this forbidden image in a worshipper's mind. Descriptions of the Queen of Heaven are also frequently framed using the language of the apologia, as many writers display an urgent desire to keep this aspect of Marian iconography alive. This chapter's journey through recusant rosary books will thus build a picture of an image of the Queen of Heaven that was adapted by writers to fit religio-political as well as devotional concerns.

The study of the poetry of Henry Constable in the previous chapter focused on the voice of a man who lived both within and outside of the nexus of the court. The voices of rosary book writers take this study further into the shadows of recusant England, but the conclusions drawn are not dissimilar. The language of recusant rosary books—like the poetry of Henry Constable—demonstrates the extent to which devotional images of the Queen of Heaven became politicized in early modern writing. Constable's work also revealed how a study of the Virgin could be a marker for confessional complexity, and in the second part of this chapter, "Harington's Rosary," I introduce the courtier poet and wit Sir John Harington, another figure whose relationship with the Virgin Mary indicates the diversity of confessions in early modern England. In 1602, Harington presented a collection of poems titled *Epigrams* to King James, arranged in the form of a gift-book that also included an engraving of the mysteries of the rosary and a rosary prayer in both Latin and English. He presented a duplicate gift-book to James's son Prince Henry in 1605. Harington's epigrams themselves evoke the confusion of the spiritual economy of Elizabethan and Jacobean England. They also reveal Harington's own confessional standpoint to be a slippery one, blending political expediency and a desire for preferment at court with often dangerous forays into Catholic devotion. Harington's own elusive relationship with the rosary epitomizes this ambiguity, particularly through the cautious language used to describe the assumption and coronation of the Virgin.

THE HISTORY OF THE ROSARY

When early modern recusant worshippers offered up rosary prayers, they were following a long-established tradition. The practice of saying the rosary dates back at least as far as the Crusades. One story of the origins of the rosary finds its roots in Dominican monastic prayer. Legend has it that in the thirteenth century Saint Dominic, in despair about his failure to convert the heretic Cathars, had retreated to a cave outside Toulouse to fast and pray. There he saw an apparition of the Virgin, a *Virgo Lactans* figure who quenched the saint's spiritual thirst with milk from her breast. Mary then gave Saint Dominic a string of beads and taught him how to say the rosary, telling him that this was a way of converting the Cathars to orthodox Christianity.[4] The rosary itself is a mesmeric devotional prayer in which the worshipper repeats 150 Hail Marys: from the fifteenth century, these have been divided into groups of ten, or decades, each decade punctuated with the Lord's Prayer. Every time a prayer is said, worshippers move a rosary bead along the string on which it is threaded, and throughout each decade they meditate on one of fifteen mysteries. The traditional fifteen mysteries of the rosary, regulated by Pope Pius V in the sixteenth century, are in three groups of five, focusing on the life of Jesus and Mary. First come the joyful mysteries: the Annunciation, the Visitation, the Nativity, the Presentation, and the Finding of Jesus in the Temple. These are followed by five sorrowful mysteries: Christ's Agony in the Garden, the Scourging, the Crowning with Thorns, the Carrying of the Cross, and the Crucifixion. Finally, there are five glorious mysteries, entitled the Resurrection, the Ascension, the Descent of the Holy Spirit, the Assumption of the Virgin, and the Coronation of the Virgin. Integral to the rosary is a belief in its power to obtain both mercy and protection from the Virgin as Queen of Heaven: the fifteen mysteries culminate in a meditation on her assumption and coronation. For every mystery, the worshipper echoes the words of the angel Gabriel as he first greets the Virgin, "Ave Maria, gratia plena," rendered as "Hail Mary, full of grace." The addition by Pius V of "Pray for us sinners now and at the hour of our death" to the reformed breviary in 1568 foregrounded the Virgin's intercessory role, imprinting further the image of the Queen of Heaven as intercessor onto the image of Mary as mother-to-be.[5]

During the English Reformation, the rosary was redeployed, becoming illegal practice instead of beloved everyday prayer. Thomas Cranmer condemned the rosary in his 1547 *Homily of Good Works*, and the practice was forbidden outright in the Edwardian Injunctions of the same year. Rosary beads, as Eithne Wilkins has commented, have a "complex value, at once numinous, aesthetic and social," and their instantly recognizable appearance made them a visual emblem of religious allegiance.[6] When Edward's sister Mary was charged with religious disobedience in 1551, she rode into London accompanied by Catholic supporters, all of whom carried black rosary beads as a symbol of defiance.[7] In Mary's own reign, rosary beads were used as a devotional aid to the illiterate, a revival of one of their prime functions in the Middle Ages.[8] Elizabeth's accession meant that reciting of the rosary was once again abolished, and beads became contraband. But the rosary clearly remained popular. In the 1590s, a group of Lancashire ministers commented despairingly that many of their parishioners were still using beads to say their prayers.[9] The State Papers of the Public Record Office in 1595 record that a carpenter and mason by the name of Greene in Derbyshire was not only constructing priest holes but also making "all the beades that liee in little boxes."[10] When a peddler by the name of Richard Cropland was arrested during the time of the Gunpowder Plot, he was carrying a range of wares for recusant buyers, including rosary beads.[11]

Perhaps the best evidence for the continued cultural relevance of the rosary is found in pejorative references by Protestant writers, many of whom satirized it as a symbol of the ignorance of the old faith. *The Lady of May*, a masque written by Sir Philip Sidney and performed at the Earl of Leicester's house in Essex on Elizabeth's 1578 progress, gave an ironic representation of Leicester as a Catholic, praying to Queen Elizabeth and not the Queen of Heaven on rosary beads.[12] Tailboys Dymoke's erotic allegorical poem *Caltha Poetarum* (The Bumble Bee; 1599) also presents a savage parody of the rosary. It is the tale of a bee, thought to be Dymoke himself, who is in love with a marigold named Marygold, an allegorical representation of both one of the queen's maids of honor and the Virgin Mary. In the poem, the bumble bee builds a chapel for his Marygold, creating a holy altar to express his idolatrous love for a secular object of desire:

> With Virgin wax he makes a hony alter,
> and on it stands the torches and the tapers,
> Where he must sing his Rosarye and Psalter,
> and pray devoutly on his holy papers,
> With book, with candlelight, with bels & clappers,
> And in the praise of Goddesse *Caltha* sing,
> That all the holy quier & Church may ring.[13]

When the bee realizes that his beloved Marygold has left him, he declares his intention to withdraw from the world and become a hermit. He makes himself rosary beads, and in the descriptions of his secular devotions Marygold becomes the Virgin of the rosary:

> He made himself a paire of holy beads,
> the fiftie Aves were of Gooseberies:
> The Pater Nosters and the holy Creeds,
> were made of red & goodly fair ripe cheries:
> Blessing his Mary gold with Ave-maries.[14]

The rosary is one of a number of Catholic signifiers that are made to look ridiculous in a poem that lampoons the trend followed by writers such as Henry Constable to use religious, especially Catholic, imagery in secular love poetry.

In Shakespeare's *Richard II* (1595), the rosary is also used as a Catholic signifier, but here its representation takes a nostalgic, rather than satirical, tone. In one of the play's most dramatic moments, the beleaguered monarch descends like Phaeton from the sky and relinquishes his crown to his cousin Bolingbroke. As he does so, Shakespeare's poet king contemplates a life away from worldly cares:

> I'll give my jewels for a set of beads,
> My gorgeous palace for a hermitage,
> My gay apparel for an almsman's gown,
> My figured goblets for a dish of wood,
> My sceptre for a palmer's walking staff,
> My subjects for a pair of carved saints
> And my large kingdom for a little grave,
> A little little grave, an obscure grave.
> (3.3.146)

With his use of "beads," Richard equates the act of saying the rosary with the simpler, solitary life of the religious hermit. The authenticity of his expression of feeling may be in doubt: Richard II is often more caught up in rhetoric than reality. The ordered anaphora of his list gives his words a sense of public declaration; Richard's speech can be seen as masking his anguish at losing his crown rather than as displaying a genuine longing for a simpler past. Shakespeare's use of the rosary is here of cultural significance, however, as it is one of a series of signifiers that Richard II uses to denote a simpler and truer life away from the court. He sets "beads" in antithesis to the "jewels" that represent the rich trappings of kingship. This reference to the rosary on one level locates Richard in the medieval era of his reign, but its deployment resonates with its use in Elizabethan times, as the rosary here denotes a crossing over from public to private life.

The opening books of *The Faerie Queene* display a similar congruence between the rosary and privacy, when Una encounters a frosty reception from the ignorant blind woman Corceca (a Latin pun on "blind heart") and her vain and foolish daughter, Abessa:

> Shee found them both in darksome corner pent;
> Where that old woman day and night did pray
> Upon her beads devoutly penitent;
> Nine hundred *Pater nosters* every day,
> And thrise nine hundred *Aves* she was wont to say.
> (1.3.13.5–9)

Spenser's contempt for the practice of saying the rosary is clear here. The blind old woman is a transparent representation of Catholicism, her rosary beads a metonym for superstition and ignorance. That Corceca sits "in eternall night" denotes not only her physical blindness but also the fate of her soul, and her frightened attempts to shut Una out show her lack of openness to Truth. But within Spenser's pejorative representation is one very telling detail. Corceca is praying the rosary in a "darksome corner," hiding away from the outside world. In different ways, Spenser's and Shakespeare's representations of the rosary show how religious reform led to its reinterpretation. As a solitary and silent form of devotion, the rosary was ideally suited to recusant England, a world full of darksome corners. It was a powerful tool that allowed the worshipper to practice his devotion to the Virgin in secret. In what Frances Dolan has termed "strategic and fluid deployments of space," the private space of the Catholic household became devotional, often reconfigured to house and hide the trappings of forbidden modes of worship, such as the rosary.[15]

The rosary was a convenient way to worship. Beads could easily be concealed; even more discreet was the rosary ring, which had ten studs for prayer around it, serving the same function as the beads themselves.[16] The rosary books studied in this chapter are all very small in size: handling the material object gives one the strong sense that, like rosary beads, they were easy to carry and easy to hide. A great deal of energy was expended in both the production and distribution of these illicit books. Some were printed on secret presses in England, while others were produced in Continental Catholic centers such as Antwerp and Douai and were subsequently ferried into England by Catholic students and priests or by merchants, who were well paid for smuggling them to isolated places on the English coast. The existence of these books is testament to the importance of the printed word to the preservation of the Catholic faith in recusant England.[17] For many they were to become surrogates for an absent Catholic priest, providing, in Ceri Sullivan's words, "all the practices which the Catholic Church would normally channel through its clergy."[18] The rosary itself was, as a consequence, repositioned, becoming, as Anne Dillon has shown, a dynamic aspect of an underground Catholicism.[19] Nathan Mitchell aptly terms this a "reframing" of the rosary, observing that one result was an amplification of the Virgin's significance as "Marian piety became emblematic of an innovative, renascent Catholicism."[20] The importance of Mary in the economy of salvation for recusant Catholics cannot be overstressed here. Through the rosary, she could be petitioned directly as an intercessor if a worshipper had no access to a priest and the sacraments. The Virgin Mary of the early modern rosary should thus be seen not as a medieval throwback but as a malleable figure reimagined for the "darksome corners" of the recusant world and given a new agency.

GARNET'S *THE SOCIETIE OF THE ROSARY*:
A TEXT IN TIME

A driving force behind the success of the rosary among the English Catholic community was the Jesuit priests, who landed on England's shores from the Catholic Continent and saw the inculcation of the Dominican rosary as integral to their mission.[21] In the 1580s, a number of missionary priests were authorized to admit English Catholics to the Dominican Society of the Rosary, known on the Continent as the Confraternity of the Rosary. Membership in the society created a sense of religious community. It was also a means via which a worshipper could be granted indulgences, and its clear rubrics of devotion could be followed without a priest. The work of one man, Henry Garnet, is of particular significance here. Garnet was Jesuit superior in England from 1586 until 1606, when he was executed for his alleged role in the Gunpowder Plot. Garnet saw the Society of the Rosary in England as a way of forging a degree of congregational homogeneity among England's diaspora of Catholic worshippers. To assist in this work, he produced a book entitled *The Societie of the Rosary* as an aid to English Catholics. What strikes one most when first encountering Garnet's book is its practical, pragmatic tone: it takes the reader on a step-by-step guide to joining the Society of the Rosary and to saying the rosary itself. It is soon clear, however, that the original rules for joining the society have been considerably relaxed. A rule, for example, that the members' names should be written in a register book has been modified by Garnet: "This maner of inrouling being not convenient in our countrey for respects too well knowne: it sufficeth that after the names be once taken of such as enter, they be torne" (sig. C7r). Garnet's *The Societie of the Rosary* is not a repetition of late medieval discourses: it is a text in time, written in full awareness of its context of reception.

The language Garnet uses to describe the Virgin similarly places her image within the milieu of recusant England. The importance of her protection is frequently emphasized, and there is absolutely no doubt about her power. She is the mother of mercy, whose goodness has the power to curb God's vengeance, and in joining the society the Catholic worshipper is given a way to connect directly with her. Garnet's awareness of the contentious nature of the Queen of Heaven's image is writ clear, as he posits that it is the duty of the Catholic to continue to pray to the Virgin in a world where her role is actively being diminished: "Heresie doth ever goe aboute to derogate unto the glory of the most soveraigne Queene of heaven and earth: so is it the part of every zealous

Catholicke with as much care and diligence, to procure to set forth, amplifie, and increase, her wonderfull praises, and most deserved honour" (sig. A6r). For the sake of "the unlearned" (sig. A6r), Garnet sets down the reasons for devotion to the Virgin, and in doing so he reconfigures the rosary from its medieval roots to embody Tridentine thinking. When he lists the "25 singular priveledges of our Blessed Lady," including her immaculate conception, the grace that is bestowed upon her, and her powers after her assumption, which exceed those of the saints, his rosary book becomes a way of disseminating Counter-Reformation values (sig. A6v).[22] Garnet emphasizes in the strongest and most passionate terms that Mary should remain in the forefront of a worshipper's mind: "In dangers, in distresses, in doubtfull cases, thinke upon Mary, call upon Mary. Let her not depart from thy mouth, let her not depart from thy hart. And that thou maiest obtaine the reliefe of her praier, doe thou not swarve from the example of her conversation. Following her, thou straiest not: calling upon her, thou despairest not: thinking upon her, thou errest not" (sig. B4v). Garnet's emotive repetition here makes it clear that using the rosary prayer is a way to combat a diminishing collective consciousness of Mary's role as intercessor.

The Societie of the Rosary can also be placed directly within a contemporary cultural context through its vivid descriptions of afflicted times that liken recusant England to the disaster of the floods of Genesis 8. The writer beseeches God that "these deadly fluddes may cease from the earth, and all creatures be restored to their former saftie"—and then proleptically figures the Virgin Mary as the rainbow that will end the flood: "This rainbow I meane to be the glorious Virgin, a most beutiful signe of God's frendship with men, & such a token of his singuler mercie. . . . Shee is in speaciall manner a rainbow against Heretickes: wheras the Church generally singeth, she hath destroyed al heresies in the wholle world" (sigs. A2v–A3r). The description of the Virgin as a "rainbow against Heretickes" bestows upon her an active role, one that is amplified by Garnet's use of military imagery. Garnet describes the Virgin as a bow, shooting forth God's arrows, that "mightily overcometh, not only her owne but also her devout clients adversaries" (sig. A5v). The rosary beads themselves "must be to our afflicted brethren instead of all maner of armour or weapons" (sig. A5v).

A militaristic depiction of the Virgin is congruent with Counter-Reformation European thought; and by this time, the rosary's relationship with military might was firmly entrenched. In the Battle of Lepanto of 1571, the Holy League won a decisive naval victory over the Ottoman Empire, a victory that was largely attributed to the rosary prayers said by Christians in Rome during the battle. This led to the instigation of the Feast of the Rosary in 1573 to celebrate Our Lady of Victory.[23] Lisa McClain views a bellicose Mary as a dominant aspect of the early modern rosary's emphasis of Marian piety, commenting on the Virgin's "reconceptualised English role as powerful warrior and intercessor through the rosary."[24] However, it would be reductive to see the Virgin of the rosary as purely a military figure. What is particularly interesting about the representation of the Virgin in recusant rosary books is how polyvalent her image is. This presents a stark contrast to the abrupt severing of "Protestant" humble handmaid and "Catholic" Queen of Heaven in Protestant writing. Garnet's text is a testament to this: his Virgin Mary encompasses both humble handmaid and Queen of Heaven, and many other personae besides. When Garnet fashions the Virgin as the mother who has power to command the son, this parries the Protestant polemic encountered earlier in this study: "She had not only an intrincicall familiaritie with the sonne of God, and was a principall scholar of his: but he vouchsafed also to be subject unto her, she having a motherly right and authoritie over him" (sig. B2v). Elsewhere, Garnet apostrophizes Mary as a mother and praises her for the reverence she shows to her son: "Who beeing subjecte unto thee, thou diddest diligently nourishe with a motherly care, and neverthelesse diddest alwaies exhibite an holy reverence unto him, as to the most high and mightie God" (sig. G1r). In *The Societie of the Rosary*, the humble Virgin of the Annunciation blends with the glorious Queen of Heaven. She is a figure of "unspeakeable humility, preferring herselfe to no creature, but alwaies ready to become the servant of all" (sig. A8r). She is saluted by the angel for her "meeke and benigne charity" (sig. L3r) but is simultaneously heaven's queen, "advaunced to the highest dignity, that could be given unto the women kind: that is to say: to bee Queene of heaven, and earth, to be next unto Almighty God, and above all creatures" (sig. L3v). Elsewhere, the Virgin is presented as a suffering mother, standing in sorrow under the cross, and, in an extrascriptural moment that foregrounds her importance as a mother, the risen Christ appears to her first: "She was the first unto whom he appeared after his gloriouse resurrection. For although of such apparition, there be no mention in the Gospell: yet of this affection to his loving Mother we need not doubt" (sig. B2v).

Garnet's popular rosary book was reprinted several times between 1593 or 1594 and 1626. In 1596 or 1597 a revised edition appeared entitled *The Societie of the Rosary. Newly Augmented*.[25] This edition includes an alternative way of saying the rosary, in which each mystery is entitled a "contemplation" and is accompanied by an extensive meditation. When it reaches the final mysteries of the rosary, weaving between Ave Marias is the language of the Song of Songs:

Arise, make haste my love my dove, my beautifull and come.
Ave Maria.
For now the winter is past, the showre is gone, and ceased.
Ave Maria.

My love thou art altogether beautifull, and no spot is in thee, come from Libanus my spouse, come from Libanus, come thou shalt be crowned.
Ave Maria.[26]

The Queen of Heaven is here a lover as well as bride, and the worshipper becomes Christ, calling the Virgin to be his heavenly spouse. It is a sensuous, beautiful meditation that culminates in a heavenly celebration of the Virgin's coronation using some of the Old Testament's most luxurious verses, from 1 Kings 2:19, "And a Throne was placed for the mother of the King, who did sitt at his right hand," to Ezekiel 16:11, "I have put a jewel on thy forehead, and earings in thy eares, and a most comely croune on thy head. Ave Maria."[27] Evocative images of the Virgin as both queen and spiritual lover are thus created. Henry Garnet's *The Societie of the Rosary* deploys the image of the Virgin in a way that reflects not only Counter-Reformation ideologies but also the cultural tensions of recusant England. She is a figure to whom the worshipper can turn in afflicted times, and she is seen in many different guises: humble handmaid, military figure, sorrowing mother, powerful intercessory Queen of Heaven, and, in the augmented version of the book, idealized beloved.

MARY AS A MODEL OF PATIENT SUFFERING

When one considers the importance of the role of women within the English recusant community, it is of little surprise that there are rosary books written with the woman reader in mind.[28] This led to an amplification of the Virgin's role in a different way, as she became a model of patient suffering with whom female readers could identify. Particularly striking examples of this can be found in two rosary books that were dedicated to women: *A Breef Directory, and Playne Way Howe to say the Rosary of Our Blessed Lady* (1576), by I. M., and *Instructions for the Use of Beads* (1589), by John Bucke.[29] The author of *A Breef Directory*, I. M., dedicates the book to his sister but expresses the hope that his works will also be read by the "many good women in Englande that honour our Lady," as "good bookes to stirre up devotion in them are scares" (sig. ¶4r).[30] I. M. encourages his readers to empathize with the Virgin's suffering. The book's meditations exhort its female reader to follow the Virgin throughout the joys and sorrows that are seen distinctly through her eyes. I. M. uses emotive language to "stirre up devotion" among his female readers. To encourage women to identify with the Virgin, he intertwines rosary devotions with meditative methods developed by the Jesuit founder Ignatius Loyola. *The Spiritual Exercises* of Ignatius Loyola are a series of meditations and prayers composed in the early 1520s in which meditators are instructed in the art of "seeing the place," envisaging an aspect of scriptural narrative with the mind's eye, and then placing themselves in the scene. They were frequently used as a spiritual and didactic aid by Catholic priests working underground in England.[31] Reading *A Breef Directory* is in many ways a similar experience to meditating on Loyola's *Spiritual Exercises*. There is a consistent use of the imperative mood as readers are repeatedly urged to "beholde" the scene that the writer lays before their eyes.

The biblical scenes themselves are frequently vividly reimagined. The horror of Christ's death is dwelt upon in graphic detail as the reader stands with Mary, empathizing with her pain: "And then as in the former, beholde his blessed mother seeing her deare sonne in a position thus cruelly tormented, whipped and scourged for thy sinnes: Call for grace and compunction, that thou maist at least shed one teare with our Ladye, to see thy Lorde and Master for thy gylt so cruelly handled: and then saye the seconde Pater noster and ten Aves" (sig. B5r). The detail with which Christ's scourging and crucifixion is described causes the reader to "see the place" from Mary's point of view. There is no turning away from vivid descriptions of Christ's body "torne with whips or roddes, the streames of bloudde freehelye trikeling downe" (sig. B5r), or of how "the weight of his body stretched the holes of his handes and feete wider and wider" (sig. C2v). Through the Loyolan methods that I. M.'s book deploys, the worshipper is invited both to identify with and to emulate the emotions of the Virgin, particularly her sorrow at the torture and death of her son.

Female empathy is also an important element of John Bucke's *Instructions for the Use of Beads*, which was dedicated to his patroness, Lady Hungerford. Bucke was chaplain to Lady Hungerford, who was the sister of Jane Dormer, the Duchess of Feria, and was living in exile in Louvain.[32] His rosary book begins with a florid introduction in which he evokes the language of the book of Exodus as he thanks his patron for his escape from "that darke Egiptiacal England (the verie sea of heresie)."[33] Bucke is frequently drawn to recusant tropes of biblical language of suffering and exile to express the times of his book's production and reception. A preoccupation with persecution underpins a representation of the Virgin Mary as a patiently suffering woman undergoing earthly trials. Both the Duchess of Feria and Lady Hungerford were viewed as significant figures among exiled Catholics and had suffered considerably for their Catholic faith. Lady Hungerford is here represented as a virtuous woman who has "endured many afflictions and grevous adversities" with patience and faith (8). Bucke's use of the word *endure* is a way of implicitly and flatteringly linking his patron's afflictions to those of the Virgin, as it is a word he frequently uses to describe Mary: "What carefull troubles and dredefull perills dyd his blessed mother endure, when it was knowen that our maister Jesus should be borne? And after he was borne a great nomber of deadlie enemies dyd dailye arise against that swete babe and her" (4). Bucke's portrayal of a suffering Mary means that he dwells with emotion on Herod's massacre of the innocents and the Holy Family's flight into Egypt:

> What terrible feare and care with paynfull labors dyd she endure travaling over hilles and dales; when she heard the cries of mothers for their children haled out of their armes and mordered before their eyes: when she dyd mete the cruell bouchers that fought to morder her dear childe by the cruell edict of wicked Herod, proclaming all male children from two yeres olde and under to be slaine? What soroufull cares and hard travalying dyd that blessed virgin endure to hyde and save her onlie sonne from the crueltie of those synfull creatures, whom her sonne came to save and kepe from hel and damnacion if they wolde accept hym? (11–12)

A female reader's relationship with the rosary is integral to Bucke's depiction of the Virgin Mary as a woman who, like his patron, endured earthly suffering. Both I. M. and John Bucke, writing books dedicated to women, are here offering consolation to their readers through the example of the Virgin's sorrows.

IMAGE AND WORD

Many rosary books also use illustrations as imaginative stimuli and are thus responding to the Council of Trent's 1563 session "On Invocation, Veneration, and Relics of Saints, and on Sacred Images," which confirmed the acceptance of visual art in devotional practice.[34] In *Meditations, of the Life and Passions of our Lord*, Gaspar Loarte stresses the power and importance of the image as a meditative tool. Loarte's advice is that the meditator should set before them "the figure or the Image . . . of the misterye which you are to meditate, the which, when you have first beholden, it shal helpe to keepe you more collected and attentive. For the memory of the Picture shall remayne as it were imprinted in your minde."[35]

The format of many rosary books is that of a series of pictures of the fifteen mysteries of the rosary, with a meditation attached. Worshippers are encouraged to gaze on the image, then meditate on its contents, imbuing the image with what they have learned from reading the text.[36] A particularly arresting example of this comes in Bucke's *Instructions*. Nestling in the back of this book is a fold-out illustration of folio size (figure 1). Entitled "Lady Hungerford's Meditacions upon the Beades," it draws the reader around the page in circular motion to gaze at illustrations of scenes from the Bible, including John the Baptist preaching, the annunciation of the Virgin, and Christ carrying the cross to Calvary, as well as the assumption and coronation of the Virgin, and Our Lady of Sorrows. Text and image fuse on the page, and visual images enrich the process of worshipping: readers are exhorted to imprint a scene on their mind's eye. The relation between physical image, mental visualization, and spiritual experience is synergistic. This is in stark contrast to, and perhaps also in protest against, Protestantism's mistrust of the image. In the middle is a drawing of the rosary itself, perhaps so that readers who did not have access to beads could at least have access to an illustration. This comes after the worshipper has read the book itself and presumably practiced saying the rosary and thus can imprint the devotional power of the words onto the images. Within these illustrations, as with John Bucke's text itself, we see how allusions to early modern recusant worship frequently intermingle with biblical and spiritual signifiers. In the bottom right-hand corner is an illustration where the setting is a chapel. The crucifix and candles on the altar can clearly be seen; a solitary worshipper kneels and is blessed by a priest. The old blends with the new, a visual realization of Bucke's synthesis of biblical language with recusant suffering.

THE QUEEN OF HEAVEN

In the center of the illustration in John Bucke's rosary book is a visual representation of the Virgin, with the infant Christ on her knee. Christ holds a chaplet in his hands, and the Virgin herself is encircled by the rosary beads, which have the visual effect of crowning her. This image

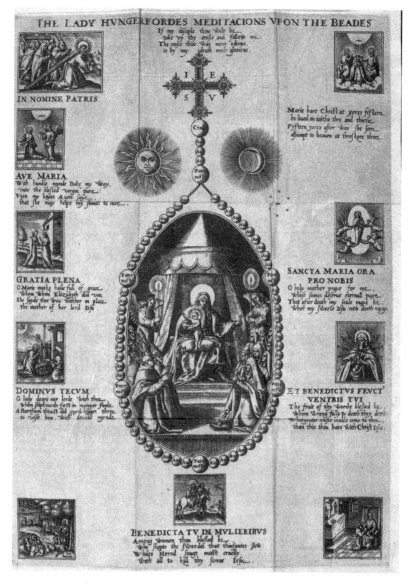

FIGURE 1. Lady Hungerford's Meditacions upon the Beades. © The British Library Board, Huth 75.

of the Virgin dominates, and one's eyes are drawn naturally and repeatedly toward it. Bucke's illustration is a visual embodiment of a reader response to rosary books, as it brings the image of the Virgin to the fore. Mary appears in many guises in rosary books, but the most powerful of all of her roles is that of heaven's queen and man's intercessor. The worshipper is effectively crowning the Virgin each time he says the rosary: to use Henry Garnet's words in *The Societie of the Rosary*, when a devout Catholic daily says his beads, he is "taking up with childly affection his most holy Mother, even corporally unto heaven and exalting and crowning her over all his holy Saintes and Angells" (sig. D5r). In contemplating the Queen of Heaven, a worshipper was going directly against state-sanctioned Protestantism. Churches, monasteries, and convents on the Catholic Continent were replete with luxurious paintings and statues of the Queen of Heaven, but a recusant worshipper had to work a little harder to connect with this aspect of the Virgin's iconography. Recusant rosary books presented a powerful solution. It is in sections on the assumption and coronation of the Virgin that some of the rosary books' most beautiful passages can be found. The combination of illustration, Loyolan methods, and sensual language gave the reader a mental image of the assumption and coronation of the Virgin that no one could destroy. It etched the image into that most darksome corner of all—the imagination.

An example is *The Garden of our B. Lady* (1619), by the Jesuit priest Sabine Chambers. In it, the reader is exhorted to see the Virgin assumed to heaven entwined with Christ as his spiritual bride: "Behold this glorious Virgin ascending, Flowing in delights, leaning upon her beloved: & with all contemplate upon our B. Saviours tender affection towards his dearest Mother, requiting (as it were) her love, who in his infancy was borne in her blessed armes, and leaned upon her; now he assisting her in this glorious triumph" (130–31). The coronation of the Virgin is introduced in terms that underline its mystic significance. Because the worshipper is about to contemplate a mystery that is beyond earthly comprehension, he is advised to keep his thoughts in heaven: "Dwell willingly in those celestiall parts with thy mind, and till thou hast accomplished thy devotion, looke not downe upon earth, nor to the distractions it beareth" (135). *The Garden of our B. Lady* uses beautiful, poetic language to imprint powerful images of the Virgin's assumption and coronation in the reader's mind. We are invited to behold Mary on the day of her coronation, "most beautifully adorned withal perfections both of mind and body, all the blessed inhabitants of Heaven attending her" (136). The Virgin is crowned in "a Diademe of glory" (136), as blessed souls in heaven sing her praises, marveling in "her beames of brightnes" (137).

A proselytizing strain underpins these evocative and sensuous descriptions. The reader is clearly instructed as to why the Virgin is being rewarded in this way—"mervaile not at the extraordinary glory she is endued with, but consider the high vocation she was called unto, and in how great a business she was imployed in this world, and how completely she performed the same" (136–37). She has received the crown in heaven, we are told, because she was "full of grace heere upon earth, and therefore must needes be full of glory in heaven" (138). Chambers adopts a didactic tone about the significance of the Virgin's grace and its relationship with her role as Queen of Heaven. *The Garden of our B. Lady* stresses the importance of praying to the Virgin as Queen of Heaven for her "potent intercession to her Sonne" (138), but it also states that a worshipper should encourage others to do the same, keeping Mary's name alive. "Lastly endeavour thou by al meanes possible, to make this Queene of glory, adored also here on earth, by drawing and exhorting as many as thou canst, to devote themselves unto her" (75). The alluring, poetic language used to describe the Virgin's assumption and coronation has a religio-political purpose. Chambers validates the coronation of the Virgin and clearly stresses the spiritual benefits enjoyed by a worshipper who appeals to the Queen of Heaven through a rosary prayer. He also encourages the devout Catholic reader to proselytize and to promote these spiritual benefits to others.

The language of *The Garden of our B. Lady*, for all its beauty and wonder, reveals that a sense of an apologia often leaked into descriptions of the Queen of Heaven in rosary books. A 1600 rosary text, *Rosarie of Our Ladie* by Thomas Worthington, president of Douai College, conveys this in a different way. After a narrative of Mary's death and burial, the worshipper is guided to meditate upon her bodily assumption: "Whereupon these so many and so excellent eye witnesses do assuredly deme, that he who tooke flesh of this immaculate bodie, hath assumpted the same into heave*n*, reunited to the soul in eternal glorie" (65). The reference to the "excelle*n*t eye witnesses" of the apostles feels like a direct attempt to lend credence to the apocryphal and extrascriptural. In a similar vein, Worthington's exposition of the coronation of the Virgin describes how the apostles, as Eyewitnesses, began to tell the story of the Virgin's bodily assumption throughout the world: "The Apostles are againe restored to the places from whence they were brought: and by them and others the death and Assumption of the most immaculate virgin, mother of God, is denounced in al parts of the world" (67).[37]

When it comes to the mystery of the coronation of the Virgin, Worthington's text follows a different line of argument; it forestalls doubters by stating that it is an event beyond mortal comprehension:

Seeing the glorie of everie Sainct in heaven is so great, as no tongue can expresse, nor the mind of man understand . . . how much lesse can the glorie of the mother of God (exalted above al the quires of Angels) be uttered or conceived by anie mortal man? But shal we therefore be silent and say nothing at al therof? Shal we also cease to thinke and meditate therof, because it so farre surmounteth both our sense and understanding? No, in no wise can we be so excused; but so much the more we are bound to rejoice, and as we can (seing we can not as we would) utter forth the praises of the mother of mercie, mother of grace, mother of life, mother of glorie, mother of God, now reigning Quene of heaven. (99)

Again, we see evidence of a text that is conscious of the times in which it is written and received, one that creates a community of worshippers who are "bound to rejoice" in the glorious mystery of the Virgin's coronation.

Praying on his beads in a "darksome corner," aided by recusant rosary books, the early modern Catholic worshipper would have had cause to imprint a number of different images of the Virgin Mary onto his mind. Here was no splintering of humble handmaid and meretricious Queen, but an image of the Virgin in which many different guises coexisted. In the fifteen mysteries of the rosary prayer, the recusant worshipper would have found the humble and obedient Mary of the Annunciation, the sorrowing mother of the Crucifixion, a military figure who could aid in the fight against heresy, and a model of devotion. But overarching all of these was the wondrous image of the Virgin as Queen of Heaven, a "mediatrix of grace" who, following her bodily assumption into heaven, had the power to intercede for man.[38] The reader of these tiny but powerful books was being exhorted not only to remember the Queen of Heaven but also to amplify her role as conduit to God in a world where priests were scarce and modes of worship hidden. The rosary books of early modern England present a reconceptualized Queen of Heaven whose power is unquestioned but who is also a figure linked with secrecy and persecution. The image of the Virgin is honored—often lyrically so—but it is also deployed as an acutely politicized construct. Through visual images and the written word, recusant rosary books urgently implored their readers to imprint the image of the Queen of Heaven in their minds, not only to guarantee its future survival, but also as a way to save their souls.

HARINGTON'S ROSARY

My setting now moves from the shadows of recusant England and back to the court, to a highly unusual deployment of a rosary prayer by one man, Sir John Harington. Harington himself is something of an enigma. Writer, courtier, and godson to the queen, he dedicated much of his life to the projection of a politically expedient outward image. One often has the feeling when reading his work that he is hiding something, and his religious beliefs are particularly hard to determine. His family background means that he shared bonds of kinship with a number of powerful and active recusant families, and his hand has been found in manuscripts of *Leicester's Commonwealth* (1584), a subversive Catholic text.[39] Yet he showed immense enthusiasm for the translation of metrical psalms that were distinctly Calvinist in tone, and he referred to himself as a "protesting Catholic Puritan."[40] Perhaps an image in one of his own poems best sums up his outlook:

As Janus first two faces had assignd him,
Of which one lookt before, t'other behinde him,
So men maie yet be founde in manie places,
that underneath one hood can beare two faces.[41]

Harington himself was something of a Janus figure, hiding his real views under a hood of polished wit. A study of his work is a search beneath this hood for subtexts, not only within the words themselves, but within the materiality of his texts and their use in social transactions. During the 1590s, Harington wrote and revised a series of 408 poems that he titled his *Epigrams*.[42] This seemingly idle and frivolous opus was presented in different carefully calculated combinations to family and powerful friends and acquaintances.[43] My focus is on one of these gift-books, which was presented in 1602 to King James: three years later, on June 19, 1605, Harington sent a copy of the same gift-book to James's eleven-year-old son, Henry, Prince of Wales. Given on the date of the king's birthday, it was clearly an attempt to reach the father as well as the son.[44] Included in the supplementary matter that accompanied these gift-books was a rosary poem in Latin and English, accompanied by an engraving illustrating the mysteries of the rosary. When this rosary poem is read in the light of both the tone of the epigrams themselves and their transmission as texts, a complex and highly politicized attitude to the image of the Virgin Mary is revealed. Whether we come any closer to knowing Harington himself, however, is questionable.

Much of Harington's output as a writer makes it easy to pigeonhole him as the Rabelaisian wit who fell in and out of his godmother's favor. His 1591 translation of the bawdy tale of Astolfo and Jocondo in *Orlando Furioso* is purported to have enraged Elizabeth so much that she banished him from court until he had translated the whole work.[45] The epigrams themselves are acidly grotesque and sharply observed.[46] They present a dystopian picture of a corrupt court, populated by cartoonish figures for whom self-seeking, promiscuity, and deception are meat and drink. The overall effect is clever, brittle, funny, and extremely unsettling. In the speaker of the epigrams, one finds a duality: a fashionable, Sidneian stance that blends a disarmingly personal—almost confessional—tone with a retreat into anonymity. Harington also uses code names,

many of which have a Martialian feel, for many of his characters, giving
the collection as a whole the feeling of one huge in-joke.[47]
What was the motivation behind Harington's presentation of these
brittle satires to King James and Prince Henry? The theatrical presentation of many of Harington's gift-books, as Jason Scott-Warren's research has shown, is indicative of a self-promoting writer who is highly
conscious of the environment of his texts' transmission. The meanings
of the poems shift in accordance with when they are presented and to
whom they are presented. When Harington gave his 1602 gift-book to
King James VI, Elizabeth's reign was coming to an end and James was
the favorite for succession. Harington's bitter and witty dissections of a
false Elizabethan court became a vehicle for indirectly glorifying the
anticipated new Stuart rule, and inveigling his way into favor.[48] When
he presented the poems to Prince Henry in 1605, their emphasis shifted
yet again. By this time, a date uncannily close to the Gunpowder Plot,
tensions between the Scots and English had tarnished the glow of optimism that had greeted James at his accession.[49] Poems about a false
Elizabethan court can be read here as a warning to the Stuart king not
to repeat Tudor mistakes.

Harington's discontent with the status quo of the world around
him sounds particularly sonorously on the subject of religion. He often
pleads for religious tolerance in a complicated world. The epigrams
themselves are carefully ordered so that every tenth poem has a religious theme. Gerard Kilroy has argued that this structure turns the collection into a mimicry of a rosary prayer, describing each tenth poem as
a "sequence of theological decades."[50] It is a persuasive reading, but
Harington's is a cynical, rather than glorious, rosary, as his tenth poems
frequently express a sense of despair at the muddied religious landscape
within which the speaker finds himself. In one poem, "Of Two Reli-
gions," a bewildered father asks his scholarly son whether he should
follow the teachings of Geneva or of Catholicism. Both seem learned to
him. The son's reply is so evasive that he seems like a mouthpiece for
Harington himself:

Sure (quoth the sonne) a man had neede be crafty
to keepe his soule and body both in saf'ty.

But both to save, this is best way to hold
die in the new, *live* if you *list* in th'old.
(212)

In fact, Harington wrote two different versions of this last line. He was, it would appear, unable to choose between *"live* in the new, *dy* if you can in th'old," and *"die* in the new, *live* if you *list* in th'old." In the gift-book presented to Prince Henry, the overwritings of this line allow the reader to see both versions, and the reader is left unsure as to whether Harington's affiliations are with the "new" or the "old" faith.[51]

Another religious poem, "A Dishe of Daynties for the Devill" (125), expresses the need for an inner, private space:

A godlie father, sitting on a draught
to do as need and nature hath us taught,
Mumbled as was his manner certayn prayers,
And unto him the Devill straight repayres,
And boldly to revile him he begins,
Alledging that such prayres were deadly sins,
And that yt proov'd he was devoyde of grace,
to speake to God from so unfitt a place.

The "godlie father" is of strong faith, however, and has the courage to confront the devil. The poem ends with his prayers ascending to heaven:

Pure prayr ascends to him that high doth sitt,
Down falls the filth for fiends of hell more fitt.

The poem has been described by T. G. A. Nelson as both "frivolous" and "impish," and it certainly seems so at first glance.[52] It is hard to draw one's mind from the bathos of the "godlie father" being confronted by Satan while on the "draught," or privy, and the unvoiced rhyme of "sitt" and "shit" at the end of the poem. Harington was no stranger to lavatory humor. He is still remembered today as the man who invented flushing jakes in his 1596 work *The Metamorphosis of Ajax*, and this poem can be seen as his own take on the scatological nature of much Reformation propaganda, fueled perhaps by Luther's own use of unsavory language in relation to the devil.

But there is a certain weight to Harington's words. Just as the scatological tone of *The Metamorphosis of Ajax* (1596) masked a savage commentary on the filth of court corruption, so Harington's poem about the priest on the privy has a serious submerged meaning.[53] We are not given specific details of the "certayn prayers" that the priest is saying, but we do know that he is reduced to mumbling them in secret, in an enclosed, private space. The word *mumbled* was often used in Protestant propaganda to describe Catholic prayers said in Latin. It may even refer specifically to the saying of the rosary: in his 1621 *The Anatomy of Melancholy*, Robert Burton describes Catholics as "praying in gibberish, & mumbling of beads," while Curione's *Pasquine in a Traunce* describes the misguided Catholic worshipper as one who "mumbled over his Beades."[54] Harington inverts the pejorative associations of the word *mumbled*, however, as his priest is the hero of the piece. Confronted by the devil, the holy man remains steadfast in his belief that his true prayers will "ascend": the only gains for the devil are the priest's "filth." In this most unlikely of environments, sin is conquered, and the man's prayers, far from damning him, are shown to be "pure" as they ascend to heaven. If the old, mumbled prayers are read as the rosary, then it is a prayer to the Virgin that is the poem's evidence of a true faith. The phrase "unfitt a place" becomes more than the jakes: it is the locus of the old faith, and a wry, scatological commentary on the manner in which Catholics renegotiated the definition of sacred space as their methods of worship were forced underground.[55]

HARINGTON AND THE VIRGIN MARY

There is clearly more to Harington than meets the eye, so it is not surprising that his attitude to the Virgin Mary is problematic and intriguing. An indication of this can be found in the Arundel-Harington manuscript, a folio volume of more than three hundred poems by writers that included Sidney, Raleigh, and Queen Elizabeth herself. The collection

was started by Harington's father and continued, clearly with great enthusiasm, by Harington himself, who transcribed many of the poems
within it. Ruth Hughey, who discovered the manuscript and subsequently edited it, comments that Harington turned it "into a kind of
commonplace book, filling its blank pages with his own compositions
and those of his friends."[56] During the period when Harington was involved in the manuscript, an anonymous poem was transcribed in
which a worshipper, echoing the Litany of Loreto, praises the Virgin as
Queen of Heaven and pleads for her intercession:

> fflower of Roses Angells joy
> Tower of David Arke of Noy
> first of sayntes whose trew protecting
> Of the younge and weake in sprite
> Makes my soule thease lynes endyte
> to thy throne her playnte dyrecting
>
> Orphan chylde alone I lye
> childlyke to thee I crye
> Queene of Heaven usde to cherishe
> Eys of grace behold I fall
> ears of pitty heare my call
> least in swaddling clowts I perishe.[57]

The Marian poem itself may feel like a medieval memory, but it functions as far more than this. Its placing within the manuscript is particularly significant. Immediately following it comes a poem entitled "Verses
made by a Catholiq; in prayse of Campion that was executed at Tyburne
for Treason and ys made knowne by Proclamation." This is "Why do I
use my paper, inke and penne," the poem attributed to the Jesuit priest
Henry Walpole. The poem to the Virgin Mary may even have been written by Campion himself, as Ruth Hughey has suggested.[58] The placing of
these two poems together can be seen as an act of resistance: as Joshua
Eckhardt has revealed, the Arundel-Harington manuscript was an example of how collectors of verse manuscripts used their collections
to recontextualize the works of others.[59] A devotional Marian poem

thus becomes, as Arthur Marotti has observed, not only a poem of consolation to anguished Catholics but also a way to "protest official oppression" and a statement of solidarity with the Catholic faith.[60]

In the inclusion of this anonymous Marian prayer in his commonplace book, Harington shows a level of allegiance to Catholic veneration of the Virgin. The only poem in the epigrams themselves to mention the Virgin Mary is difficult to decode, however. Entitled "In Prayse of Two Worthy Translations, Made by Two Great Ladies," it is a paean to Mary Sidney, Countess of Pembroke, and Mary Talbot, Countess of Shrewsbury:

> My soule one only Mary doth adore,
> onely one Mary doth injoy my hart,
> yet hath my Muse found out two Maries more,
> that merit endles prayse by dew desart,
> Two Maries that translate with divers art,
> two subjects rude and ruinous before,
> both having noblesse great and bewties store,
> Nobless and bewty to their works impart.
> Both have ordayn'd against Deaths dreadfull Dart
> a Shield of fame induring evermore
> both works advaunce the love of sacred lore,
> Both help the souls of sinners to convart.
> Their learned payn I prayse, heer costly Alms
> A Colledge this translates, the tother Psalms.
>
> (227)

This is a neatly turned piece of praise, in which Harington clearly distinguishes between the sacred and the secular. His wife, Mary, a regular character in his poetry, is the one who will continue to "injoy" his heart, the two "Maries" of the poem deserve his "prayse"—but the use of "soule" in the first line would appear to indicate that the Mary whom he adores is the Virgin. The poem has immortality as its theme, claiming that both of these great ladies have achieved fame, allowing them to conquer "Deaths dreadfull Dart." Harington clarifies in his final line that his use of translations in reference to each of the titular Marys is different—one is translating, or transforming, a college through her benefactions (Mary Talbot had donated funds to St. John's College Cambridge), while the other has translated psalms. This refers to Mary Sidney's involvement in translations of the Psalms, a work that was influenced by the Protestant Geneva Bible and the commentaries of John Calvin and Théodore de Bèze. Within a poem that praises Protestant translations of the Psalms, Harington appears to profess his adoration of the Virgin, albeit in a muffled way. Harington viewed Henry Constable as an intimate friend, and in places this poem bears an uncanny similarity to the Constable sonnet "To the Countesse of Shrewsburye" discussed in the previous chapter, suggesting an exchange of creative ideas between the two men.[61] Constable's sonnet also presents the Countess of Shrewsbury as an object of admiration and also uses the Virgin as a vehicle for praise of women who bear her name.

HARINGTON'S "FIFTEEN SEVERAL DISTICKS"

The most overt reference to the Virgin in Harington's gift-book comes in the rosary poem "Fifteen several disticks on the fifteen divisions." This takes the form of a series of Latin couplets, or "disticks," followed by a translation, also in couplets.[62] A spiritual poem in Latin sees Harington flirting with danger: as Steven May comments, "Any treatment of religious subjects in classical metres would necessarily have savoured of Catholicism."[63] A poem that would not be out of place in one of the rosary books examined in the first section of this chapter appears in the most unexpected of settings. The existence of this rosary prayer in Harington's gift-book signals that the practice of saying the rosary was still recognized and understood, and it is not too much of a leap of faith to see this as an indication of how recusant rosary books were reaching some of the most influential households. The "disticks" display direct, uncomplicated devotion to the Virgin, and their tone is entirely different from that of the epigrams. Harington here creates his own spiritual garland, the poem coming full circle with the controversial opening words of the rosary prayer—"Haile full of grace"—repeated at its beginning and end.

Alongside the poem is an engraving of the mysteries of the rosary, where each picture corresponds to one of the poem's elegiac couplets. The opening of the poem, with its use of *picture*, leaves the reader in no doubt as to its integral relationship with the illustration that accompanies it:

The blessed virgins picture first hath place
to whom thus Gabriel saith. Haile full of grace.

Each couplet of the poem corresponds to a different picture in the engraving; the reader is thus guided through the fifteen mysteries step by step. This turns the implied reader of Harington's rosary into a worshipper, and the effect of reading this poem is remarkably similar to that of reading a recusant rosary book. It is as if Harington, like rosary writers such as Henry Garnet and John Bucke, wants both to educate his readers on how to say the rosary and to encourage them to use the accompanying images as an *aide memoire*. He seems to be encouraging both the Protestant King James and his pious Protestant son to commit a Catholic prayer to memory by reading it in a meditative way. If the warnings the preceding poems sounded of a spiritually barren Elizabethan age are taken into consideration, then a complex plea for tolerance emerges. Harington's use of a Catholic prayer can also be viewed as a powerful reminder to James and Henry of their own familial links to Catholicism, especially as within the *Epigrams* is a poem lamenting the death of Mary Queen of Scots.[64] Harington's motives may be muddied, but it is clear that this most slippery of subjects was sailing very close to the wind indeed.

The inclusion of the "disticks" in this gift-book is perhaps the work of a serial risk taker, but when it comes to representations of the Virgin's assumption and coronation Harington retreats under a hood of political expediency. The Catholic rosary books studied in the first part of this chapter all regard the assumption and coronation of the Virgin as the triumphant climax of the fifteen mysteries. Harington's "disticks," however, strike a note of caution, as the speaker becomes more evasive. Turning first to the Latin, one sees the shift from active to passive:

Creditur et mater caelis assumpta supernis,
Supra virgineos sola beata choros.

The use of the passive voice in *creditur* (it is believed) has a very different effect from the powerful *credo* of the Nicene and Apostles' creeds of the liturgy, and the result is that the speaker distances himself from his contentious subject matter. The translation is even more cautious:

And after all theis things it is presumed,
The blessed virgin was to heaven assumed.

While "The blessed virgin was to heaven assumed" certainly covers *mater caelis assumpta*, it omits that it was to the "highest" heavens (*supernis*) that the Virgin was assumed. Harington here gives very little attention to the second of the two Latin lines: because the Virgin is not raised to the highest heights of heaven, she is not necessarily "supra virgineos . . . choros." The Latin *supra* holds associations of excelling someone; the omission of it from the translation implies that the Virgin has not quite become Queen of Heaven.

The rosary ends with the Virgin Mary crowned in glory as Queen of Heaven, but Harington's final "distick" shies away from crowning the Virgin in both Latin and English versions. Instead, the reader is encouraged to contemplate the end of the speaker's own life, when he will salute the Virgin in heaven:

Da mihi finitae pater o post tempora vitae,
Illi cum sanctis dicere semper. Ave.

This is Englished as

God graunt me, when my life hath run the race
to say to her with saynts. Haile full of grace.

The speaker hopes ultimately to be placed alongside the saints, but he, like them, is below the Virgin in heaven's hierarchy. In both English and Latin, this could be seen as dangerous enough, as it gives a vision of heaven that privileges the Virgin, but it is still a significant step back from a rosary prayer. Mary is not directly referred to as the Queen of Heaven interceding for men on earth, although the description of her as "full of grace" is a potent one. Harington's inclusion of a rosary poem is potentially incendiary, but he strikes a cautious and pragmatic note when it comes to the assumption and coronation of the Virgin.

In her brilliant assessment of the "puzzle of Harington's own religion," Debora Shuger observes that "his respect for tradition is high enough to allow belief, if not in purgatory and the Assumption, at least in their possibility." This view on the Virgin's assumption is not one to be dismissed. As Shuger argues, although Harington may himself be a minor figure, it is possible "to discern reflections of his moderate Catholic Protestantism across the spectrum of Elizabethan society"—so much so, that her whimsical use of "Haringtonian" to describe this confessional standpoint presents itself with considerable authority.[65] Certainly, reading Harington's *Epigrams* is as good a way as any to attempt to understand the complexity of the religious climate in the 1590s and early 1600s. It leaves us with many different versions of the man himself: a self-seeking courtier on the make, a man dispirited with the schismatic effects of the Reformation whose most sincere plea was for religious tolerance, and a writer who used his work as a veiled gesture of his own Catholic sympathies. Harington's "Fifteen Disticks" and their accompanying engraving are uncannily similar to recusant rosary books. When they are viewed in the context of the timing and implied readers of the 1605 gift-book, and the poems criticizing religious confusion and corruption that preceded them, the audacity of this inclusion of a rosary prayer becomes breathtaking. In his own way, Harington was politicizing the image of the Virgin of the rosary just as much as the Catholic writer of a rosary book. However, the language used to depict the most passionate and contentious elements of the rosary—the assumption and coronation of the Virgin—shows Harington hiding, Janus-like, beneath a hood of pragmatism. We find ourselves once again in evasive company.

CHAPTER 7

The Assumption and Coronation
in the Poetry of Robert Southwell

He died
As one that had been studied in his death
To throw away the dearest thing he owed,
As 'twere a careless trifle.

                                        —*Macbeth* 1.4.8–11

On February 21, 1595, the crowds flocked to Tyburn to witness the brutal theatrical spectacle of a man being hung, drawn, and quartered. The man on the scaffold threw a rosary to a friend in the watching crowd and prayed for the intercession of the Virgin Mary. He faced his death, it is said, with mildness and dignity, and when the hangman held up his severed head he was met with silence rather than jeering cries. The man was the Jesuit priest Robert Southwell.[1] He had come to England from Rome in 1586, and up until his arrest in 1592 he had been a driving force behind London's underground Catholic movement and one of the state's most wanted men. When he finally succeeded in capturing him, Queen Elizabeth's sadistic priest-hunter Richard Topcliffe boasted that "I never did take so weighty a man."[2] Southwell was not only a Jesuit priest but also a poet, whose verse caused something of a stir among the University Wits. But although he spent much of his time in the houses of rich and influential recusant families, he was no gentleman poet, composing sonnets "to his mistress' eyebrow."³ For Southwell, the roles of priest and poet combined, and he wrote only sacred verse, displaying an exemplary post-Tridentine view of art's didactic and sacred purpose. His zealous vindication of sacred verse was also expressed in a virulent response to the secular love poetry of the period. Southwell declared that poets who make "the follies and feyninges of love the customary subject of theire base endeavors" were guilty of abusing both their talents and poetry itself.⁴ As Southwell's biographer Anne Sweeney has appositely commented: "The creation of poetry for its own sake was not his end: saving souls was."⁵

Before he arrived in England, Southwell was a prefect of an elite group called the Sodality of the Virgin in Rome. Members of the Sodality made an act of consecration to the Virgin in which they promised faithful service to her as "my Queen, my Advocate, and my Mother."⁶ In this chapter, I will explore Southwell's own poetic relationship with the Virgin through an analysis that focuses on his two poems on her assumption and coronation: the Latin "Poema de Assumptione BVM" and the later English work "The Assumption of Our Lady," which formed part of a sequence of poems on the life of the Virgin. If we are to see the image of the Virgin as a symbol that is capable of sustaining many referents, then this is encapsulated in Southwell's verse. In both poems he invests the Virgin with a complex identity that is by turns militaristic and devotional, didactic and personal. In spite of this, Southwell's representation of the Virgin is often strikingly characterized by a sense of absence, as he deploys contrast and antithesis to describe what the Virgin is *not*.

My discussion is grouped around the four areas of polemics, beauty, love, and death. I begin by examining Southwell's polemical poetic voice through a focus on "Poema de Assumptione BVM," a poem that follows Counter-Reformation paradigms in its presentation of the Virgin as a warrior. In spite of this, Mary is for the most part a mute and elusive presence in this poem and is overshadowed by Death, a personified figure through which Southwell engages vividly with the language of female ugliness. An awareness of the Virgin's absence from this poem underpins the next section of the chapter, which is a discussion of beauty. In his frequent vicious satires on Petrarchan love poetry, Southwell warns against the lures of secular beauty, but his poems, perhaps surprisingly, do not leave the reader with a strong sense of the Virgin as beauty's sacred archetype. The third section of the chapter takes love as its theme and focuses on Southwell's English sequence of poems that intertwine the lives of Christ and the Virgin. Here Southwell marshals a number of poetic methods to create a nuanced sacred parody that both celebrates the Virgin and educates the reader about her cosmological significance. "The Assumption of Our Lady" forms the culmination of this sequence: for all its sophisticated rhetoric and joyful expressions of love, this poem ultimately reveals a sense of absence in its depiction of the Virgin that chimes with the elusiveness of her presence elsewhere in Southwell's work. The final section of the chapter focuses on images of death; here, I will show how Southwell's use of iconography of the Virgin's intact form at her assumption in both poems is integral to the way in which his poetry intersects with the cult of martyrdom, as it can be set in stark contrast to images that connote his own anticipated death.

On the eve of his departure to England, Southwell wrote: "I am sent indeed into the midst of wolves."[7] This was not hyperbole: England at this time was a dangerous place for a Catholic to be. In 1581, the Act to retain the Queen's Majesty's Subjects in their due Obedience was passed by Parliament. It meant that to convert from Protestantism to Catholicism, or to reconcile to Catholicism, was deemed treason, and enormous penalties were imposed by the state for nonattendance at church. Under the statute of 1585, to be a seminary priest or a Jesuit in England, or even to assist a priest in any way, became a treasonous offense.[8] The line between "martyr" and "traitor" had become dangerously blurred.[9] One of Southwell's very real fears was that he would be arrested as a political traitor before he had had the chance to prove his pastoral mettle as a priest. His fears were well founded. From the moment he arrived in England, he was plunged into the terrifying cat-and-mouse game of Jesuit and pursuivant and was nearly captured several times. An excerpt from one of his letters evokes the raw fear engendered by this: "The pursuivants were rampaging all round the house. . . . I heard them shouting and breaking down the woodworking and sounding the walls in search of hiding places. But after a few hours, thanks to

God's goodness, they failed to find me although there was only a thin partition and not a wall that separated me from them."[10] Although the odds seemed stacked against him, Southwell did manage to avoid the pursuivants for six years, and, in doing so, he was able to leave the legacy of writing that was so integral to his mission. For all their flashes of literary brilliance, Southwell's poems suggest a practical ministerial purpose. Written both to teach and to give comfort to English Catholics, they form part of what Geoffrey Hill has memorably described as the "absolute reasonableness of Robert Southwell," crafted by a man who was "meticulously practical in his conduct of missionary matters."[11] Southwell's poems were in the main circulated in manuscript, copied and passed from household to household: revived interest in the circulation of manuscripts has led to an awareness of the significance of his poetry to England's Catholic community.[12] It is no coincidence that the function of these poems is similar to that of the recusant rosary books studied in the previous chapter. Southwell's companion on his fatal mission was Henry Garnet, the rosary's champion, and the two men were friends as well as colleagues. Garnet's *The Societie of the Rosary* was written in Southwell's lifetime and was printed on the same secret press as Southwell's prose work *An Epistle of Comfort.*[13] Southwell's readership extended beyond the recusant community, however. After his death, printed and manuscript versions of his poetry were widely circulated. As Robert Miola has argued, Southwell's poetry was able to evoke different meanings for different communities of readers.[14] A volume of Southwell's verse entitled *Saint Peters Complaint, With Other Poemes* was first published in March 1595; in various forms, this had run into fifteen editions by 1636.[15] Brian Cummings comments that there is something uncanny about the way in which its title page bears the name of the printer only, the "erased signature" of the work's Catholic author making Southwell a clandestine presence.[16] Overtly Catholic references—such as to the Virgin's assumption—were also omitted from published, Protestant, editions of Southwell's verse.[17]

In spite of its popularity in the years immediately following his death, Southwell's poetry subsequently languished for a long time in the literary shadows.[18] Monographs written in the first half of the twentieth century advanced scholarly research but often tended to be hagiographical in tone, unsurprising when one considers the narrative arc of the Jesuit poet's life.[19] Hagiography aside, an approach that focuses on biographical details seems appropriate for the poet who viewed his works as part of his mission—but there is always a danger that an appreciation of the quality of the verse might become subsumed by details about the man. From the mid-twentieth century, a number of studies began to privilege Southwell's poetry over details of his life and death. This has led to a fruitful exploration of Southwell's cultural significance in terms of a Counter-Reformation or Baroque aesthetic. An early exponent of this, Pierre Janelle, in his 1935 book, *Robert Southwell the Writer*, perceived in Southwell's work a move from a concettist style that reflected his Jesuit education to a more direct style that evolved as he stayed in England.[20] Later critics such as Joseph Scallon and Anthony Raspa have laid further emphasis on the Continental influences upon Southwell's verse, while Peter Davidson has memorably placed the Jesuit poet at the vanguard of a "universal Baroque" that he sees as permeable, supranational and supraconfessional.[21] The blend of Counter-Reformation influences with an evocation of the English Catholic experience is potently realized in Southwell's representations of the Virgin's assumption and coronation.

The supraconfessional appeal of Southwell's poetry is also often foregrounded by scholars. Much emphasis has been made on Southwell's influence on other works: he had, to use the memorable words of F. W. Brownlow, an "audience of writers."[22] Louis Martz's influential *The Poetry of Meditation* (1954) positioned Southwell as a prime exponent of the sacred parody but viewed his work as flawed, seeing the Jesuit poet as the influencer of others rather than the finished product himself.[23] Later critics have deemed Southwell as worthy of study in his own right.[24] Alison Shell's *Catholicism, Controversy and the Literary Imagination* (1999) argued persuasively for Southwell's canonical importance on the strength of the quality of his writing.[25] As Shell has shown, Southwell's effect on a range of writers including Thomas Lodge, Edmund Spenser, and John Donne was extensive.[26] Ben Jonson was famously to observe "that Southwell was hanged yett so he had written that piece of his, the Burning Babe, he would have been content to destroy many of his."[27] There has even been vigorous discussion about Southwell's influence on Shakespeare's work. When Southwell wrote, "Still finest wits are stilling Venus' rose," he was clearly delivering a call to arms to the secular poet to write sacred verse, but it has also been suggested that he was alluding to Shakespeare's *Venus and Adonis* and that the initials "W. S." in Southwell's prose dedication to his extended poem *Saint Peters Complaynt* stand for "William Shakespeare."[28] This debate has served to inch Southwell a little more to the mainstream, and his poetry can judiciously be viewed as a body of work that mounts a credible challenge to the fashionable Petrarchan love poetry of the courtier poet.[29] Southwell's representation—or as I will argue, nonrepresentation—of the Virgin is integral to a Counter-Petrarchan discourse that should be viewed as much more than the product of the zeal and claustrophobia of recusant England.

MARIAN POLEMICS

In the margins of a letter to his friend Jan Dekkers, Southwell wrote a Latin metrical prayer to the Virgin Mary, a tiny, anguished reworking of the *Salve Regina* where, in a begging tone, he implores the Virgin to come to his aid:

O virgo clemens et pia
O genetrix altissimi
Succure mihi Maria
Vae Vae Vae
Misero mihi vae
Nisi Succurras Maria
Vae vae nihil nisi vae
Quia privabo gloria.[30]

———

[O Virgin, merciful and pious,
O Mother of the Most High,
Come to my aid, Mary.
Woe, woe, woe
to wretched me, woe,
unless you come to my aid, Mary.
Woe, woe, nothing except woe,
as I shall be deprived of your glory.]

It is an evocative indication of the importance of the Virgin Mary within Southwell's ministry. The Sodality of the Virgin, the elite group of which Southwell was prefect in Rome, has been described by Anthony Raspa as "a kind of Marian youth corps."[31] There were strong proselytizing and militaristic elements to the act of consecration that Sodalists made to the Virgin, with many pledging to defend Marian doctrines to the point of death.[32] Southwell the priest was, as Anne Sweeney observes, "honour bound to engage in Marian apologetics."[33] It is therefore unsurprising that Southwell the poet expressed this Marian devotion via a polemical poetic voice.

Southwell's Latin epyllion on the Virgin's assumption and coronation, "Poema de Assumptione B[eatae] V[irginis] M[ariae]," can be seen as an expression of this proselytizing, polemical zeal. Composed while Southwell was still in Rome, it is an ambitious work in its scope.[34] The opening thirty-eight lines are rather like *Paradise Lost* in miniature, as Southwell attempts to encapsulate both the fall from Eden and Lucifer's jealousy. After this, the focus of the poem narrows to the point of the Virgin's death and assumption. It depicts the fury and bewilderment of Death, who is personified as a foul and disease-ridden hag. The pure and perfect Virgin has succeeded in overcoming Death and her retinue. Death calls her nobles together, fearing that her realm is in danger. The poem then becomes a Stygian court case, which debates whether the Virgin was immaculately conceived and is therefore exempt from the corruption of mortality. As counsel for the prosecution, Death argues that as Mary was born mortal, God has no right to exempt her from laws that have been in place since Adam's fall. The angel Gabriel then speaks as counsel for the defense on behalf of a mute Virgin Mary:

Id Christi genetricis erat sponsaeque tonantis,
Ut pura infectos transiret sola per artus,
Communique carens culpa, mala debita culpa
Haud ferret. Nullis Deus est nisi sontibus ultor.
(92)

———

[It was the property of Christ's mother and of the Thunderer's
    spouse,
that she alone, untainted, passes by infected limbs.

And, lacking that shared guilt, she does not endure
the evil debts of guilt. To none except the guilty is God an avenger.]

The speeches of the prosecution and defense concluded, God pro-
nounces his verdict, that the spirit of the Virgin should rise up to the
stars. The poem ends swiftly and in a blaze of glory; Mary is assumed
into heaven and takes her seat as its queen. Death, showing all the impotent fury of the defeated, takes flight.

Emphasizing the importance of Latin as a medium for the Baroque
world, Peter Davidson asserts that this poem is an example of the "oppositional status" of the recusant Catholic and a direct channel for
Continental influence in England.[35] It is a poem that can be viewed as
oppositional in a number of other ways. Its use of the language of the
court case is highly theatricalized, reflecting, as Davidson and Sweeney
observe, the "controversialist tone and linguistic virtuosity" of Jesuit
productions.[36] Indeed, Sweeney persuasively reads this poem as a
specific poetic expression of a Reformation debate, with Death playing
the Protestant role and Southwell's Gabriel embodying "plainer rhetoric" as he lucidly expounds tenets of the Catholic faith.[37] The setting is
all-important here: by transplanting theology into the court, Southwell's poem reflects the controversies surrounding the assumption of
the Virgin.

REPRESENTATION BY ABSENCE:
SOUTHWELL AND THE VIRGIN'S BEAUTY

What is most interesting about this poem, however, is that the Virgin
does not speak on her own behalf in this court case. In fact, she does
not speak at all. Adding to this sense of absence is the fact that in spite
of the poem's title, the actual assumption of the Virgin is dealt with
very swiftly indeed:

Annuit Omnipotens. Divum sonat aula triumphis,
Virgo poli regina sedet, mors victa fugatur.

(93)

——

[The Almighty nodded in assent, and the courtyard of the gods
resounded with triumphs
As the Virgin Queen of Heaven took her seat, and conquered
Death was put to flight.]

It is possible to see the poem as structurally flawed and uneven, particularly as it devotes far more time to the hysterical rantings of Death than to the Virgin's assumption and coronation.[38] The swiftness of the Virgin's assumption is, however, in line with Southwell's ephemeral representation of the Virgin as a whole in this poem. She is first introduced with militaristic imagery and described as *vindex* (46), a champion or punisher, who is able to defeat Death's entourage:

Donec virgo, suae vindex generosa parentis,
Se rabido victrix objecit prima furori
Mortis, et imperii saevas convellere leges
Orsa, satellitium mortis superavit, et ipsi
Terrorem incussit dominae, quod corporis aequa
Temperies, vegetique artus, et vivida virtus
Lethiferis aditum praecluderet integra morbis.

(89)

——

[Until the Virgin, kindly champion of her own ancestry,
Was the first to cast herself as conqueror into the path of
the ravenous fury
Of Death, and having uprooted the savage statutes
Of her authority, overcame Death's entourage. She shook fear
Into Lady Death herself, moreover, because her body's balanced
Constitution, her vigorous limbs, and her lively virtue—
Intact as it was—prevented the approach of death-bringing
diseases.]

The imagery is redolent of Southwell's Sodality training, but after this dramatic introduction there is actually little sense of the Virgin's physical presence within the poem.

The Virgin's absence becomes even more marked when it is set in
contrast to the memorable and repulsive physical presence of Death,
who is personified as a woman. In his foul descriptions of Death,
Southwell spares no blushes:

> Hic Annosa sedet canis mors horrida saetis,
> Os macie, taboque genas confecta, cavisque
> Immersos fossis oculos et livida circum
> Dentes labra gerens turpique patentia rictu.
>
> (89)
>
> ———
>
> [Here sits aged Death, savage with hoary bristles,
> Her mouth afflicted with emaciation, her cheeks with putridity,
>   and into
> Hollow pits are sunk her eyes, and around her teeth
> Her bruised lips spread into a filthy grimace.]

Death's decayed and corrupt body is here suggestive of the syphilitic, an
outward emblazoning of inward sin, in contrast to the purity, sweetness,
and beauty of the Virgin Mary.[39] Southwell's use of contrasting images of
the female body to represent ideological and theological oppositions is
not mobilizing imagery of female bodies; rather, it is entering into a discourse that already existed. John Bale's *The Image of Both Churches,* for
example, used the image of the body to represent the true church as pure,
in opposition to the feminized, diseased false Catholic religion, epito-
mized in the body of the Whore of Babylon, who was capable of "infect-
ing men's eyes, ears, and understandings."[40] In Southwell's work, Bale's
model is subverted. Death—and by inference the Protestant disregard of
the Virgin's assumption—is here seen as the diseased object, with the
Virgin, a metonym for Catholic belief, as the pure alternative.

Southwell's prosopopeiac representations of Death also reveal a
misogynistic anxiety about women as objects of sexual desire. "Poema
de Assumptione BVM" ultimately reveals the Virgin as an elusive, absent figure, represented more by contrast to Death than in her own
right. Death "belches out terrible noises," while the Virgin remains fascinatingly mute. This representation by absence is a pattern that South-

well repeats elsewhere in his poems, particularly if one examines how he expresses—or rather does not express—the Virgin's beauty. There is little doubt that Southwell was both fascinated and repelled by poetic representations of beauty, as his writing returns again and again to a criticism of the Petrarchan secular poetic aesthetic. The satires on Petrarchism that occur in Southwell's verse are concomitant with his declared intention to use his talents for sacred, rather than secular, ends. In Southwell's verse, invective against courtly love frequently disintegrates into misogyny about the deceptive power of a woman's beauty.

"What joy to live," for example, sees Southwell deploying the Petrarchan and Sidneian oxymoron, as the speaker suffers a range of contrary emotions—"I frye in freesing cold." However, the longing expressed in this poem is not for a woman but for a release from the prison of earthly existence. Southwell's *contemptus mundi* finds its most vehement expression in an invective against representations of earthly beauty:

Heere bewty is a bayte that swallowed choakes
A treasure sought still to the owners harmes
A light that eyes to murdring sightes provokes
A grace that soules enchaunts with mortall charmes.
(46)

The use of anaphora here adds a tinge of hysteria to the poem's misogynistic invective, and the strikingly unforgiving metaphor for beauty as a "bayte that swallowed choakes" is not dissimilar to the one used by Shakespeare in Sonnet 129, where his mistress is evoked as "a swallow'd bait / On purpose laid to make the taker mad."[41] While Petrarch's poetry sees love as an ennobling pathway to God, Southwell here bluntly foregrounds a view that English sonnet sequences, by ennobling earthly beauty, are not pursuing a Petrarchan agenda of spiritual elevation.

Saint Peters Complaynt also mounts a concerted criticism of Petrarchism. The poem's speaker, St. Peter himself, is full of reproach for denying Christ, but much of his vitriol is directed at the maid who has asked him whether he knows Christ.[42] Here the speaker uses language that is uncannily reminiscent of Southwell's own withering contempt for the tyrant mistress. Peter bemoans that just like other men in the

Bible—David, Solomon, and Samson—he has been brought down "with wordes of woman's spight" (71). This complaint disintegrates into a blistering invective against deceiving beauty:

> O women, woe to men: traps for their fals,
> Still actors in all tragicall mischaunces:
> Earthes necessarie evils, captiving thralls,
> Now murdring with your tongs, now with your glances.
>
> (72)

The Petrarchan descriptions of women's murdering tongues and glances are an example of the many warnings that Southwell's verse sounds against the traps and lures of secular female beauty, but what examples of sacred beauty does he employ to counteract this? As prefect of the Sodality, Southwell pledged allegiance to the Virgin in a manner not dissimilar to the chivalrous knight to his lady.[43] One might therefore have expected him to translate this chivalry into his poetry, conceptualizing the Virgin as an idealized alternative to the shallow and dangerous beauties of the earthly woman. Henry Constable followed this path, but while Southwell's poems create a critique of secular Petrarchan poetry that is even more vehement than Constable's, his own representations of the Virgin's beauty often seem fleeting and ephemeral.[44]

In *Saint Peters Complaynt*, Southwell counters his own vitriolic criticism of women's deceiving beauty with an extended deployment of Petrarchan language directed not at the Virgin but at Christ himself. A brief mention in Luke's Gospel (Luke 22:61) is amplified to an apostrophe to the beauty of Christ's eyes:

> These blazing Comets, lightning flames of love,
> Made me their warming influence to know;
> My frozen hart theyr sacred force did prove,
> Which at their lookes did yeeld like melting snow.
>
> (74)

Southwell here places himself comfortably within the idiom, sustaining the apostrophe to Christ's eyes for fourteen stanzas, and his semantic field is consistently that of contemporaneous amorous verse.[45] This Baroque beautifying of a feminized Christ is not in itself out of the ordinary, but when the sustained misogyny of Southwell's anti-Petrarchan invective is taken into consideration, it is possible to observe a homoerotic impulse at this point. This is not wild conjecture; biographers treat with sensitivity the young Southwell's intense relationship with Jan Dekkers, the young man who persuaded him to become a Jesuit rather than a Carthusian.[46] That a homoerotic instinct, however submerged, may lie behind Southwell's reticence when it comes to poetic representations of the Virgin's beauty is a reading that should not be disregarded.

LOVE: SOUTHWELL'S SEQUENCE OF POEMS
ON THE VIRGIN AND CHRIST

It would be grossly distorting, of course, to claim that the Virgin is not a presence at all in Southwell's poetry, but it is striking to note how frequently she is represented through absence and contrast. An awareness of this ultimately disrupts rather than dislodges the maxim that Mary is constructed in Southwell's verse as a figure who inspires devotion. During his mission in England, Southwell wrote a sequence of fourteen poems intertwining the lives of the Virgin and Christ that culminated in a poem on the Virgin's assumption and coronation.[47] Within his sequence, Southwell does engage with a seemingly more traditional lexis drawn from Elizabethan love poetry to describe the Virgin. In the penultimate poem in the sequence, "The Death of Our Ladie," the Virgin's beauty is described using extravagant imagery in relation to her eyes:

Her face a heaven two planettes were her eyes
Whose gracious light did make our clearest day
But one such heaven there was and loe it dyes
Deathes darke Eclipse hath dymmed every ray.
Sunne hide thy light, thy beames untymely shine
Trew light sith wee have lost we crave not thine.
(11)

Gary Waller has justly quoted the final lines of this poem as evidence that Southwell was redirecting Petrarchan rhetoric of the court from a secular to a sacred love object.[48] Pilarz similarly observes that "finally Southwell has found an object worthy of the lavish adulation that secular poets waste, from his perspective, on the women they love."[49] The metaphor of Mary's face as a "heaven" whose eyes shoot out beams of "gracious light" can certainly be seen as a sacred deployment of Petrarchan language. It is worthy of note, however, that this is far briefer than the fourteen-stanza apostrophe to Christ's eyes in *Saint Peters Complaynt* and also comes in a poem that ultimately mourns the Virgin's absence rather than celebrating her presence.

With some degree of qualification, therefore, it is possible to see the Virgin as an object of love in Southwell's sequence, but it would be reductive to view the poems purely in this way. Southwell's representation of the Virgin is here functioning on a number of levels. The structure of the poems, particularly the way in which they culminate in descriptions of the Virgin's assumption and coronation, strongly echoes that of a rosary prayer.[50] Like Henry Garnet's book *The Societie of the Rosary*, Southwell's sequence can be seen as offering a spiritual lifeline to England's recusant community, working to support Garnet's liturgies.[51] The sequence also devotes entire poems to the Virgin's immaculate conception and her perpetual virginity: these poems can be read as a didactic tools, educating the reader about the Virgin's significance. An English Catholic was living in a world where the role of the Virgin in the economy of salvation had been marginalized, but Southwell here presents an arresting alternative by celebrating Mary's overwhelming cosmological significance. Her power is foregrounded through descriptions of her as a figure able to transcend temporal boundaries. In "The Visitation," Southwell reveals this through a proleptic glimpse. The poem retells the biblical narrative of Mary visiting Elizabeth and the child leaping in her womb (Luke 1:39–41) and commences by addressing Mary thus:

Proclaymed Queene and mother of a god
The light of earth the Soveraigne of Saints
With Pilgrimm foote upp tyring hils she trod
And heavenly stile with handmayds toyle acquaints.

(6)

Southwell here simultaneously represents Mary as the Queen of Heaven, interceding for sinners in glory, and the young pregnant "handmaid" on the arduous journey to visit her cousin. Mary's role as Queen of Heaven thus conquers time. This fascination with temporal paradoxes does not only teach the reader about the Virgin's cosmological significance. It is also an integral part of the rhetorical nature of the sequence and as such is another of the methods employed by Southwell to counteract secular love poetry. The sequence itself is a virtuosic display of poetic wit. Constructed with a skillful eye on sophisticated rhetoric, the poems abound in conceits, paradoxes, and aphorisms; through them, Southwell demonstrates to the secular poet that his skills could be put to better, sacred, use.[52]

These elements combine in the final poem of the sequence, "The Assumption of Our Lady," which condenses the final two mysteries of the rosary, the assumption and coronation of the Virgin. Here, the language of love blends with numerous examples of poetic wit and sophistication in a poem that foregrounds an aspect of the Virgin's cosmological significance no longer present in Protestant worship:

If sinne be captive grace must finde release
From curse of synne the innocente is free
Tombe prison is for sinners that decease
No tombe but throne to guiltles doth agree
Though thralles of sinne lye lingring in their grave
Yet faultles cors with soule rewarde must have.

The daseled eye doth dymmed light require
And dying sightes repose in shrowdinge shades
But Eagles eyes to brightest light aspire
And living lookes delite in loftye glades
Faynte winged foule by ground doth fayntly flye
Our Princely Eagle mountes unto the skye.

Gemm to her worth spouse to her love ascendes
Prince to her throne Queene to her heavenly kinge
Whose court with solemne pompe on her attends
And Quires of Saintes with greeting notes do singe

Earth rendreth upp her undeserved praye
Heaven claymes the right and beares the prize awaye.
(11–12)

This is a self-consciously rhetorical poem. Its first two stanzas are a series of antitheses that juxtapose the Virgin's sinless body, rising to heaven, with the heavy, sluggish body of concupiscent man. In the opening lines, Southwell's antitheses force the reader to dart back and forth, from "sinne" to "grace," "tombe" to "throne," "sinners" to "guiltles" in a manner that recalls stichomythia. The stichomythic effect continues in the second stanza. Here, concupiscent man is represented in the first two lines using the synecdoche of the "daseled eye" and imagery of light and darkness—"dymmed light" and "shrowdinge shades." The eyes of sinful man are shown to be as frail and feeble as his body and too weak for the dazzling light of God's love. This is a Southwellian commonplace: images of mists and shadows in his poetry often reveal that the eyes of the fallen man are unable to encounter external representations of God's brightness.[53]

In Southwell's poem, man's feeble eyes are juxtaposed in the second stanza with the eyes of the Virgin, who is metaphorically represented as an eagle: "But Eagles eyes to brightest light aspire." Southwell's use of the eagle metaphor condenses a number of associations. It both anticipates Mary's regal stature as Queen of Heaven, seen in the image of "Our Princely Eagle," and foregrounds her sinless state: compared with sinful man, her vision is strong, pure, and clear. It was believed that the eagle could look at the sun without blinking; James McDonald and Nancy Pollard Brown gloss the phrase "loftye glades" as "beams of the clear light of heaven," commenting that the word *glades* had, at the time, associations with flashes of lightning and tails from comets.[54] The Virgin's eyes are thus set in direct contrast to the dazzled eyes of sinful man. The use of the eagle is also an allusion to another biblical text traditionally associated with the Virgin's assumption—that of the vision of the Woman Clothed with the Sun, who, in escaping from a dragon, is transformed: "And there were given to the woman two wings of a great eagle, that she might fly into the desert" (Rev. 12:14). There is a sense overall in Southwell's poem that the Virgin is being lifted out of a world of concupiscence in a way that is similar to the escape from the dragon in Revelation. The submerged allusion to the Woman Clothed with the Sun in Southwell's eagle metaphor can be read as a Catholic reclamation of this complex biblical symbol.

The use of the metaphor of the eagle also anticipates the swiftness and lightness of Mary's assumption into heaven. This occurs in the third and final stanza of the poem, which becomes lush, lyrical, and beautiful. The allusion to the Song of Songs in "spouse to her love ascendes" connects the imagery of this stanza with the Bible's most evocative of love poems. The contrasts between the Virgin and concupiscent man recede from view. As the poem anticipates the Virgin's coronation, as she ascends "Queene to her heavenly kinge," the dualities expressed in the poem shift to ones of congruence between the Virgin, variously represented as "gemm," "spouse," "prince," and "Queene," and the heavenly treasures that await her—"worth," "love," "throne," and "kinge." The imagery is that of a love poem, and in the swiftness and lightness of tone one is reminded of the Virgin's assumption into heaven in Southwell's earlier Latin poem.

Up until this point in the poem we have been witnessing Mary's assumption, and the poem's swiftness of movement has meant that we have been, to a certain extent, traveling with her. But in the final couplet the perspective of the poem shifts, and we are left behind:

Earth rendreth upp her undeserved praye
Heaven claymes the right and beares the prize awaye.

The image of the Virgin as the personified earth's "undeserved praye" who is borne away into heaven strikes an uneasy, almost predatory note, particularly after the lush beauty of the lines that have preceded it. Southwell is asking the reader to contemplate man's unworthiness compared with the Virgin here—but these lines can also be read as a commentary on the dark ages of the end of the sixteenth century, a time in which such images of the Virgin's assumption and coronation had been ripped out of the liturgy. It is the Virgin's triumph—but is it ours? We remain on the dark ground, shut off from the blazing light of heaven. Noting the overall celebratory tone of the poem, Waller observes Southwell's triumphalist stance against a Protestant universe that had "been emptied of superstition."[55] But while this poem undoubtedly trumpets the Virgin's cosmological significance, its end is also about loss, as Southwell does not allow the reader to share in this triumph.

For all its deployment of language associated with spiritual love, Southwell's "The Assumption of Our Lady" ends with the Virgin disappearing from view. The poem commenced with a conditional "if"; from the start, Southwell is showing his awareness that the assumption and coronation of the Virgin represent a contentious subject, an argument to be won. Anthony Cousins has observed that Southwell "mingles the culture of post-Tridentine Europe with that of his homeland," a view that seems particularly pertinent here.[56] The absence of the Virgin at the end of the poem sharpens the politicized subtext of her representation, and its last two lines have all the resonance of recusant verse of exile and tears. On the surface, this poem is far less polemical than the Latin "Poema de Assumptione BVM," but beneath the surface is an equally acute awareness of the contentious nature of the image of the Virgin's assumption and coronation. Brownlow says of Southwell's most famous poem, "The Burning Babe," that it begins with a vision and ends with a disappearance.[57] The same could be said of "The Assumption of Our Lady," which also leaves the speaker and the reader isolated and alone at its end.

IMAGES OF DEATH

In his English assumption poem, Southwell's description of the Virgin's body forms a striking image:

Though thralles of sinne lye lingring in their grave
Yet faultles cors with soule rewarde must have.

These lines encapsulate the movement of the whole poem—the swift flight of the Virgin's assumption and the sluggish torpor of sinful readers, who are ultimately left to "lye lingring in their grave." Inherent in the image of the Virgin's "faultles cors" is the belief not only that Mary's body is free from sin but also that it has not been polluted or penetrated by disease or wounds. This study has frequently observed how belief in the Virgin's immaculate flesh is strongly associated with belief in her assumption into heaven; it is a pattern vividly evoked, for example, in the medieval *Golden Legend*. In Southwell's verse, descriptions of the Virgin's pure flesh take on a particularly personal resonance. My final exploration of Southwell's poetic depictions of the Virgin takes death as its theme and centers on the way in which this image of purity of the Virgin's body contrasts with a constant motif of fragile and vulnerable flesh that runs through Southwell's poetry. Through this juxtaposition, Southwell deploys the image of the Virgin to intersect with English Catholic experiences in a different way, by obliquely invoking the experience of martyrdom.

This contrast is best demonstrated through analysis of a single poem. One of the ways in which Southwell's sequence of poems on the Virgin and Christ departs so radically from the Dominican rosary is that the crucifixion of Christ is not included within it. Instead, the vulnerability of Christ's human flesh is represented in a poem entitled "The Circumsision." Here, the reader is encouraged to look through images of the baby Christ's body, wounded in a Jewish ritual, to the crucifixion of Christ. The Virgin thus shifts from the concerned mother of her infant son to the *Mater Dolorosa* who experiences her crucified adult son's pain with a synaesthetic intensity. The effect is similar to that of the *pentimento* in painting, where one can see a visible trace of another, earlier painting beneath the layers of paint on the canvas:

With weeping eyes his mother rev'd his smart
If bloode from him, teares rann from her as fast
The knife that cutt his fleshe did perce her hart
The payne that Jesus felt did Marye tast.
(7)

The image of the knife cutting Mary's heart alludes to St. Luke's Gospel, where Simeon prophesies that Mary herself will become a martyr with the words "And thy own soul a sword shall pierce" (Luke 2:35). In the twelfth century, Bernard of Clairvaux connected this prophecy with the bitter laments of the *Mater Dolorosa*, grieving at the foot of her son's cross, and exhorted worshippers to emulate Mary's spiritual martyrdom.[58] Southwell's image also encapsulates the contrast between the Virgin and Christ. The knife that cuts Christ's flesh is here real—but it pierces the Virgin's heart metaphorically. While the son's martyred body is broken, penetrated, and frail, the mother's remains pure and intact, leaking only tears, which have cleansing and purifying properties.[59] Southwell's representation of Mary's physical flesh as unscarred by wounds or disease is made all the more powerful by its marked contrast to the fragile flesh of her son, mutilated first by his circumcision and ultimately by his brutal death.

If we look deeper into the *pentimento* of Christ's broken and vulnerable human flesh, it is also possible to see the image of the poet's own body, mutilated at Tyburn. In acknowledging this, one is not simply instilling the text with a macabre mental image of Southwell's execution, and neither does this detract from the practicality of his mission: Southwell was not actively seeking his own death. Students at the English College in Rome were instructed not to seek immediate martyrdom in a manner that could be deemed suicidal. Effectively functioning priests were an integral part of the future of Catholicism in England, and the length of Southwell's mission in England is a testament to this.[60] However, Southwell's awareness of his own likely martyrdom frequently breaks through his works. His prose work *An Epistle of Comfort*, for example, is alive with contemporaneous language of torture and execution: "Let our adversaryes therefore loade us with the infamous titles of traytours, and rebels. . . . So lett them drawe us uppon hurdles, hange us, unbowel us alyve, mangle us, boyle us, and sett our quarters uppon their gates, to be meate for the byrdes of the ayre, as they use to handle rebels: we wil aunswere them as the Christians of former persecutions have done."[61] Southwell's poems, as Brian Cummings observes, "suggest beyond themselves, without directly uttering it, the persecutory context of the poet's death."[62] The virtuosic poem "Christ's bloody sweat" finds Southwell's speaker exhorting God to make him a martyr in an impassioned apostrophe:

> O sacred Fire come shewe thy force on me
> That sacrifice to Christe I maye retorne
> If withered wood for fuell fittest bee

If stones and dust yf fleshe and blood will burne
I withered am and stonye to all good.
A sacke of dust a masse of fleshe and bloode.
(17)

In the image of "a masse of fleshe and bloode" is a reiteration of Christ's presence in the Eucharist, presented with a rich economy that is characteristic of Southwell's poetic style. Within this image is also an acknowledgment of the physical frailty of human flesh; it is one of many examples of the motif of broken and battered bodies that runs through Southwell's poetry. As Peter Davidson has brilliantly shown, this poem typifies Southwell's encoded use of allusion, with covert references to death on the scaffold; in *imitatio Christi*, Southwell here both accepts and anticipates his own death.[63]

At Southwell's trial, the chief justice of the Queen's Bench, John Popham, baited him with accusations of hubris for stating that at thirty-three he was the same age as Jesus. Southwell's reply was that he was "a worme of the earth, and the work and creature of Christ, his maker."[64] But the link between the death of a Catholic martyr and the death of Christ is hard to ignore. In the line "that sacrifice to Christe I maye retorne," Southwell conceptually conflates his own anticipated martyrdom with that of Christ. Geoffrey Hill has commented that the "object contemplated" for Southwell in Ignatian meditational practice "was most frequently and formally the Passion of Christ; but there can be little doubt that for Southwell it was also his own almost inevitable martyrdom."[65] The execution of an Elizabethan priest had, to use Brownlow's words, an "implied script" of a Passion play only recently forbidden, as the martyr became "the central figure in a reenactment of the passion and crucifixion of Christ, complete with bystanders, apostles, soldiers and faithful women."[66] Southwell's awareness that his own earthly life was likely to end, like Christ's, in an undignified and brutal penetration of frail human flesh is painfully evoked in his poetry.

While Southwell was in Rome, he witnessed the emotional outpouring that followed the execution of Edmund Campion in 1581. This was part of a powerful propaganda machine, overturning the Protestant narrative of traitor on the scaffold into one of triumph for the

Catholic martyr.[67] The circulation of accounts of the death of martyrs such as Campion, both orally and in manuscript, was pivotal to the cult of the martyr, but art also had a role to play in this narrative.[68] In 1583, Nicolò Circignani painted the chapel walls of the English College in Rome with thirty-five frescoes, which depicted ancient and contemporary English martyrs. Circignani's visual depiction of Campion's death shows the executioners in Roman dress, vividly conflating Campion's martyrdom with the martyrdom of Christ.[69] Campion's face, like those of all the martyrs in Circignani's images, shows a stillness and calm. The paintings are an exercise in the *ars moriendi*. Thomas Freeman has observed that a martyr's stoicism in the face of terrible pain created a Christocentric model, paralleling the early modern martyr with not only Christ but also the martyrs of the early Christian Church and creating a "potent propaganda for their own cause."[70] As tutor at the college at the time, Southwell would have seen these paintings every day, and they became psychological and spiritual preparation for martyrdom.[71]

Art—in the form of poetry—also contributed to the memorialization of Campion in England. A number of poems were written about Campion's death: the most notable was Henry Walpole's eulogy "Why do I use my paper, inke and penne," which was circulated prolifically in manuscript form. This poem, as the previous chapter showed, had an important place in Sir John Harington's manuscript collection. In a poem that ironically itself functions as a way of keeping Campion's memory alive, Walpole claims that the "paper, inke and penne" that he uses to write his poem are in fact inadequate. It is Campion's martyred blood that becomes the ink of the poem, speaking as eloquently as the man himself, as his execution serves "to write those precious guiftes in bloode."[72] Campion's body here intersects with language as Walpole uses his poetic skills to beautify and empower the mangled flesh of the martyr.[73] Southwell's works present similar paradoxes of beautiful savagery. "The Flight into Egypt," a poem that forms part of Southwell's sequence on the lives of the Virgin and Christ, focuses on the cruelty of Herod's massacre of the innocents. Here in this poem is the Southwellian motif of broken flesh, as the slashed throats of the slaughtered babies become "fayre garlandes," singing the praise of a savior they are forbidden to name:

O blessed babes, first flowers of Christian springe
Who though untimely cropt fayre garlandes frame
With open throats and silent mouthes you singe
His praise whome age permits you not to name.
(9)

As he stood on the scaffold and faced his death with patience and heroism, Robert Southwell was already public property. He must have been aware that his every word and move would construct a narrative that would be told and retold. It is reported that he repeated three times the prayer uttered by many Catholic martyrs, "In manus tuas, Domine, commendo spiritum meum" (Into thy hands, Lord, I commend my spirit).[74] Thus his dying words echoed those of Christ (Luke 23:46). But he was also heard to pray to the Virgin: "Sancta Maria Mater Dei, et omni Sancti Dei orate et intercedite pro me" (Holy Mary, mother of God, and all the Saints, pray and intercede for me).[75] In doing so, he was using the name of the Virgin to foster a sense of community and identity among English Catholics.[76] A few years after Southwell's death, in 1605 and later in 1607, the recusant composer William Byrd published his *Gradualia*, a collection of music for Catholic liturgical devotions. Kerry McCarthy has persuasively explored links between Southwell and Byrd, observing that both Southwell's sequence and Byrd's *Gradualia* created "sacred epigrams," which followed the techniques of contemplation cultivated by the rosary and Ignatian meditation to provide succor to English Catholics.[77] Included in the *Gradualia* was the motet "In Manus Tuas," the setting for which is a conflation of the titular prayer with "Sancta Maria, Mater Dei, ora pro nobis." It is thought that this unliturgical conflation of phrases from the Compline short responsory with the Marian prayer was an occluded message of remembrance of the words spoken on the scaffold by martyrs such as Southwell and Henry Garnet.[78] Byrd's motet, like Walpole's poem and Circignani's frescoes, is an example of the integral role that art could play in the construction of the narrative of martyrology. Southwell's own poems, awash with beautifully crafted allusions of the frailty of human flesh and circulated widely in print and manuscript after his death, ultimately functioned in a similar way. They became, to use Marotti's phrase, his "literary remains," combining with the traditional martyrological narrative of heroism on the scaffold to keep the poet's memory alive.[79]

Southwell's poetic representations of the Virgin's assumption are integral to this discourse. If we look again at Southwell's descriptions of the Virgin's assumption and his repeated evocations of death and the frail human body, the comparisons become stark. The Virgin is presented as pure and intact, a paradigm not only of sexual purity but also of the physical purity of the body: her physical flesh is unscarred by wounds or disease. In "Poema de Assumptione" she is described as terrifying Death because her pure body shuts off access to deadly disease. The contrast between this and the repeated motif of fragile and mutilated flesh in Southwell's poetry is dramatic. Southwell's imagery of the physical vulnerability of the human flesh is a way of exploring what Caraman describes as a "seam of meditation that time and time again brought him comfort," that God allowed human flesh to be mutilated and mangled only to make it perfect and beautiful in its second casting in heaven.[80] As Southwell wrote in his prose piece *An Epistle of Comfort*: "And for our bodyes, they shalbe of most comely & gracious feature, bewteous and lovely, healthful without al weaknes, alwais in youth flower and prime of theyr force, personable of shape, as nimble as oure thought, subject to noe penall impression, uncapable of greefe, as cleere as christall, as brighte as the Sunne, and as able to finde passage thorough heaven, earth, or any other material stopp, as in the liquid and yeldinge ayre."[81] The Virgin's body needs no second casting. In "Poema de Assumptione," the troop of personified diseases that accompanies Death makes a last request that it be allowed to dissolve Mary's body: "Demum acrius instat / Ut saltem extinctum liceat dissolvere corpus" (93; At last, it urges with particular avidity that it should at least be permitted to give the body dissolution). God does not grant permission, and the Virgin rises to heaven, escaping putrefaction and decay. In "The Assumption of Our Lady," the description of her body as a "faultles cors" underlines how the Virgin rises to heaven inviolate.

Southwell also demonstrates how Mary's death is painless, explicitly contrasting it with both the death of Christ and his own anticipated end. In "The Death of Our Ladie," the Virgin's death is compared to man's: "Death was to her a frende to us a foe," and perhaps an awareness of the way in which the Virgin's painless death contrasts with Southwell's motif of broken flesh gives added impetus to the Petrarchan language that this same poem uses to present the Virgin's beauty. In "Poema de Assumptione," Southwell gives God the following words:

et violenta doloris
Vis nulla impediat, sit summa exire voluptas.
(93)

———

[And may no violent pang of pain
Impede her. May her greatest delight be to die.]

The Elizabethan traitor's death of hanging, drawing, and quartering represented an appalling violation of human flesh, which was emasculated, disembowelled, and ultimately dismembered. Nothing could be further from the perfection and beauty of the Virgin's intact body as she is painlessly assumed to heaven to become its queen. Southwell's poetry often shies away from descriptions of the Virgin's physical beauty, but through her intact flesh at her assumption he finds a way to express the Virgin as wholly and purely beautiful.

Iconography of the assumption and coronation of the Virgin in Southwell's poetry is personal, polemical, and devotional. His pragmatic poetry was written actively to encourage devotion to the Virgin through its embodiment of Tridentine values and its repeated affirmation of her cosmological significance. But although many of his poems are shot through with a blazing sense of devotion, Southwell does not consistently conceptualize Mary as an idealized alternative to the secular beauties he so savagely satirizes. This adds to the sense that when examining Southwell's relationship with the Virgin, one frequently encounters imagery that connotes separateness and absence. It is there in "Poema de Assumptione BVM," which presents a mute and ultimately evasive picture of the Virgin, and in "The Assumption of Our Lady," a poem that leaves the reader ultimately alone. It could be argued that in his constant references to the Virgin's absence this Counter-Reformation, Baroque poet presents us with poetry that is in fact English indeed, speaking for a sense of loss felt by recusant Catholics. I began this chapter with the story of Southwell's death because his is so often a story that is told in reverse.[82] He landed on England's shores in 1586 in the almost certain knowledge that his mission would end in martyrdom. Southwell's work reveals an awareness of this through its overriding preoccupation with man's physical fragility and mortality, one that has a profound effect upon his very complex portrayal of the Virgin. One of his most sustained representations of Mary's beauty is that of her immaculate flesh as she is assumed into heaven, escaping painful death and earthly putrefaction. The Virgin's separateness from man is thus foregrounded, and her triumph over death—swift, beautiful, and too pure for the eyes of sinful man—is revealed as radically different from Southwell's own.

Epilogue

What's past is prologue.

—*The Tempest*, 2.1.245

This study of early modern confessions began at St. Paul's Cross and ended at Tyburn. In London today, these are both still tourist attractions. St. Paul's Cross itself is no longer there, destroyed by Puritans during the first Civil War. Instead, the magnificent Baroque confection of St. Paul's Cathedral looms over a jumble of cafés, souvenir shops, and restaurants. It is still a busy spot, but it feels resolutely secular: in the heart of London's financial district, runners weave in and out of tourists, bankers walk with mobile phones jammed against their ears, and overflowing pubs tip lunchtime drinkers out onto the street. Around the corner from the cathedral itself, however, is an echo of the past. An evangelical bookshop stands abutted by a hairdresser and a sports retailer. It is located, with perhaps a certain irony, on Ave Maria Street, the place where in the Middle Ages monks would stop to pray to the Virgin on the Corpus Christi procession to the cathedral. A journey of just ten minutes on London's Underground takes the tourist to the crossroads that was once known as Tyburn. Now it is Marble Arch, a nineteenth-century London landmark that stands proudly but rather uneasily on a busy traffic island. New layers of conflict have been placed over Tyburn's gruesome past. Today, police keep a watchful eye over a fluid community of homeless immigrants, a reminder of the suffering and conflict that exist just below the tourist gloss of England's capital city. On the spot where the gallows once stood is a small plaque, a memoriam to Tyburn's bloody tree. Three fragile young trees grow around it to symbolize the three gallows themselves. They form a small, sad memory that feels engulfed by the roar of traffic all around. London is a city where the past constantly leaks into the present.

The journey from St. Paul's to Tyburn is not far in terms of distance, but the confessional journey of this study, from the Protestant polemic of the pulpit to the Catholic devotion of the Jesuit mission, has been a long one. It has encompassed a spectrum of many confessional shades, from apostasy and conversion to elusive confessional standpoints. My analysis of iconography of the assumption and coronation of the Virgin has provided an insight into the complexity of belief systems in early modern England, showing how representations of the Queen of Heaven reflected the often confrontational ideologies of their creator and were frequently expressions of religio-political concerns. This study does not deny that during the reigns of Elizabeth I and James I Catholicism moved from the mainstream to the margins. With this shift, a set of universally accepted belief systems that privileged the Virgin as mediatrix were lost. But a growing body of evidence refutes previously held maxims that iconography of the Virgin simply disappeared in the Reformation: the reality is much more complex. Indeed, the marginalization of the Virgin's image made it more political, more polemical, particularly in the case of extrascriptural aspects of Mariology such as the assumption and coronation.

I have shown how excoriations of the Virgin as Queen of Heaven from the pulpit and in religious tracts led to a reimagining of this once beloved image. The result was the construction of a sham Queen of Heaven, a figure who, like the Whore of Babylon, was a metonym for a feminized, demonized Catholic Church and a disorderly Catholic woman. I have described the overt and covert presence of the sham Queen of Heaven in the writings of Curione and Spenser, but her presence must surely be felt in other works. The effect of this enforced polarization was one of dislocation rather than clarity. The vilified Queen of Heaven was viewed in anti-Catholic writing as a wholly different character from the revered humble handmaid—and yet they are part of the same image. This tension between *ancilla Domini* and *Regina Coeli* fueled a complex Catholic retrenchment that presented the Queen of Heaven as much more than a militaristic figure: instead, the medieval memory of the plurisignant image of the Virgin was re-formed and invested with new exigencies. The transformation I have documented presents further evidence of the way the image of the Virgin has adapted and changed over the centuries. It is a testament to the infinite variety of Mary as a symbol that a study of her image has encountered so many diverse aspects of early modern culture, from the relationship between breastfeeding and religious instruction to the cult of martyrdom. Through the writings of Sir John Harington, Henry Constable, and Aemilia Lanyer, the Virgin's image intersected with court politics and discourses on gender. Moreover, in very different ways, recusant rosary books and the poetry of Robert Southwell have revealed that iconography of the Virgin played a significant role in the formulation of a Counter-Reformation aesthetic that was governed by the peculiarities of the English Catholic experience. In a study that argues for the continued cultural and ideological relevance of the Virgin in Elizabethan and Jacobean culture, this diversity forms perhaps the most persuasive argument of all.

Overarching all of this has been an awareness that history is porous, that early modern representations of the Queen of Heaven can be situated in dialogue with medieval iconography. This sense of the past as prologue looks forward as well as back. Later representations of the Virgin's assumption and coronation do not come out of nowhere. In very different ways, ripples of familiar conflicts and tropes pass through modern culture, as writers still strive to contain the Virgin Mary. In 2013 on the stage of London's Barbican Theatre, the actress Fiona Shaw sits silently in a glass box, a living embodiment of a statue of the Virgin Mary. She is serene and still, as theatergoers cluster around her, pointing, staring, taking pictures with their phones. The audience return to their seats and Shaw begins to speak. She speaks and speaks for the next ninety minutes, as emotive, painful, angry words are placed in the mouth of a mute icon. She is Mary the mother of Jesus, Mary the mother of a man executed for terrorism, performing a visceral, brilliant evocation of what it is like to be left behind. Colm Tóibín's monologue *The Testament of Mary* was a critical success in America as well as England, but the play's Broadway run was short-lived. It closed after only two weeks because of noisy protests outside the theater from evangelical Christian groups who deemed it blasphemous. The Virgin is still today a figure who can elicit an impassioned response.

The controversy that surrounds the figure of the Virgin is not exclusively concerned with artistic representation. Twenty-first-century theological debates on Mary's role often express a tension between the two roles of Queen of Heaven and humble handmaid that feels uncannily familiar. The image of the Virgin may be constantly changing, but it would appear that the polarities established by Reformation thinking are still a matter for dispute. On one evangelical Protestant website dedicated to answering biblical questions there is an emphatic denial of the Queen of Heaven's existence that rewrites the anxieties of the pulpit at St. Paul's Cross: "There is no queen of heaven. There has never been a queen of heaven. There is most certainly a King of Heaven, the Lord of hosts, Jehovah. He alone rules in heaven. He does not share His rule or His throne or His authority with anyone. The idea that Mary, the mother of Jesus, is the queen of heaven has no scriptural basis whatsoever, stemming instead from proclamations of priests and popes of the Roman Catholic Church." Mary is described instead as a humble handmaid, "a godly young woman greatly blessed in that she was chosen to bear the Savior of the world."[1]

The gulf between the Marian paradigms of *ancilla Domini* and *Regina Coeli* remains a focus of debate in modern Catholic writing. In her excellent study *Missing Mary*, the feminist writer and academic Charlotte Spretnak grapples with Mary's identity within modern-day confessions. Spretnak's deep-seated belief in Mary's cosmological significance is clear; terming herself a "Marian Catholic," she levels an accusation against the Catholic Church that, since Vatican II, it has sought to modernize itself by shrinking the influence and profile of the Virgin.[2] She comments that "progressive" intellectuals in the Catholic Church "tend to consider any glorification of the Nazarene village woman as 'Queen of Heaven' to be theologically regressive and even dangerously reactionary—or, at very least, in poor taste."[3] The book laments the absence of Mary's "larger, cosmological presence," which is embodied in the symbolic figure of the Queen of Heaven.[4] Spretnak's discussion on the splintering of the image of the Virgin into either "Nazarene House-wife" or "Queen of Heaven" would be at home in many chapters of my own study of early modern writings. Nicholas Ayo brilliantly encapsulates this debate as "the polarization of those who would maximise Mary and those who would minimise her."[5] Similarly debating the ramifications of Vatican II for the shift from the "high Mariology" of the *Regina Coeli* to the "low Mariology" of the *ancilla Domini*, Ayo presents the reader with an open-ended story: "There may indeed be an overall development in this zig-zag course, but one ought never to believe that today's theology is the last word. A high Mariology may live to serve the faithful again, but it will be renewed and purified. Theologies do not die; they are transformed and then rediscovered."[6]

Perhaps the figure of the Virgin Mary will never be free from controversy, and perhaps the role of Queen of Heaven is the most controversial of all. To use the words of the theologian Nathan Mitchell: "Imagining this slave girl crowned 'Queen of Heaven' is like imagining Jesus—crowned with thorns and co-crucified with criminals on the crossbeam of state-sponsored capital punishment—as the ultimate revelation of God's power, wisdom and divinity. Both images are subversive, transgressive."[7] *Subversive* and *transgressive* are powerful words and seem to sit more lightly on the male form of Christ than they do on the female form of Mary. At the core of this lie issues of gender: the relationship between the Virgin's identity and female identity. The tensions that exist between the archetypes of humble handmaid and Queen of Heaven resurface in many representations of women in today's society: the stay-at-home mother versus the working mother, the Jihadi bride versus the Western teenager, the female priest—even female bishop—versus the stalwart churchgoer who struggles to find a biblical precedent for women in a position of public religious authority. A debate about the Queen of Heaven is a debate about perceptions of female power.

The very first words in this study were about the Virgin's shrine at Walsingham, and it is at Walsingham where I end. The words of the "The Walsingham Ballad" create a topography of iconoclastic destruction. At Walsingham today, the East Window of the medieval priory church stands alone in the grounds as a ruined arch, a dramatic reminder

of times past. Walsingham itself is no longer a spiritually barren place,
however. Hundreds of years after the Reformation, the shrine under-
went two separate revivals, Anglican and Catholic, and the two now
exist comfortably side by side.[8] At the end of May every year, a little bit
of Seville or Cordoba comes to this tiny and remote Norfolk village as it
plays host to its annual pilgrimage.[9] Open-air ceremonies are held under
the shadow of the ruined arch: a site of destruction has become a site of
celebration. The Virgin's roles of *ancilla Domini* and *Regina Coeli* combine here. The shrine's strongest connection is with the annunciation
of the Virgin: the medieval pilgrimage site was one where, in the eleventh century, the noblewoman Lady Richeldis saw a vision of the Holy
House. However, the statue of the Virgin that forms the focus of a pilgrimage to Walsingham is one of Mary crowned as heaven's queen. As
part of the pilgrimage celebrations it is this statue that, adorned with
flowers, is processed around the streets of the village by clergy and
pilgrims.

The past seeps into the present in different ways here. On the wel-
come page of the Anglican shrine's website is the following warning:
"The statue of Our Lady of Walsingham is much-loved. It is important
to understand that the statue is simply a focus for devotion—a visual
aid—and not something to be worshipped in itself."[10] The language deployed is a salutary reminder of the human propensity to blur the
boundaries between image and prototype. Its awareness of man's
proneness to idolatry feels uncannily familiar in its sensibilities. The
pilgrimage itself is also a microcosm of confessional complexity. It
comes under the umbrella of the Church of England and is therefore
not a Catholic celebration. The pilgrims are Anglo-Catholic, members
of the High Church body of the Church of England, and the services
embody the love of ceremony and ritual that are the hallmarks of this
branch of Anglicanism. The Walsingham pilgrimage has veneration of
the Virgin at its heart, and the modes of worship it espouses are too
much for some. Outside the abbey grounds stand a knot of protesters,
railing against the "popery" of all they see around. They carry placards:
one quotes Ezekiel 14:6, exhorting the pilgrims to repent and turn from
idols, while another is entitled "Genealogy of Mariology," following a
path of female goddesses, Isis, Ashtoreth, Ceres, and Diana, which leads

to "Mary Worship," here described as "Apostate Christianity." The protesters deliver impassioned homilies, the sounds of which occasionally cut through the rosary prayers being said by pilgrims inside.

The overwhelming feeling on a Walsingham pilgrimage, however, is one of joy. There is in fact a curiously tolerant coexistence between protesters and worshippers; the protesters are so much of a regular feature that one feels their absence would be missed. Conducting interviews with today's pilgrims, Simon Coleman and John Elsner described the Walsingham pilgrimage as a "playful embrace" of medieval traditions, commenting that "more than one pilgrim, including clergy, has actually described the experience as akin to going to a funfair."[11] This is an extraordinarily apt description. The Walsingham pilgrimage is a glorious jamboree, a paradox of overwhelmingly moving spirituality and a carnival atmosphere, of sincerity of purpose and an infectious party spirit. It is a pilgrimage of picnic baskets and pushchairs. All walks of life are here, young and old, elaborately attired clergy worshipping alongside congregation members in tracksuits and trainers. There are cakes and ale for all. How appropriate that it is the Virgin, enthroned and crowned, meekly obeying the words of an angel, who forms the focal point of this most glorious, most contradictory of celebrations.

NOTES

INTRODUCTION

1. David Norbrook and H. R. Woudhuysen, eds., *The Penguin Book of Renaissance Verse, 1509–1659* (1992; repr., London: Penguin, 2005), 531.

2. In the early seventeenth century, the ballad was copied into Constance Aston Fowler's verse miscellany, Huntington Library MS HM 904. It is thought that it had been circulated for many years before this, however. See Helen Hackett, *Virgin Mother, Maiden Queen: Elizabeth I and the Cult of the Virgin Mary* (Basingstoke: Palgrave, 1995), 159, and Norbrook and Woudhuysen, *Renaissance Verse*, 820n250.

3. The protest elements of the poem are discussed by Alison Shell in *Oral Culture and Catholicism in Early Modern England* (Cambridge: Cambridge University Press, 2007), 90–91.

4. A list of the Virgin's appearances in the Bible can be found in Chris Maunder, "Mary in the New Testament and Apocrypha," in *Mary: The Complete Resource*, ed. Sarah Jane Boss (Oxford: Oxford University Press, 2007), 12.

5. Sigmund Freud, *The Interpretation of Dreams*, trans. James Strachey (London: George Allen and Unwin, 1954), 292–93 and 306–8.

6. Simon Coleman, "Mary: Images and Objects," in Boss, *Mary*, 400.

7. Pierre Du Moulin, *Father Cotton a Jesuite* (London: John Barnes, 1614), 38. Du Moulin was a Huguenot who held an international reputation as a reformist thinker. He spent long periods of his life in England, where he gained the preferment of King James. Brian G. Armstrong and Vivienne Larminie, "Du Moulin, Pierre (1568–1658)," in *ODNB*.

8. Thomas Tuke, *New Essayes: Meditations, and Vowes Including In Them The Chiefe Duties Of A Christian* (London: N[icholas] O[kes], 1614), 254–55.

9. Sally Cunneen, *In Search of Mary: The Woman and the Symbol* (New York: Ballantine, 1996), xv, xxi. A similar viewpoint is expressed by Averil Cameron. See "The Cult of the Virgin in Late Antiquity: Religious Develop-

222

ment and Myth Making," in *The Church and Mary: Studies in Church History*, ed. R. N. Swanson (Woodbridge: Ecclesiastical History Society, 2004), 20.

10. Brian Cummings and James Simpson, eds., *Cultural Reformations: Medieval and Renaissance in Literary History* (Oxford: Oxford University Press, 2010), 3.

11. Throughout this study, my use of the term *iconography* refers to modes of representation associated with the Virgin rather than exclusively to the visual image.

12. For the origins of the nickname, see Margaret Aston, *England's Iconoclasts* (Oxford: Oxford University Press, 1988), 133n24.

13. J. C. Dickinson, *The Shrine of Our Lady of Walsingham* (Cambridge: Cambridge University Press, 1956), 43.

14. Danielle Clarke, "The Iconography of the Blush: Marian Literature of the 1630s," in *Voicing Women: Gender and Sexuality in Early Modern Writing*, ed. Kate Chedgzoy, Melanie Hansen, and Suzanne Trill (Pittsburgh, PA: Duquesne University Press, 1996), 111–28.

15. For a history of decline and decay, often termed a Protestant-Whig narrative, see A. G. Dickens, *The English Reformation*, 2nd ed. (London: B. T. Batsford, 1989). J. J. Huizinga, *The Waning of the Middle Ages* (1924; repr., New York: Anchor, 1954), also fostered the concept of decline: the influence of this is discussed by Margaret Aston in a chapter entitled "Huizinga's Harvest," in *Faith and Fire: Popular and Unpopular Religion, 1350–1600* (London: Hambledon, 1993), 146–47. Revisionist disruptions of the narrative of decline and decay include J. J. Scarisbrick, *The Reformation and the English People* (Oxford: Basil Blackwell, 1984); Eamon Duffy, *The Stripping of the Altars: Traditional Religion in England, c. 1400–c. 1580*, 2nd ed. (New Haven, CT: Yale University Press, 2005); and Christopher Haigh, "The Continuity of Catholicism in the English Reformation," *Past and Present* 93 (1981): 37–69. See also Patrick Collinson, *The Religion of Protestants: The Church in English Society, 1559–1625* (Oxford: Oxford University Press, 1982), chap. 5; Arnold Pritchard, *Catholic Loyalism in Elizabethan England* (London: Scolar Press, 1979); and Peter Lake, "Anti-Popery," in *Conflict in Early Stuart England*, ed. Richard Cust and Ann Hughes (London: Longman, 1989), 72–106. I am aware that the term *revisionist* is reductive, but its use in reference to a school of thought that has revealed the longevity and complexity of England's Reformation is fruitful in terms of this study. For a more historiographically nuanced view, see *England's Long Reformation, 1500–1800*, ed. Nicholas Tyacke (London: UCL Press, 1998), 1–4.

16. John Bossy, *The English Catholic Community, 1570–1850* (London: Darton, Longman and Todd, 1975); Christopher Haigh, *Reformation and*

Resistance in Tudor Lancashire (Cambridge, Cambridge University Press, 1975); Alexandra Walsham, *Church Papists: Catholicism, Conformity and Confessional Polemic in Early Modern England* (Woodbridge: Boydell Press, 1999).

17. Gillian Woods, *Shakespeare's Unreformed Fictions* (Oxford: Oxford University Press, 2013), 5.

18. Louise Imogen Guiney's anthology, *Recusant Poets* (London: Sheed and Ward, 1938), remains a fruitful collection of Catholic writing. A similar anthology of prose is A. C. Southern, ed., *Recusant Prose, 1559–1582* (London: Sands, 1950). The publications of the Catholic Record Society also form a valuable resource, while the Jesuit historian Philip Caraman has produced a number of excellent monographs on Catholic writers and public figures in the time of Elizabeth and James.

19. Robert S. Miola, *Early Modern Catholicism* (Oxford: Oxford University Press, 2007). John Saward, John Morrill, and Michael Tomko, eds., *Firmly I Believe and Truly: The Spiritual Tradition of Catholic England* (Oxford: Oxford University Press, 2011), is a wide-ranging anthology that traces Catholic writing from 1483 to the present day.

20. Alison Shell, *Catholicism, Controversy and the Literary Imagination* (Cambridge: Cambridge University Press, 1999), 18; Arthur F. Marotti, *Religious Ideology and Cultural Fantasy: Catholic and Anti-Catholic Discourses in Early Modern England* (Notre Dame, IN: University of Notre Dame Press, 2005); Arthur F. Marotti, ed., *Catholicism and Anti-Catholicism in Early Modern English Texts* (Basingstoke: Macmillan, 1999); Sophie Read, *Eucharist and the Poetic Imagination in Early Modern England* (Cambridge: Cambridge University Press, 2013); Brian Cummings, *The Literary Culture of the Reformation: Grammar and Grace* (Oxford: Oxford University Press, 2002).

21. Susannah Brietz Monta, *Martyrdom and Literature in Early Modern England* (Cambridge: Cambridge University Press, 2005), 2.

22. Frances E. Dolan, *Whores of Babylon: Catholicism, Gender, and Seventeenth-Century Print Culture* (Ithaca, NY: Cornell University Press, 1999).

23. The most prominent proponents of occluded messages in Shakespeare have been Richard Wilson, *Secret Shakespeare: Studies in Theatre, Religion and Resistance* (Manchester: Manchester University Press, 2004), and Clare Asquith, *Shadowplay: The Hidden Beliefs and Coded Politics of William Shakespeare* (New York: Public Affairs, 2005). More multidimensional discussions of Shakespeare's Catholic leanings can be found in Peter Milward, *Shakespeare's Religious Background* (London: Sidgwick and Jackson, 1973), 15–67, and *The Catholicism of Shakespeare's Plays* (Southampton: Saint Austin Press, 1997). For religio-political allegories, see Julia Reinhard Lupton, *Afterlives of*

the Saints: Hagiography, Typography, and Renaissance Literature (Stanford, CA: Stanford University Press, 1996). Edited by Richard Dutton, Alison Findlay, and Richard Wilson, *Lancastrian Shakespeare* is a two-volume collection of essays that capitalizes on the possibility of Shakespeare's Catholic Lancastrian connections while encompassing a variety of viewpoints on Shakespeare's faith. See *Lancastrian Shakespeare*, vol. 1, *Theatre and Religion*, and vol. 2, *Region, Religion and Patronage* (Manchester: Manchester University Press, 2003). The variegated nature of the religious context of Shakespeare's times has been further explored in Alison Shell, *Shakespeare and Religion* (London: Arden, 2010), Brian Cummings, *Mortal Thoughts: Religion, Secularity and Identity in Shakespeare and Early Modern Culture* (Oxford: Oxford University Press, 2013), and David Scott Kastan, *A Will to Believe: Shakespeare and Religion* (Oxford: Oxford University Press, 2014).

24. See Jeffrey Knapp, *Shakespeare's Tribe: Church, Nation, and Theater in Renaissance England* (Chicago: University of Chicago Press, 2002), 119; Louis Montrose, "The Purpose of Playing," *Helios* 7 (1980): 51–74; G. Woods, *Shakespeare's Unreformed Fictions*; and Stephen Greenblatt, *Shakespearean Negotiations* (Oxford: Oxford University Press, 1988).

25. Diarmaid MacCulloch, "Mary and Sixteenth-Century Protestants," in Swanson, *Church and Mary*, 214; Tina Beattie, *Eve's Pilgrimage: A Woman's Quest for the City of God* (London: Burns and Oates, 2002), 138. A similar view is expressed by Hilda Graef in *Mary: A History of Doctrine and Devotion*, rev. ed. (Notre Dame, IN: Ave Maria Press, 2009), 289.

26. Frances A. Yates, "Queen Elizabeth as Astraea," *Journal of the Warburg Institute* 10 (1947): 75. See also Roy Strong, *Gloriana: The Portraits of Queen Elizabeth I* (London: Thames and Hudson, 1987), and Robin Headlam Wells, *Spenser's "Faerie Queene" and the Cult of Elizabeth* (London: Croom Helm, 1983), 17.

27. Louis Montrose, *The Subject of Elizabeth: Authority, Gender, and Representation* (Chicago: University of Chicago Press, 2006), 107; Hackett, *Virgin Mother*.

28. For examples of this, see Miri Rubin, *Mother of God: A History of the Virgin Mary* (London: Penguin, 2009), 378; Barry Spurr, *See the Virgin Blest: The Virgin Mary in English Poetry* (Basingstoke: Palgrave Macmillan, 2007), 35; Jaroslav Pelikan, *Mary through the Centuries* (New Haven, CT: Yale University Press, 1996), 161.

29. David Underdown, "Yellow Ruffs and Poisoned Possets: Placing Women in Early Stuart Political Debate," in *Attending to Early Modern Women*, ed. Susan D. Amussen and Adele F. Seeff (Cranbury, NJ: Associated University Presses, 1998), 232.

30. Elizabeth Mazzola, *The Pathology of the English Renaissance: Sacred Remains and Holy Ghosts* (Leiden: Brill, 1998), 4–7.

31. See Regina Buccola and Lisa Hopkins's introduction in *Marian Moments in Early Modern British Drama* (Aldershot: Ashgate, 2007), 1–17.

32. Ruben Espinosa, *Masculinity and Marian Efficacy in Shakespeare's England* (Farnham: Ashgate, 2011). Other explorations of Marian echoes include Sid Ray, *Mother Queens and Princely Sons: Rogue Madonnas in the Age of Shakespeare* (New York: Palgrave Macmillan, 2012), and Susan Dunn-Hensley, "Return of the Sacred Virgin," in *Walsingham in Literature and Culture from the Middle Ages to Modernity*, ed. Dominic Janes and Gary Waller (Farnham: Ashgate, 2010), 185–97. Walsingham itself has played an important part in scholarship linking images of the Virgin with fragmentation and loss. See Gary Waller, *Walsingham and the English Imagination* (Farnham: Ashgate, 2011).

33. Gary Waller, *The Virgin Mary in Late Medieval and Early Modern English Literature and Popular Culture* (Cambridge: Cambridge University Press, 2011), 135. In *A Cultural Study of Mary and the Annunciation* (London: Pickering and Chatto, 2015), Waller takes a broader interdisciplinary approach, tracing the intellectual and psychological structures underpinning the Annunciation story from the patristic period to the Enlightenment.

34. Arthur F. Marotti, "Marian Verse as Politically Oppositional Poetry in Elizabethan England," in *Religious Diversity and Early Modern English Texts*, ed. Arthur F. Marotti and Chanita Goodblatt (Detroit, MI: Wayne State University Press, 2013), 25–54.

CHAPTER 1. THE VIRGIN'S ASSUMPTION AND
CORONATION THROUGH THE AGES

1. It is important to note that it was not until 1950 that the assumption of the Virgin was defined as official dogma, by Pope Pius XII in the Apostolic Constitution *Munificentissimus Deus*. Marina Warner describes this, and the celebrations that greeted it, as "the climax of centuries of tradition." See *Alone of All Her Sex: The Myth and the Cult of the Virgin Mary* (1976; repr., New York: Vintage, 1983), 92.

2. For a survey of apocryphal writings of the second century, see *Mary in the New Testament*, ed. Raymond E. Brown et al. (London: Geoffrey Chapman, 1978), 241–82, and J. K. Elliot, "Mary in the Apocryphal New Testament," in *The Origins of the Cult of the Virgin Mary*, ed. Chris Maunder (London: Burns and Oates, 2008), 59–60.

3. For different translations, see Elliot, "Mary," 59. More detailed descriptions of the contents of the *Protoevangelium* are in Rubin, *Mother of God*, 10–11, and Spurr, *See the Virgin Blest*, 7–9.

4. A caveat to this comes in John Mcguckin's observations that we cannot wholly dismiss cultic devotion to the Virgin in Christianity's early centuries. See "The Early Cult of Mary and Inter-Religious Contexts in the Fifth-Century Church," in Maunder, *Origins*, 1–22.

5. Tina Beattie, "Mary in Patristic Theology," in Boss, *Mary*, 80.

6. Stephen J. Shoemaker, *Ancient Traditions of the Virgin Mary's Dormition and Assumption* (Oxford: Oxford University Press, 2002).

7. Eva de Visscher, "Marian Devotion in the Latin West in the Late Middle Ages," in Boss, *Mary*, 192.

8. Mary Clayton, *The Apocryphal Gospels of Mary in Anglo-Saxon England* (Cambridge: Cambridge University Press, 1998), 3.

9. Before the Council of Ephesus, August 15 was the occasion of a feast called the Memory of Mary, celebrated in Palestine and the Byzantine Empire. See Shoemaker, *Ancient Traditions*, 116.

10. Stephen J. Shoemaker, "Marian Liturgies and Devotion in Early Christianity," in Boss, *Mary*, 141.

11. For more detailed versions of the different stories of the Virgin's assumption, see Clayton, *Apocryphal Gospels*, 24–61.

12. Warner, *Alone*, 104–5.

13. Henry Mayr-Harting, "The Idea of the Assumption of Mary in the West, 800–1200," in Swanson, *Church and Mary*, 88.

14. Julia Kristeva, "Stabat Mater," in *The Female Body in Western Culture*, ed. Susan Rubin Suleiman (Cambridge, MA: Harvard University Press, 1986), 106.

15. Sarah Jane Boss, "The Development of the Virgin's Cult in the High Middle Ages," in Boss, *Mary*, 161.

16. Donna Spivey Ellington, *From Sacred Body to Angelic Soul: Understanding Mary in Late Medieval and Early Modern Europe* (Washington, DC: Catholic University of America Press, 2001), 107–8.

17. Visscher, "Marian Devotion," 180.

18. Ibid., 186.

19. Boss, "Development," 160.

20. Clarissa W. Atkinson, *The Oldest Vocation: Christian Motherhood in the Middle Ages* (Ithaca, NY: Cornell University Press, 1991), 162.

21. Victor Turner and Edith Turner, *Image and Pilgrimage in Christian Culture: Anthropological Perspectives* (Oxford: Basil Blackwell, 1978), 143.

22. Mayr-Harting, "Idea of the Assumption," 86–87.

23. *Elisabeth of Schönau: The Complete Works*, trans. Anne L. Clark, preface by Barbara Newman (New York: Paulist Press, 2000), 5. Further citations are to page numbers in this edition and are given parenthetically in the text.

24. Diarmaid MacCulloch, *A History of Christianity* (London: Penguin Books, 2009), 394.

25. Mayr-Harting, "Idea of the Assumption," 109; Rubin, *Mother of God*, 137.

26. Kristeva, "Stabat Mater," 105.

27. This argument is discussed in more depth by Jean-Marie R. Tillyard in "The Marian Issues," in *Studying Mary*, ed. Adelbert Denaux and Nicholas Sagovsky (London: Continuum, 2007), 10.

28. Although Mary's immaculate conception did not become dogma until 1854, I frequently refer to it in this study, as, like the Virgin's assumption, it was a belief that had been in currency since late antiquity. The relationship between Mary's bodily assumption and her immaculate conception is discussed by Matthew Levering in *Mary's Bodily Assumption* (Notre Dame, IN: University of Notre Dame Press, 2015), 136–37. See also Caroline Walker Bynum, *Fragmentation and Redemption: Essays on Gender and the Human Body in Medieval Religion* (New York: Zone, 1991), 210–12, and Ellington, *From Sacred Body*, 106.

29. Warner, *Alone*, 99–100.

30. Turner, *Image and Pilgrimage*, 154–55.

31. Caroline Walker Bynum, *Jesus as Mother: Studies in the Spirituality of the High Middle Ages* (Berkeley: University of California Press, 1982).

32. See Shoemaker, *Ancient Traditions*, 12–13, and Levering, *Mary's Bodily Assumption*, 126.

33. Warner, *Alone*, 121–33.

34. E. Ann Matter, *The Voice of My Beloved: The Song of Songs in Western Medieval Christianity* (Philadelphia: University of Pennsylvania Press, 1990), 154.

35. Ibid., 166; Pelikan, *Mary through the Centuries*, 139; Boss, "Development," 159.

36. Herbert L. Kessler and Johanna Zacharias, *Rome 1300: On the Path of the Pilgrim* (New Haven, CT: Yale University Press, 2000), 66, 142.

37. *Acheropita* is a term for a sacred image that, it was believed, was produced by divine intervention.

38. Hans Belting, *Likeness and Presence: A History of the Image before the Era of Art*, trans. Edmund Jephcott (Chicago: University of Chicago Press, 1994), 327.

39. John Mirk, *Festial*, ed. Susan Powell, 2 vols. (Oxford: Oxford University Press, 2011), 2:200. Further citations are to page numbers in this edition and are given parenthetically in the text.

40. Judy Ann Ford, *John Mirk's "Festial": Orthodoxy, Lollardy and the Common People in Fourteenth-Century England* (Cambridge: D. S. Brewer Press, 2006), 13.

41. John N. King, *Tudor Royal Iconography: Literature and Art in an Age of Religious Crisis* (Princeton, NJ: Princeton University Press, 1989), 196.

42. Gail McMurray Gibson, *The Theatre of Devotion: East Anglian Drama and Society in the Late Middle Ages* (Chicago: University of Chicago Press, 1989), 171–73. The initial identification was made by J. B. L. Tolhurst in "The Hammer-Beam Figures of the Nave Roof of St. Mary's Church, Bury St. Edmunds," *Journal of the British Archaeological Association*, 3rd ser., 25 (1962): 70.

43. King, *Tudor Royal Iconography*, 197.

44. Hackett, *Virgin Mother*, 29–34.

45. A further example of this is a statue of the Virgin in Long Melford Church in Suffolk, which was bedecked in precious jewels and cloth. See D. Dymond and C. Paine, eds., *The Spoil of Long Melford Church: The Reformation in a Suffolk Parish* (Ipswich: Salient, 1992), 13–14.

46. Jacobus de Voragine, *The Golden Legend*, trans. William Granger Ryan, with an introduction by Eamon Duffy (1993; repr., Princeton, NJ: Princeton University Press, 2012), 464. Further citations are to page numbers in this edition and are given parenthetically in the text.

47. The intensity of Marian devotion in England's East Anglia is explored in G. Gibson, *Theatre of Devotion*, 144. The play's principal source was *The Golden Legend*, but it also incorporated elements of *Transitus* narratives. Stephen Spector, ed., *The N-Town Play*, 2 vols. (Oxford: Oxford University Press, 1991), 2:527.

48. Spector, *N-Town Play*, 1:387–409 (400). Further citations are to page numbers in this edition and volume and are given parenthetically in the text.

49. *The Assumption of the Virgin*, in *The York Plays: A Critical Edition of the York Corpus Christi Play as Recorded in British Library Additional MS 35290*, ed. Richard Beadle, 2 vols. (Oxford: Oxford University Press, 2009 and 2013), 424–35. Further citations are to page numbers in this edition and are given parenthetically in the text.

50. *The Coronation of the Virgin*, in Beadle, *York Plays*, 436–41. Further citations are to page numbers in this edition and are given parenthetically in the text.

51. Joanna Dutka, *Music in the English Mystery Plays*, Early Drama, Art, and Music Reference Series (Kalamazoo, MI: Medieval Institute Publications, 1980), 7.

52. Ibid., 68.

53. Ibid., 88; Spector, *N-Town Play*, 2:531–32.

54. Richard Rastall, *The Heaven Singing: Music in Early English Religious Drama*, 2 vols. (Cambridge: D. S. Brewer, 1996), 1:246.

55. John Stevens, "The Music of Play XLV: The Assumption of the Virgin," in Beadle, *York Plays*, 465–74.

56. Beadle, *York Plays*, 2:434–35.

57. Kerry McCarthy, *Liturgy and Contemplation in Byrd's Gradualia* (New York: Routledge, 2007), 3. McCarthy's research shows how the work of the recusant composer William Byrd reshapes this medieval tradition.

58. Magnus Williamson, ed., *The Eton Choirbook Facsimile and Introductory Study* (Oxford: DIAMM [Digital Image Archive of Medieval Music], 2010), iv.

59. Warner, *Alone*, 115.

60. David J. Allinson, "The Rhetoric of Devotion," PhD diss., Exeter University, 1998, 38. See also Williamson, *Eton Choirbook*, iv.

61. Ford, *John Mirk*.

62. Margaret Aston, *Lollards and Reformers: Images and Literacy in Late Medieval Religion* (London: Hambledon, 1984), 168.

63. Desiderius Erasmus, *Colloquies*, trans. N. Bailey, 2 vols. (1526; repr., London: Reeves and Turner, 1878), 2:5.

64. MacCulloch, "Mary and Sixteenth-Century Protestants," 195–96.

65. Bynum, *Jesus as Mother*, 16–17.

66. Christine Peters, *Patterns of Piety: Women, Gender and Religion in Late Medieval and Reformation England* (Cambridge: Cambridge University Press, 2003), 96.

67. Song of Songs 4:8, from *The Vulgate Bible, Douay-Rheims Translation*, ed. Swift Edgar and Angela M. Kinney, 6 vols. (Cambridge, MA: Harvard University Press, 2011), 3.

68. Elizabeth Clarke, *Politics, Religion and the Song of Songs in Seventeenth-Century England* (Basingstoke: Palgrave Macmillan, 2011), 89.

69. Martin Luther, *Works*, ed. Jaroslav Pelikan and Helmut T. Lehmann, 55 vols. (Saint Louis, MO: Concordia Publishing House, 1956), 21:327, 329.

70. Beth Kreitzer, *Reforming Mary: Changing Images of the Virgin Mary in Lutheran Sermons of the Sixteenth Century* (Oxford: Oxford University Press, 2004). See also Pelikan, *Mary through the Centuries*, 163.

71. Bridget Heal, *The Cult of the Virgin Mary in Early Modern Germany* (Cambridge: Cambridge University Press, 2007), 284, 114–15.

72. Merry E. Wiesner-Hanks, "Luther and Women: The Death of Two Marys," in *Disciplines of Faith*, ed. Jim Obelkevich, Lyndal Roper, and Raphael Samuel (London: Routledge and Kegan Paul, 1987), 303. Wiesner-Hanks discusses similar concepts in *Women and Gender in Early Modern Europe* (Cambridge: Cambridge University Press, 2008), 214.

73. Kreitzer, *Reforming Mary*, 141; Heal, *Cult of the Virgin.*

74. Rubin, *Mother of God*, xxv.

75. Trevor Johnson, "Mary in Early Modern Europe," in Boss, *Mary*, 363–65.

76. Keith P. Luria, "Popular Catholicism and the Catholic Reformation," in *Early Modern Catholicism*, ed. Kathleen M. Comerford and Hilmar M. Pabel (Toronto: University of Toronto Press, 2002), 119.

77. Bridget Heal, "Marian Devotion and Confessional Identity in Sixteenth-Century Germany," in Swanson, *Church and Mary*, 225.

78. Ellington, *From Sacred Body.*

79. Paul Williams, "The English Reformers and the Blessed Virgin Mary," in Boss, *Mary*, 253.

80. Beadle, *York Plays*, 2:431; Claire Cross, "Excising the Virgin Mary from the Civic Life of Tudor York," *Northern History* 39 (2002): 279–84.

81. Andrew Willet, *Synopsis Papismi* (London: Thomas Orwin for Thomas Man, 1592), 403.

82. Ibid., 402.

83. William Perkins, *A Warning Against the Idolatrie of the Last Times* (Cambridge: John Legate, 1601), 174, 175.

CHAPTER 2. THE QUEEN OF HEAVEN IN PROTESTANT RELIGIOUS DISCOURSE

1. See Susan Wabuda, *Preaching during the English Reformation* (Cambridge: Cambridge University Press, 2002), 26–27, 63. Wabuda also observes a tendency among historians to presume that sermons were rare before the Reformation, commenting that although there were many obstacles to preaching, the homily was in fact an important part of late medieval devotion. The popularity of Mirk's *Festial*, which I explored in the previous chapter, indicates the significance of the vernacular sermon in the Middle Ages.

2. It is not known how long a cross stood on this site, but there are records of public assemblies there from the thirteenth century. It was demolished in 1643. See Millar MacLure, *The Paul's Cross Sermons, 1534–1641: An Introductory Survey* (Toronto: University of Toronto Press, 1958), 3–19.

3. Patrick Collinson, *The Birthpangs of Protestant England: Religious and Cultural Change in the Sixteenth and Seventeenth Centuries* (Basingstoke: Macmillan, 1988), 20.

4. Thomas Platter, *Thomas Platter's Travels in England, 1599*, trans. Clare Williams (London: Jonathan Cape, 1937), 177.

5. John Donne, *Sermons*, ed. G. R. Potter and E. M. Simpson, 10 vols. (Berkeley: University of California Press, 1953–62), 10:133. Arnold Hunt gives an imaginative reconstruction of the noises at St. Paul's Cross in *The Art of Hearing: English Preachers and Their Audiences* (Cambridge: Cambridge University Press, 2010), 62–63. See also Emma Rhatigan, "Preaching Venues: Architecture and Auditories," and John Craig, "Sermon Reception," both in *The Oxford Handbook of the Early Modern Sermon*, ed. Peter McCullough, Hugh Adlington, and Emma Rhatigan (Oxford: Oxford University Press, 2011), 104–5 and 183–85.

6. This attitude is inherent in MacLure, *Paul's Cross Sermons*, William Fraser Mitchell, *English Pulpit Oratory from Andrewes to Tillotson* (London: S. P. C. K., 1932), and John Wheatley Blench, *Preaching in England in the Late Fifteenth and Sixteenth Centuries: A Study of English Sermons, 1450–c.1600* (Oxford: Basil Blackwell, 1964).

7. Lori Anne Ferrell and Peter McCullough, eds., *The English Sermon Revised: Religion, Literature, and History, 1600–1750* (Manchester: Manchester University Press, 2000), 3.

8. Ibid., 10.

9. Lori Anne Ferrell, *Government by Polemic: James I, the King's Preachers, and the Rhetorics of Conformity* (Stanford, CA: Stanford University Press, 1998), 8.

10. For a discussion of the term *public sphere*, see Tony Claydon, "The Sermon, the 'Public Sphere' and the Political Culture of Late Seventeenth-Century England," in Ferrell and McCullough, *English Sermon Revised*; and Peter Lake and Michael Questier, *The Antichrist's Lewd Hat: Protestants, Papists and Players in Post-Reformation England* (New Haven, CT: Yale University Press, 2002), 335–76.

11. Tessa Watt, *Cheap Print and Popular Piety, 1550–1640* (Cambridge: Cambridge University Press, 1991); Alexandra Walsham, *Providence in Early Modern England* (Oxford: Oxford University Press, 1999); Patrick Collinson,

"Biblical Rhetoric: The English Nation and National Sentiment in the Prophetic Mode," in *Religion and Culture in Renaissance England*, ed. Claire McEachern and Debora Shuger (Cambridge: Cambridge University Press, 1997), 30.

12. Lake and Questier, *Antichrist's Lewd Hat*, chap. 9.

13. Bryan Crockett, *The Play of Paradox: Stage and Sermon in Renaissance England* (Philadelphia: University of Pennsylvania Press, 1995), 55. Other studies into the rhetorical nature of the sermon include Peter Mack, *Elizabethan Rhetoric: Theory and Practice* (Cambridge: Cambridge University Press, 2002), chap. 8, and Andrew Pettegree, *Reformation and the Culture of Persuasion* (Cambridge: Cambridge University Press, 2005), chap. 2.

14. Hunt, *Art of Hearing*, 16; Crockett, *Play of Paradox*, 50–52.

15. James Rigney, "Sermons into Print," in McCullough, Adlington, and Rhatigan, *Oxford Handbook*, 202. For the transition of sermons from an oral delivery into print, see also Hunt, *Art of Hearing*, chap. 3.

16. Craig, "Sermon Reception," 189–93.

17. Ian Green, *Print and Protestantism in Early Modern England* (Oxford: Oxford University Press, 2000), chap. 1. See also Patrick Collinson, Arnold Hunt, and Alexandra Walsham, "Religious Publishing in England, 1557–1640," in *The Cambridge History of the Book in Britain*, vol. 4, *1557–1695*, ed. John Barnard and D. F. McKenzie with Maureen Bell (Cambridge: Cambridge University Press, 2002), 29–66.

18. Graef, *History of Doctrine*, 79, 87.

19. Erasmus, *Colloquies*, 2:278.

20. John Craig, "Jewel, John (1522–1571)," in *ODNB*.

21. John Jewel, *Certaine Sermons Preached Before the Queenes Majestie, and at Paule's Crosse* (London: Christopher Baker, 1583), sig. 8r.

22. Patrick Collinson, *From Cranmer to Sancroft* (New York: Hambledon Continuum, 2006), 158–59.

23. John Bridges, *The Supremacie of Christian Princes Over All Persons Throughout Their Dominions* (London: Henrie Bynneman, for Humfrey Toye, 1573), 404–5. Further citations are by page number to this edition and are given parenthetically in the text.

24. William Charke, *An Answeare for the Time, unto that foule, and wicked Defence of the censure, that was giuen vpon M. Charkes booke* (London: Thomas Dawson and Tobie Smith, 1583), sig. H1r. Further citations are by page number to this edition and are given parenthetically in the text.

25. Richard L. Greaves, "Charke, William (d. 1617)," in *ODNB*.

26. Hugh Latimer, *Sermons*, ed. George Elwes Corrie (Cambridge: Cambridge University Press, 1844), 383–84, 515.

27. See Maunder, "Mary," 63; Richard Price, "Theotokos: The Title and Its Significance in Doctrine and Devotion," in Boss, *Mary*, 31.

28. John Boys, *An Exposition of the Dominical Epistles and Gospels Used in our English Liturgie Throughout The Whole Yeare* (London: Felix Kyngston for William Apsley, 1610), 147.

29. William Richardson, "Boys, John (*bap.* 1571, *d.* 1625)," in *ODNB.*

30. Other works by William Perkins that present the Virgin as an overbearing mother include *Of the Right Knowledge of Christ Crucified* (Cambridge: John Legate, 1596), sig. C1v; *An Exposition of the Symbole or Creed of the Apostles According to the Tenour of the Scriptures* (Cambridge: John Legate, 1595), 124; *A Reformed Catholike* (Cambridge: John Legate, 1598), sig. ¶3v, and *Satans Sophistrie Answered by Our Saviour Christ and in Divers Sermons Further Manifested* (London: Richard Field for E. E., 1604), 121.

31. William Perkins, *A Golden Chaine: or The Description of Theologie Containing the Order Of The Causes of Salvation and Damnation* (Cambridge: John Legate, 1600), 263.

32. Ibid., 650.

33. William Perkins, *The Combat Betweene Christ and the Divell Displayed: or A Commentarie Upon the Temptations of Christ* (London: Melchisedech Bradwood for E. E[dgar], 1606), 47.

34. Kenneth Gibson, "Downham [Downame], George (*d.* 1634)," in *ODNB.*

35. George Downame, *A Treatise Concerning Antichrist Divided into Two Bookes* (London: Cuthbert Burbie, 1603), 57.

36. Ibid., 96. There are no recorded entries in the *Oxford English Dictionary* for *assiance*, which possibly has the meaning of "assurance" here.

37. This is considered in more detail by Christopher Lee in *1603: A Turning Point in British History* (London: Headline, 2003), 218–21.

38. Maureen M. Meikle, "A Meddlesome Princess: Anna of Denmark and Scottish Court Politics, 1589–1603," in *The Reign of James VI*, ed. Julian Goodare and Michael Lynch (East Lothian: Tuckwell Press, 2000), 126–40. Meikle shows that Anna exerted considerable influence over her husband, particularly in the Scottish court. It is generally understood, however, that Anna's Catholicism was a more private and more elusive affair. See Peter McCullough, *Sermons at Court: Politics and Religion in Elizabethan and Jacobean Preaching* (Cambridge: Cambridge University Press, 1998), 170, 178–82.

39. Helen Hackett has highlighted the relationship between "queen" and "mother" with an observation that Elizabeth's greeting to Mary of Luke 1:43 as "the mother of my Lord" uses an expression that can also mean "queen-

mother" in the Old Testament. See *Virgin Mother*, 22–23. The title of queen mother, or *gebirah*, was one bestowed on the mothers of rulers of Judah in the Old Testament.

40. The famous Shakespearean quote about Margaret of Anjou comes from *3 Henry VI*, 1.4.111. Kavita Mudan, "'A Queen in Jest': Queenship and Historical Subversion in Shakespeare's *3 Henry VI* and *Richard III*," in *Representations of Elizabeth I in Early Modern Culture*, ed. Alessandra Petrina and Laura Tosi (Basingstoke: Palgrave Macmillan, 2011), 244–56.

41. Leonie Frieda, *Catherine de Medici* (London: Phoenix, 2003), 287; Katherine Crawford, "Catherine de Medicis and the Performance of Political Motherhood," *Sixteenth Century Journal* 31, no. 3 (2000): 658.

42. John Knox, *The First Blast of the Trumpet Against The Monstruous Regiment of Women* (Geneva: J. Poullain and A. Rebul, 1558), sig. C2r.

43. Ibid., sig. F1r.

44. Montrose, *Subject of Elizabeth*, 1 and passim. See also Carole Levin, "'We Shall Never Have a Merry World While the Queene Lyveth,'" in *Dissing Elizabeth*, ed. Julia M. Walker (Durham, NC: Durham University Press, 1998), 77–95.

45. John Aylmer, *An Harborowe for Faithfull and Trewe Subjectes Agaynst the Late Blowne Blaste, Concerninge the Governme[n]t of Wemen* (London: John Day, 1559), sig. Q3v. Helen Hackett notes that although Aylmer's work was written to engender loyalty to the Protestant Queen Elizabeth it is "somewhat half-hearted as a defence of female monarchy." See Hackett, *Virgin Mother*, 49. For representations of Elizabeth as a mother, see Lena Cowen Orlin, "The Fictional Families of Elizabeth I," in *Political Rhetoric, Power, and Renaissance Women*, ed. Carole Levin and Patricia A. Sullivan (Albany: State University of New York Press, 1995), 84–110, and Christine Coch, "'Mother of My Contreye': Elizabeth I and Tudor Constructions of Motherhood," *English Literary Renaissance* 26, no. 3 (1996): 423–50. Mary Tudor also blended the language of queenship with maternal metaphors in her denunciation of the Wyatt rebellion of 1554. See Anna Whitelock, *Mary Tudor: England's First Queen* (London: Bloomsbury, 2009), 215.

46. Louis Montrose, "Shaping Fantasies: Figurations of Gender and Power in Elizabethan Culture," *Representations* 2 (Spring 1983): 61–94; Helen Hackett, "The Rhetoric of (In)fertility: Shifting Responses to Elizabeth I's Childlessness," in *Rhetoric, Women and Politics in Early Modern England*, ed. J. Richards and A. Thorne (New York: Routledge, 2007), 149–71.

47. Katherine Eggert, *Showing Like a Queen: Female Authority and Literary Experiment in Spenser, Shakespeare and Milton* (Philadelphia: University of Pennsylvania Press, 2000), 3 and passim.

48. Susan Ackerman, "'And the Women Knead Dough': The Worship of the Queen of Heaven in Sixth Century Judah," in *Gender and Difference in Ancient Israel*, ed. Peggy L. Day (Minneapolis: Fortress Press, 1987), 109–24.

49. In my use of the term *exemplum* rather than *type* I am following the lead of Mary Morrissey, who lucidly makes the distinction between the two. Morrissey observes that a *type* is an event in history designed by God to refer to a future event rather than a comparison made in hindsight. She concludes that "Israel is compared to England by an *exemplum* or *example*, a far looser form of comparison with obvious hortatory uses." See Mary Morrissey, "Elect Nations and Prophetic Preaching: Types and Examples in the Paul's Cross Jeremiad," in Ferrell and McCullough, *English Sermon Revised*, 51.

50. Hunt, *Art of Hearing*, 294.

51. Lake and Questier, *Antichrist's Lewd Hat*, 335–76. See also Walsham, *Providence*, 281–325; Collinson, *Birthpangs of Protestant England*, 10.

52. Michael McGiffert, "God's Controversy with Jacobean England," *American Historical Review* 88 (1983): 1153. See also Collinson, "Biblical Rhetoric," 19.

53. MacLure, *Paul's Cross Sermons*, 120.

54. Thomas M. McCoog, "Martin, Gregory (1542?–1582)," in *ODNB*.

55. William Fulke, *A Defense of the Sincere and True Translations of the Holie Scriptures into the English Tong* (London: Henrie Bynneman for George Bishop, 1583), 467–68.

56. Ibid., 470. Santes Pagninus (1470–1536) was a Dominican biblical scholar who developed a Latin translation of the Hebrew Bible.

57. There are many other examples of commentary linking the queen of heaven of Jeremiah with the Virgin Mary, including Thomas Knell, *A Declaration of Such Tempestuous, and Outrageous Fluddes* (London: William How, 1571), sig. D3v–D4r; Thomas Jackson, *Judah Must into Captivitie* (London: Printed by I. Haviland, 1622), 91–92, and George Benson, *A Sermon Preached at Paules Crosse the Seventh of May, M.DC.IX* (London: H. L[owns] for Richard Moore, 1609), 58.

58. James Bisse, *Two Sermons Preached, the One at Paules Crosse the Eighth of Januarie 1580. The Other, at Christe Churche in London on the Same Day in the After Noone* (London: Thomas Woodcocke, 1581), sigs. G8v, H1r.

59. Henry Barrow, *A Brief Discoverie of the False Church* (Dort[?]: 1590[?]), 81.

60. Ibid., 82.

61. Patrick Collinson, "Barrow, Henry (c.1550–1593)," in *ODNB*. Barrow's life was fictionalized in David Edgar's play *Written on the Heart*, first

performed by the Royal Shakespeare Company in 2011. The play explores Barrow's relationship with Launcelot Andrewes, who was instrumental in his imprisonment for separatism. At one point in Edgar's play, Barrow is seen smashing a window of the Virgin Mary with a hammer.

62. Henry Greenwood, *The Race Celestial, or, A Direct Path to Heaven* (London: N. O. for Henry Bell, 1609), 15–16.

63. The first recorded use of this proverb is in 1571. See Robert William Dent, *Proverbial Language in English Drama Exclusive of Shakespeare, 1495–1616: An Index* (Berkeley: University of California Press, 1984), 438.

64. For an exploration of this early Marian cult, see Shoemaker, "Marian Liturgies and Devotion," 132. A debate about the existence of the Collyridians is developed in Geoffrey Ashe, *The Virgin: Mary's Cult and the Re-emergence of the Goddess* (London: Penguin, 1976), 150–52, and Michael Carroll, *The Cult of the Virgin Mary: Psychological Origins* (Princeton, NJ: Princeton University Press, 1986), chap. 2.

65. John Jewel, *A Defence of the Apologie of the Churche of Englande, Conteininge an Answeare to a certaine Booke lately set foorthe by M. Hardinge* (London: Henry Wykes, 1567), 312–13.

66. Ibid., 313. The word *boulte* refers to a method of sieving flour by passing it through a bolting cloth.

67. Dolan, *Whores of Babylon*.

68. Jewel, *Defence of the Apologie*, 313.

69. Willet, *Synopsis Papismi*, 403. Willet's antipapist guide ran into five different editions. See Anthony Milton, *Catholic and Reformed: The Roman and Protestant Churches in English Protestant Thought, 1600–1640* (Cambridge: Cambridge University Press, 1995), 13.

70. Willet, *Synopsis Papismi*, 404.

71. J. F. Merritt, "Tuke, Thomas (1580/81–1657)," in *ODNB*.

72. Tuke, *New Essayes*, 254–55.

73. Alexandra Walsham, "Bell, Thomas (*b. c.*1551, *d.* in or after 1610)," in *ODNB*.

74. Thomas Bell, *The Woefull Crie of Rome Containing a Defiance to Popery* (London: T[homas] C[reed] for William Welby, 1605), 70. Further citations are to page numbers in this edition and are given parenthetically in the text.

75. John Calvin, *A Harmonie Upon The Three Evangelists, Matthew, Mark and Luke*, trans. E. P. (London: Thomas Dawson, 1584), 35. Further citations are to page numbers in this edition and are given parenthetically in the text.

CHAPTER 3. SHAM QUEENS OF HEAVEN

1. The event is relayed in John Phillips, *The Reformation of Images: Destruction of Art in England, 1535–1660* (Berkeley: University of California Press, 1973), 75, and Aston, *England's Iconoclasts*, 173.

2. Latimer, *Sermons*, 55.

3. Ibid., 393–95, 403.

4. *The Oxford English Dictionary* reports the first instance of this use of the word *sibyl* in Robert Greene's *Menaphon*, published in 1589; "Sibyl, n.," OED Online, March 2017, Oxford University Press, http://www.oed.com/view /Entry/17915.

5. Bernard McGinn, "Teste David cum Sibylla: The Significance of the Sibylline Tradition in the Middle Ages," in *Women of the Medieval World: Essays in Honour of John H. Mundy*, ed. Julius Kirshner and Suzanne Wemple (Oxford: Basil Blackwell, 1985), 6–35.

6. Aston, *England's Iconoclasts*, 394 and passim.

7. John Bale, *The Image of Both Churches*, in *Select Works of John Bale, D.D.*, ed. Henry Christmas (1545[?]; repr., Cambridge: Cambridge University Press, 1849).

8. Shell, *Catholicism, Controversy*, 31.

9. Hackett, *Virgin Mother*, 70.

10. In the preface to the second edition of *The Stripping of the Altars*, Duffy recalls his "startled pleasure" on spotting four people in a London tube-carriage reading his book (xvi).

11. Ibid., 459.

12. Sir Philip Sidney, *The Major Works*, ed. Katherine Duncan-Jones (1989; repr., Oxford: Oxford University Press, 2002), 217.

13. My research in this chapter focuses on the Queen of Heaven, an image perceived as oppositional in Protestant writing, but it would be grossly misrepresentative to claim that images were not part of Protestant visual and literary culture. Although Patrick Collinson's use of the term *iconophobia* to describe the religious atmosphere of Protestant England post-1580 still holds a certain currency, more recent scholarship has qualified his thesis. Tessa Watt suggests a fluid adaptation rather than wholesale destruction of images, while David J. Davis has shown that images were still used in religious works. See Collinson, *Birthpangs of Protestant England*, 115–19; Watt, *Cheap Print and Popular Piety*, and David J. Davis, *Seeing Faith, Printing Pictures: Religious Identity during the English Reformation* (Leiden: Brill, 2013).

14. James R. Siemon, *Shakespearean Iconoclasm* (Berkeley: University of California Press, 1985), 3.

15. Ernest B. Gilman, *Iconoclasm and Poetry in the English Reformation* (Chicago: Chicago University Press, 1986), 45.

16. A more detailed account of the early history of iconoclasm can be found in Michael O'Connell, *The Idolatrous Eye: Iconoclasm and Theatre in Early Modern England* (Oxford: Oxford University Press, 2000), chap. 2, and Aston, *England's Iconoclasts*, 47–61.

17. Aston, *England's Iconoclasts*, 221.

18. The history of iconoclasm in England's Reformation is charted by Duffy, *Stripping of the Altars*, chaps. 11–17.

19. It is also worth noting that the continuing presence of relics in early modern England meant that polemic against the image as relic was still germane. See *Relics and Remains*, ed. Alexandra Walsham, *Past and Present*, suppl. 5 (Oxford: Oxford University Press, 2010), 126.

20. The homily is part of *The Second Book of Homilies*, which first appeared in 1563. For authorship, see Ashley Null, "Official Tudor Homilies," in McCullough, Adlington, and Rhatigan, *Oxford Handbook*, 360, and John Griffiths's preface to *Book of Homilies* (1560; repr., Vancouver: Regent College, 2008), facsimile of the 1859 Oxford University Press edition of *The Two Books of Homilies Appointed to Be Read in Churches*, xxii and xxxi–xxxii. Further citations to the *Book of Homilies* are to page numbers in this edition and are given parenthetically in the text.

21. See Crockett, *Play of Paradox*, 15, and Ian Green, "Preaching in the Parishes," in McCullough, Adlington, and Rhatigan, *Oxford Handbook*, 138–39.

22. Marotti, *Religious Ideology*, 37.

23. Huston Diehl, *Staging Reform, Reforming the Stage: Protestantism and Popular Theater in Early Modern England* (Ithaca, NY: Cornell University Press, 1997).

24. Ibid., 160.

25. Marnix van St. Aldegonde, *The Bee Hive of the Romishe Church*, trans. George Gylpen (London: Thomas Dawson, 1579). The ESTC records five reprints of this text between 1579 and 1636.

26. Ibid., 252.

27. Michael Carroll, *Madonnas That Maim: Popular Catholicism in Italy since the Fifteenth Century* (Baltimore: John Hopkins University Press, 1992), 2.

28. Ibid., 52–66.

29. Peter Hughes, "Curione, Celio Secondo," in *Dictionary of Unitarian and Universalist Biography*, ed. Unitarian Universalist History and Heritage Society, http://uudb.org/articles/celiosecondocurione.html.

30. Celio Secondo Curione, *Pasquine in a Traunce a Christian and Learned Dialogue (Contayning Wonderfull and Most Strange Newes Out of*

Heaven, Purgatorie and Hell), trans. W. P. (London: Wyliam Seres, 1566[?]). Further citations are to page numbers from this edition and are given parenthetically in the text.

31. John W. Spaeth, Jr., "Martial and the Pasquinade," *Transactions and Proceedings of the American Philological Association* 70 (1939): 242–43.

32. Ibid., 246.

33. Joseph L. Black, ed., *The Martin Marprelate Tracts* (Cambridge: Cambridge University Press, 2008), lxiii.

34. A detailed discussion of the identity of W. P., with sources, can be found in Letizia Panizza, "Pasquino among Anglican Reformers," in *Ex Marmore: Pasquini, pasquinisti, pasquinate nell'Europa moderna. Atti del colloquio internazionale, Lecce-Otranto, 17–19 novembre 2005,* ed. Chrysa Damianaki, Paulo Procaccioli, and Angelo Romano (Rome: Vecchiareli Editore, 2006), 407–12. Panizza here concludes that the polemicist William Punt is the most likely translator. However, an introductory poem to the text, written by Bernard Garter, names the translator William Page in a poem that puts the translator on a par with the author for influence. William Page's name also appears on the frontispiece of a surviving copy of the 1566 edition, which is housed at Cambridge University Library. Other frontispieces, however, name the translator simply as W. P. The ESTC entry for both the 1566 and 1584 editions lists the translator as William Page but suggests as other candidates William Painter, the writer and translator, and William Phiston, a translator who was known to have Calvinist sympathies.

35. Anne Overell, *Italian Reform and English Reformations, c.1535–1585* (Aldershot: Ashgate, 2008), 189, 200.

36. Panizza, "Pasquino among Anglican Reformers," 411.

37. For the significance and popularity of Elizabethan polemical dialogues, both Protestant and Catholic, see Antoinina Bevan Zlatar, *Reformation Fictions: Polemical Protestant Dialogues in Elizabethan England* (Oxford: Oxford University Press, 2011).

38. Timothy Cook uses the term *Beata Virgo* to evoke Curione's descriptions of grandiose decorated statues of the Queen of Heaven. This apt and useful phrase is one that I adopt in this chapter. See Timothy Cook, "Gabriel Harvey, 'Pasquill,' Spenser's Lost 'Dreames,' and *The Faerie Queene*," *Yearbook of English Studies* 7 (1977): 80.

39. The word *Dogge* is probably a reference to the Doge of Venice, and by implication to the riches given to the Catholic Church by state authorities.

40. Thomas Mason, *Christs Victorie over Sathans Tyrannie* (London: George Eld and Ralph Blower, 1615), 386.

41. Ibid.

42. For a detailed exploration of this motif, see Shell, *Catholicism, Controversy,* 29–32.

43. Jane Grogan, *The Persian Empire in English Renaissance Writing, 1549–1622* (Basingstoke: Palgrave Macmillan, 2014).

44. Cook, "Gabriel Harvey."

45. Edmund Spenser and Gabriel Harvey, *Three Proper, and Wittie, Familiar Letters: Lately Passed Betweene two Universitie Men* (London: H. Bynneman, 1580), 41.

46. Andrew Hadfield, *Edmund Spenser: A Life* (Oxford: Oxford University Press, 2012), 88–102.

47. For links between Spenser and the book of Revelation, see John E. Hankins, "Spenser and the Revelation of St John," *PMLA* 60 (1945): 364–81; Michael O'Connell, *Mirror and Veil: The Historical Dimension of Spenser's "Faerie Queene"* (Chapel Hill: University of North Carolina Press, 1977), 39; Anthea Hume, *Edmund Spenser, Protestant Poet* (Cambridge: Cambridge University Press, 1984), 72.

48. Hume, *Edmund Spenser, Protestant Poet,* 90.

49. Wells, *Spenser's Faerie Queene,* 32–33. Hackett also observes that the phrase "mayden Queene" was often used by panegyrists of Elizabeth I. See *Virgin Mother,* 218–20.

50. Sayre N. Greenfield, *The Ends of Allegory* (Newark: University of Delaware Press, 1998), 17, 41.

51. Harry Berger, *The Allegorical Temper: Vision and Reality in Book II of Spenser's "Faerie Queene"* (New Haven, CT: Yale University Press, 1957), 122–23.

52. Grogan, *Persian Empire,* 94.

53. John N. King, *Spenser's Poetry and the Reformation Tradition* (Princeton, NJ: Princeton University Press, 1990), 91–97. See also Marotti, *Religious Ideology,* 37 and 226n19, and Aston, *England's Iconoclasts,* 468.

54. Stuart Clark, *Vanities of the Eye: Vision in Early Modern European Culture* (Oxford: Oxford University Press, 2007); O'Connell, *Idolatrous Eye,* 10; Gilman, *Iconoclasm and Poetry,* 201.

55. David Lee Miller, *The Poem's Two Bodies: The Poetics of the 1590 "Faerie Queene"* (Princeton, NJ: Princeton University Press 1988), 82–83.

56. Anthony Munday, *A Second and Third Blast of Retrait from Plaies and Theaters* (London: Henrie Denham, 1590), 95–96.

57. D. Miller, *Poem's Two Bodies,* 85. On the relationship between the reader and the world of the poem, Miller observes that "a certain formal reciprocity among poet, protagonist and reader, or between the represented action and the act of representation, must be a constant and integral dimension of the allegory, part of its mirroring system," 13.

58. Theresa M. Krier, *Gazing on Secret Sights: Spenser, Classical Imitation, and the Decorums of Vision* (Ithaca, NY: Cornell University Press, 1990), 134.

59. Waller, *Virgin Mary*, 120.

60. The many dethronements and repeals of destabilizing female rule in Spenser's text are explored by Katherine Eggert in *Showing Like a Queen*.

61. Margaret Miles, *Image as Insight: Visual Understanding in Western Christianity and Secular Culture* (Boston: Beacon Press, 1985), 107.

62. Claire McEachern, *The Poetics of English Nationhood, 1590–1612* (Cambridge: Cambridge University Press, 1996), 45.

63. The ESTC records that *Of the Ende of This World* was reprinted ten times between 1577 and 1583.

64. Sheltco à Geveren, *Of the Ende of This World, and Second Coming of Christ*, trans. Thomas Rogers (London: Henry Middleton, for Andrew Maunsell, 1582), sigs. B4r, B5v.

65. Ibid., sig. B5v.

66. William Haller and Malleville Haller, "The Puritan Art of Love," *Huntington Library Quarterly* 5, no. 2 (January 1942): 235–72.

67. Mazzola, *Pathology*, 106.

CHAPTER 4. THE VIRGIN MARY AND THE GODLY
PROTESTANT WOMAN

1. Thomas Becon, *The Catechism of Thomas Becon* (1564; repr., Cambridge: Cambridge University Press for the Parker Society, 1844), 369. The biblical source for this is Luke 2:19.

2. Suzanne W. Hull, *Chaste, Silent and Obedient: English Books for Women, 1475–1640* (San Marino, CA: Huntington Library, 1982), ushered in a wave of feminist criticism that considered this prescriptive model. Other examples include Ann Rosalind Jones, *The Currency of Eros: Women's Love Lyric in Europe, 1540–1620* (Bloomington: Indiana University Press, 1990), 12; Michelle Osherow, *Biblical Women's Voices in Early Modern England* (Farnham: Ashgate, 2009), 3–5. Similar ideologies had earlier been mapped by Ruth Kelso in *Doctrine for the Lady of the Renaissance* (Urbana: University of Illinois Press, 1956), 44–52.

3. This analogy between household and state is discussed by Susan D. Amussen in *An Ordered Society: Gender and Class in Early Modern England* (New York: Basil Blackwell, 1988).

4. Elaine Beilin, *Redeeming Eve: Women Writers of the English Renaissance* (Princeton, NJ: Princeton University Press, 1987), xix.

5. Robert Cleaver, *A Godlie Forme of Householde Government for the Ordering of Private Families* (London: Felix Kingston for Thomas Man, 1598), 230.

6. Margaret Mikesell, "The Place of Vives's *Instruction of a Christen Woman* in Early Modern English Domestic Book Literature," in *Contextualizing the Renaissance: Returns to History. Selected Proceedings from the 28th Annual CEMERS Conference*, ed. Albert H. Tricomi (Turnhout: Brepols, 1999), 105–6.

7. Juan Luis Vives, *The Instruction of a Christen Woman*, trans. Richard Hyrde, ed. Virginia Walcott Beauchamp, Elizabeth H. Hageman, and Margaret Mikesell (1529; repr., Urbana: University of Illinois Press, 2002), lxxvii. Further citations are to page numbers in this edition and are given parenthetically in the text.

8. Margo Todd, *Christian Humanism and the Puritan Social Order* (Cambridge: Cambridge University Press, 1987), 53–56.

9. Gail Kern Paster, *The Body Embarrassed: Drama and the Disciplines of Shame in Early Modern England* (Ithaca, NY: Cornell University Press, 1993), 24.

10. Ralph Houlbrooke, *Church Courts and the People during the English Reformation, 1520–70* (Oxford: Oxford University Press, 1979), 80.

11. Peter Stallybrass, "Patriarchal Territories," in *Rewriting the Renaissance: The Discourses of Sexual Difference in Early Modern Europe*, ed. Margaret W. Ferguson, Maureen Quilligan, and Nancy J. Vickers (Chicago: University of Chicago Press, 1986), 127.

12. Mikesell, "Place of Vives's *Instruction*," 105.

13. Vives, *Instruction*, lxxxvii. For a list of amendments in the 1585 edition, see *Instruction*, 184–88. Amendments include several emendations from "our lady" to "the virgin mary" or simply "Mary."

14. Amussen, *Ordered Society*, 35–37; Lawrence Stone, *The Family, Sex and Marriage in England, 1500–1800* (London: Penguin, 1977), 100–101. The Protestant ideal of marriage, propounded by the *Homily on the State of Matrimony*, was that marriage was "instituted of God." See Griffiths, *Homilies*, 500.

15. Todd, *Christian Humanism*, 105–11.

16. See David Underdown, "The Taming of the Scold," in *Order and Disorder in Early Modern England*, ed. Anthony Fletcher and John Stevenson (Cambridge: Cambridge University Press, 1985), 116–36.

17. William Whately, *A Bride Bush or Wedding Sermon* (London: William Jaggard for Nicholas Bourne, 1619), 43.

18. Although this form of punishment was first entered into a city record in northern England in 1620, Lynda E. Boose has cited striking literary evidence

244 Notes to Pages 113–121

for the existence of the scold's bridle before that date. See "Scolding Brides and Bridling Scolds: Taming the Woman's Unruly Member," *Shakespeare Quarterly* 42, no. 2 (Summer 1991): 198, 200–201.

19. Lisa Jardine, *Still Harping on Daughters: Women and Drama in the Age of Shakespeare* (Brighton: Harvester Press, 1983), chap. 4.

20. Joseph Swetnam, *The Arraignment of Lewde, Idle, Froward, and Unconstant Women* (London: George Purslowe for Thomas Archer, 1615), sig. F4v.

21. For responses to Swetnam's text, see Katherine Usher Henderson and Barbara F. McManus, eds., *Half Humankind: Contexts and Texts of the Controversy about Women in England, 1540–1640* (Urbana: University of Illinois Press, 1985), 11–20.

22. Swetnam, *Arraignment*, sig. G4r.

23. See Barbara Kiefer Lewalski, *Writing Women in Jacobean England* (Cambridge, MA: Harvard University Press, 1993). Lewalski focuses on different ways in which writers of the Jacobean period resisted this ideal.

24. Karen Raber, *Dramatic Difference: Gender, Class, and Genre in the Early Modern Closet Drama* (Newark: University of Delaware Press, 2001), 216. See also Lynette McGrath, *Subjectivity and Women's Poetry in Early Modern England* (Burlington: Ashgate, 2002), 2, 100, and Wendy Wall, *The Imprint of Gender: Authorship and Publication in the English Renaissance* (Ithaca, NY: Cornell University Press, 1993), 279–340.

25. Dorothy Leigh, *The Mothers Blessing* (London: John Budge, 1616), 16–17. Further citations are to page numbers in this edition and are given parenthetically in the text.

26. Jocelyn Catty, "Leigh, Dorothy (*d.* in or before 1616)," in *ODNB*.

27. See Jeanne Shami, "Women and Sermons," in McCullough, Adlington, and Rhatigan, *Oxford Handbook*, 164–67.

28. Henry Smith, *A Preparative to Marriage* (London: Thomas Orwin for Thomas Man, 1591), 51.

29. Marie B. Rowlands, "Recusant Women, 1560–1640," in *Women in English Society, 1500–1800*, ed. Mary Prior (London: Methuen, 1985), 149–80.

30. Henry Garnet, *A Treatise of Christian Renunciation* (London: Fr. Garnet's First Press, 1593), sig. F2r.

31. Catharine Gray, "Feeding on the Seed of the Woman: Dorothy Leigh and the Figure of Maternal Dissent," *English Literary History* 68, no. 3 (Fall 2001): 574.

32. Ibid., 563.

33. Ibid., 574.

34. In 1978, the historian A. L. Rowse used the information from these diaries as evidence that Lanyer was the Dark Lady of Shakespeare's sonnets, an assertion that has subsequently been refuted. See David Bevington, "A. L. Rowse's Dark Lady," in *Aemilia Lanyer: Gender, Genre, and the Canon*, ed. Marshall Grossman (Lexington: University Press of Kentucky, 1998), 10–28.

35. Lanyer's bold dedications are discussed by Lewalski in *Writing Women*, 219–26.

36. Leeds Barrol, "Looking for Patrons," in Grossman, *Aemilia Lanyer*, 30.

37. Barbara K. Lewalski, "Of God and Good Women: The Poems of Aemilia Lanyer," in *Silent but for the Word: Tudor Women as Patrons, Translators and Writers of Religious Works*, ed. Margaret Patterson Hannay (Kent, OH: Kent State University Press, 1985), 207.

38. Aemilia Lanyer, *The Poems of Aemilia Lanyer, Salve Deus Rex Judaeorum*, ed. Susanne Woods (Oxford: Oxford University Press, 1993), 297–302. Further citations are to line numbers in this edition and are given parenthetically in the text.

39. The rhetorical nature of this section of the poem is discussed by Lyn Bennett in *Women Writing of Divinest Things: Rhetoric and the Poetry of Pembroke, Wroth and Lanyer* (Pittsburgh, PA: Duquesne University Press, 2004), 177–96.

40. Gary Kuchar, "Aemilia Lanyer and the Virgin's Swoon: Theology and Iconography in *Salve Deus Rex Judaeorum*," *English Literary Renaissance* 37, no. 1 (December 2007): 47–48.

41. Theresa M. DiPasquale, *Refiguring the Sacred Feminine: The Poems of John Donne, Aemilia Lanyer, and John Milton* (Pittsburgh, PA: Duquesne University Press, 2008), 135.

42. Brian Cummings, ed., *The Book of Common Prayer* (Oxford: Oxford University Press, 2011), 112.

43. Waller, *Cultural Study*, 64–65.

44. Calvin, *Harmonie*, 35.

45. Gary Waller discusses the relationship between Annunciation traditions and Gabriel's masculine authority in *Cultural Study*, 38–39.

46. Achsah Guibbory, "The Gospel According to Aemilia: Women and the Sacred," in Grossman, *Aemilia Lanyer*, 194.

47. The controversy that arises from these translations and interpretations is discussed by Nicholas Ayo in *The Hail Mary: A Verbal Icon of Mary* (Notre Dame, IN: University of Notre Dame Press, 1994), 42–44.

48. Susanne Woods discusses the influence of Protestant and Catholic imaginative writing on Lanyer's work, in *Lanyer: A Renaissance Woman Poet*

(Oxford: Oxford University Press, 1992), 131. See also Lewalski, *Writing Women*, 233.

49. Parallels between the countess and the Virgin are discussed by Di-Pasquale, *Refiguring the Sacred Feminine*, 143.

50. As Janet Mueller has suggested, the feminized meek Christ is the figure that most resembles the conduct-book woman. Janet Mueller, "The Feminist Poetics of *Salve Deus Rex Judaeorum*," in Grossman, *Aemilia Lanyer*, 112. A similar view of the feminized Christ is expressed in Jacqueline Pearson's essay "Women Writers and Women Readers," in Chedgzoy, Hansen, and Trill, *Voicing Women*, 46.

51. Susanne Woods argues that the stylistic debt Lanyer's writing methods owes to Catholic religious writing, particularly the lavish descriptions of Christ's body, can be seen as a way of appealing to Queen Anna and Arbella Stuart. S. Woods, *Renaissance Woman Poet*, 127.

52. Guibbory, "Gospel According to Aemilia," 206.

53. Naomi J. Miller, "(M)other Tongues: Maternity and Subjectivity," in Grossman, *Aemilia Lanyer*, 151.

Chapter 5. The Queen of Heaven and the Sonnet Mistress

Sections of an earlier version of this chapter appeared in *Poetry and the Religious Imagination: The Power of the Word*, ed. Francesca Bugliani Knox and David Lonsdale (Farnham: Ashgate, 2015). I am grateful to the editors and the press for their permission to reproduce the material.

1. Arthur F. Marotti, " 'Love Is Not Love:' Elizabethan Sonnet Sequences and the Social Order," *English Literary History* 49, no. 2 (Summer 1982): 396–428. See also Ann Rosalind Jones and Peter Stallybrass, "The Politics of *Astrophil and Stella*," *Studies in English Literature, 1500–1900* 24, no. 1 (Winter 1984): 53–68. Heather Dubrow's reminder that the Petrarchan sonnet can be viewed as addressing sexual and gender as well as courtly politics is salutary. *Echoes of Desire: English Petrarchism and Its Counterdiscourses* (Ithaca, NY: Cornell University Press, 1995), 86 and passim.

2. Ceri Sullivan, "Constable, Henry (1562–1613)," in *ODNB*.

3. Joan Grundy observes that Constable was "of considerably higher rank than such poets as Spenser, Daniel, or Drayton." See Henry Constable, *The Poems of Henry Constable*, ed. Joan Grundy (Liverpool: Liverpool University Press, 1960), 20.

4. Ibid., 15.

5. The source for this is a letter written by close friend Pierre du Moulin, which says that Constable "has killed his father from sorrow." See John Bossy, "A Propos of Henry Constable," *Recusant History* 6 (1962): 231–32.

6. MS Dyce 44, fols. 12–43. For more on manuscript sources, see Constable, *Poems*, ed. Grundy, 50.

7. See Constable, *Poems*, ed. Grundy, 60–63.

8. Marotti, " 'Love Is Not Love,' " 407. A second edition of *Diana*, published in 1594, featured five other sonnets by Constable, eight by Sir Philip Sidney, and a further forty-one sonnets that are unassigned.

9. Henry Constable, *Diana: The Sonnets and Other Poems*, ed. William Carew Hazlitt (London: Basil Montagu Pickering, 1859), v.

10. The source for these sonnets is British Library, Harleian MS 7553, fols. 32–40. The poems were first attributed to Constable by Thomas Park in 1812, when they appeared in his *Harleian Miscellany*. See Constable, *Poems*, ed. Grundy, 53.

11. Hazlitt made this observation in Constable, *Diana*, vi. Joan Grundy begged to differ, describing Constable's best sacred poems as works that "far surpass the secular ones"; Constable, *Poems*, ed. Grundy, 82. An indication of the views of later scholarship is the placing of the sacred poem "To St Mary Magdalen" in Norbrook and Woudhuysen, *Penguin Book*, 536. More recent anthologies have cited several examples of Constable's work, with a commentary on his life. See Miola, *Early Modern Catholicism*, 187–92, and Saward, Morrill, and Tomko, *Firmly I Believe*, 177–80.

12. Shell, *Catholicism, Controversy*, 122–26; Helen Hackett, " 'The Art of Blasphemy?' Interfusions of the Erotic and the Sacred in the Poetry of Donne, Barnes and Constable," *Renaissance and Reformation* 28, no. 3 (2004): 27–51; Gary Kuchar, "Henry Constable and the Question of Catholic Poetics: Affective Piety and Erotic Identification in the Spiritual Sonnets," *Philological Quarterly* 85, nos. 1–2 (Winter 2006): 69–90.

13. In "Henry Constable, 1562–1613," in *Recusant Poets*, 306, Guiney dates the "Spirituall Sonnettes" at around 1593.

14. Ilona Bell, *Elizabethan Women and the Poetry of Courtship* (Cambridge: Cambridge University Press, 1998), 108–13.

15. Ibid., 2. See also Catherine Bates, *The Rhetoric of Courtship in Elizabethan Language and Literature* (Cambridge: Cambridge University Press, 1992), 7. For Petrarchism in writing to the queen, see Michael R. G. Spiller, *The Development of the Sonnet: An Introduction* (London: Routledge, 1992); Leonard Foster, *The Icy Fire: Five Studies in European Petrarchism* (Cambridge:

Cambridge University Press, 1969), 122–47; Philippa Berry, *Of Chastity and Power: Elizabethan Literature and the Unmarried Queen* (London: Routledge, 1989), 61–165; Louis Montrose, "Celebration and Insinuation: Sir Philip Sidney and the Motives of Elizabethan Courtship," *Renaissance Drama* 8 (1977): 3–35, and *"Eliza, Queen of Shepheardes* and the Pastoral of Power," *English Literary Renaissance* 10 (1980): 153–82; Leonard Tennenhouse, "Sir Walter Ralegh and the Literature of Clientage," in *Patronage in the Renaissance*, ed. Guy Fitch Lytle and Stephen Orgel (Princeton, NJ: Princeton University Press, 1981), 235–58.

16. Constable, *Poems*, ed. Grundy, 138. Further citations are to page numbers in this edition and are given parenthetically in the text.

17. For Elizabeth's role as *belle dame*, see Susan Doran, "Why Did Elizabeth Not Marry?," in Walker, *Dissing Elizabeth*, 35–36.

18. Hackett, *Virgin Mother*, 151, and "Art of Blasphemy?," 42. Stephen Greenblatt has evocatively shown the extent to which the word *purgatory* still held strong imaginative associations in *Hamlet in Purgatory* (Princeton, NJ: Princeton University Press, 2001).

19. See Helen Wilcox, Richard Todd, and Alasdair MacDonald, eds., *Sacred and Profane* (Amsterdam: VU University Press, 1996), xii–xiii and passim, and Stephen Hamrick, *The Catholic Imaginary and the Cults of Elizabeth, 1558–1582* (Burlington, VT: Ashgate, 2009).

20. John Carey, *John Donne: Life, Mind and Art* (1981; repr., London: Faber and Faber, 1983), 37–59; Paul J. C. M. Franssen, "Donne's Jealous God and the Concept of Sacred Parody," in Wilcox, Todd, and MacDonald, *Sacred and Profane*, 153. See also Shell, *Catholicism, Controversy*, 122, and Hackett, "Art of Blasphemy?"

21. See Constable, *Poems*, ed. Grundy, 235.

22. Shell, *Catholicism, Controversy*, 124.

23. Atkinson, *Oldest Vocation*, 130–31; A. A. MacDonald, "Contrafacta and the *Gude and Godlie Ballatis*," in Wilcox, Todd, and MacDonald, *Sacred and Profane*, 33; Roger Boase, *The Origin and Meaning of Courtly Love: A Critical Study of European Scholarship* (Manchester: Manchester University Press, 1977), 83–86.

24. Kristeva, "Stabat Mater," 106.

25. In *Virgin Mother*, Hackett gives a number of examples of the use of Catholic terminology in encomia to the queen, including images of the Virgin, 146–51, 200–201.

26. For the theoretical development of the sacred parody, see Louis Martz, *The Poetry of Meditation*, rev. ed. (New Haven, CT: Yale University Press, 1962), 184–93.

27. Links between the sacred parody and Jesuit aesthetics are discussed by Pierre Janelle in *Robert Southwell the Writer: A Study in Religious Inspiration* (Clermont-Ferrand: Vallier; New York: Sheed and Ward, 1935), 254–67.

28. Southwell's poem can be found in *St Robert Southwell: Collected Poems*, ed. Peter Davidson and Anne Sweeney (Manchester: Carcanet Press, 2007), 32. Herbert's poem "A Parodie" is in *The English Poems of George Herbert*, ed. C. A. Patrides (London: Dent, 1974), 187. Patrides observes that *parody* is used by Herbert "in the musical sense of providing new words for a familiar tune" (209–13).

29. Warner, *Alone*, 20.

30. See Nicholas Sander, *Rise and Growth of the Anglican Schism*, trans. David Lewis (1585; repr., London, Burns and Oates, 1877), 23–27. Elizabeth's legitimacy was also denied in the propaganda war waged by followers of Mary Queen of Scots.

31. See James Emerson Phillips, *Images of a Queen: Mary Stuart in Sixteenth-Century Literature* (Berkeley: University of California Press, 1964), 24, 29–30.

32. Sir Philip Sidney, *Major Works*, ed. Duncan-Jones, 182.

33. Robert Miola comments on the Neoplatonic elements of this sonnet in *Early Modern Catholicism*, 191. Counter-Reformation Neoplatonic concepts are discussed by Erica Veevers in *Images of Love and Religion: Queen Henrietta Maria and Court Entertainments* (Cambridge: Cambridge University Press, 1989), 75–109.

34. Franssen, "Donne's Jealous God," and Gary A. Stringer, "Some Sacred and Profane Contexts of John Donne's 'Batter My Hart,'" both in Wilcox, Todd, and MacDonald, *Sacred and Profane*, 150–62 and 173–83, respectively.

35. Colleen McDannell and Bernhard Lang, *Heaven, a History* (New Haven, CT: Yale University Press, 1988), 156–67.

36. Guiney, *Recusant Poets*, 259. Further citations are to page numbers in this edition and are given parenthetically in the text.

37. Saward, Morrill, and Tomko, *Firmly I Believe*, 170.

38. Margaret Miles, *A Complex Delight: The Secularization of the Breast, 1350–1750* (Berkeley: University of California Press, 2008), 9.

39. The significance of descriptions of Elizabeth as a nursing mother are discussed in Doran, "Why Did Elizabeth Not Marry?," 139; Hackett, *Virgin Mother*, 4, and Catherine Loomis, *The Death of Elizabeth I: Remembering and Reconstructing the Virgin Queen* (Basingstoke: Palgrave Macmillan, 2010), 71–72. King James similarly described himself as a nursing father, using the biblical source Isaiah 49:23: "And Kings shalbe thy nourcing fathers, and Quenes shalbe thy nources."

40. The painting and its significance are discussed by Sarah Jane Boss in *Empress and Handmaid: Nature and Gender in the Cult of the Virgin Mary* (London: Cassell, 2000), 26.

41. E. Clive Rouse, *Medieval Wall Paintings* (1968; repr., Princes Risborough: Shire Publications, 1991), 60. Rouse gives the example of a fourteenth-century Last Judgment scene in North Cove, Suffolk, where the Virgin bares both breasts in supplication to Christ.

42. Salvador Ryan, "The Persuasive Power of a Mother's Breast," *Studia Hibernica* 32 (2002–3): 59–74.

43. Michael P. Carroll, "Pilgrimage at Walsingham on the Eve of the Reformation: Speculations on a 'Splendid Diversity' Only Dimly Perceived," in Janes and Waller, *Walsingham in Literature*, 36.

44. Jean Calvin, *Tracts and Treatises on the Reformation of the Church*, trans. Henry Beveridge, 7 vols. (Edinburgh: Oliver and Boyd, 1844), 1:317.

45. Susan Signe Morrison, *Women Pilgrims in Late Medieval England* (London: Routledge, 2000), 33; Bynum, *Fragmentation and Redemption*, 102–14.

46. Bethan Hindson, "Attitudes towards Menstruation and Menstrual Blood in Elizabethan England," *Journal of Social History* 43, no. 1 (Autumn 2009): 89–114.

47. Thomas Raynalde, *The Birth of Mankind*, ed. Elaine Hobby (1560; repr., Farnham: Ashgate, 2009), 72.

48. Marilyn Yalom, *A History of the Breast* (London: Harper Collins, 1997), 69–70, 84–85. In 1622, the dowager Countess of Lincoln, Elizabeth Clinton, published a short tract on breastfeeding in which she gave reasons why every woman should nurse her child, citing a number of examples of biblical women who had nursed their children: Elizabeth Clinton, *The Countesse of Lincolnes Nurserie* (Oxford: John Lichfield, and James Short, 1622). Queen Anna, wife of James I, proudly breastfed her own children, expressing her distaste at the thought of wet-nursing, as it would mingle royal blood with the blood of a subject. See Morwenna Rendle-Short and John Rendle-Short, *The Father of Child Care: Life of William Cadogan (1711–1797)* (Bristol: John Wright and Sons, 1966), 26.

49. Paster, *Body Embarrassed*, 39, 83.

50. Yalom, *History of the Breast*, 37.

51. William Tyndale, *The Obedience of a Christen Man* (Antwerp: Hans Luft [Hoochstraten], 1528), fol. xxiiiv.

52. Griffiths, *Homilies*, 187.

53. Antoine Arnauld, *Le Franc Discours, Faithfully Englished* (London: James Roberts, 1602), 122.

54. Yalom, *History of the Breast*, 40.

55. Boss, *Empress and Handmaid*, 26–72.

56. Peters, *Patterns of Piety*, 74.

57. Yalom, *History of the Breast*, 49–90; Miles, *Complex Delight*, 10–19; Bynum, *Fragmentation and Redemption*, 85–87. Gary Waller contends that this sexualization became intertwined with iconography of the Virgin in the Middle Ages, leading to an unease, even revulsion, at the image of the *Virgo Lactans*. See "The Virgin's 'Pryvytes': Walsingham and the Late Medieval Sexualisation of the Virgin," in Janes and Waller, *Walsingham in Literature*, 126.

58. For associations of the image with humility, see Spurr, *See the Virgin Blest*, 27, and Warner, *Alone*, 202–5. In *Women Pilgrims*, Signe Morrison refutes, correctly I feel, Marina Warner's assertion that the suckling Virgin was purely a sign of humility, 33.

59. Boss, *Empress and Handmaid*, 26.

60. Dolan, *Whores of Babylon*, 112–14.

61. Richard Crashaw's own striking use of *Virgo Lactans* imagery is worthy of note for the radical difference it presents between the attitudes of father and son. In his sensual poem 'Blessed Be the Paps which Thou Hast Sucked,' the speaker posits that the Virgin herself will gain spiritual nourishment only from sucking from the blood in Christ's side. The poem culminates in the controversial image "The Mother then must suck the Son." See *The Complete Poetry of Richard Crashaw*, ed. George Walton Williams (New York: New York University Press, 1972), 14.

62. Scribianus's work was in fact written in appreciation of another text about the *Virgo Lactans* by the renowned Southern Netherlandish scholar Justus Lipsius, who, deeply moved by his experiences at Halle, wrote *De Virgo Hallensis* (1604), in which he underlined his belief in the statue's thaumaturgic power. See Marissa Bass, "Justus Lipsius and His Silver Pen," *Journal of the Warburg and Courtauld Institutes* 70 (2007): 157–94.

63. William Crashaw, *The Jesuites Gospel* (London: E. A. for Leonard Becket, 1610), sig. C2r. Further citations are to page numbers in this edition and are given parenthetically in the text.

64. Guiney, *Recusant Poets*, 267.

65. Ibid., 211.

CHAPTER 6. A GARLAND OF AVES

1. Throughout this chapter, *rosary* will refer both to the prayers said and to rosary beads, the material object that is used to mark those prayers. Lisa McClain's comment that "English Catholics in the late sixteenth and early

seventeenth centuries probably conceived of no separation in meaning, and they used the term indiscriminately to refer to either the material item or the liturgical exercise," is pertinent here. *Lest We Be Damned* (New York: Routledge, 2004), 83.

2. John Gerard, *The Autobiography of an Elizabethan*, trans. Philip Caraman (1951; repr., London: Longmans, Green, 1965), 117–19.

3. The rosary books referred to in this chapter are Henry Garnet, *The Societie of the Rosary* (London[?]: Henry Garnet's secret press, [1593 or 1594]); John Bucke, *Instructions for the Use of the Beades* (Louvain, 1589); I. M., *A Breefe Directory, and Playne Way Howe to Say the Rosary of Our Blessed Lady* (Bruges Flandrorum: excudebat Hu. Holost. [i.e., London: W. Carter and J. Lion], 1576); Sabine Chambers, *The Garden of our B. Lady. Or a Devout manner, How to Serve Her in Her Rosary* ([St. Omer], 1619); and Thomas Worthington, *Rosarie of Our Ladie, Otherwise Called Our Ladies Psalter* (Antwerp: Joannem Keerbergium, 1600). Further citations are to signature numbers (for Garnet and I. M.) or page numbers (for Bucke and Chambers) in these editions and are given parenthetically in the text.

4. Eithne Wilkins, *The Rose-Garden Game: The Symbolic Background to the European Prayer Beads* (London: Victor Gollancz, 1969), 38. The story of Saint Dominic's vision was not in currency until the fifteenth century. A different story of the origins of the rosary is that it was developed by the Carthusian Dominic of Prussia. See Anne Dillon, "Praying by Number," *History* 88, no. 291 (July 2003): 458.

5. Warner, *Alone*, 306–7.

6. Wilkins, *Rose-Garden Game*, 51.

7. Whitelock, *Mary Tudor*, 153.

8. Eamon Duffy, *Fires of Faith: Catholic England under Mary Tudor* (New Haven, CT: Yale University Press, 2009), 17.

9. Haigh, *Reformation and Resistance*, 222.

10. Patrick McGrath, *Papists and Puritans under Elizabeth I* (London: Blandford Press, 1967), 265; Henry Foley, ed., *Records of the English Province of the Society of Jesus*, 7 vols. (London: Burns and Oates, 1879), 5:470.

11. A. L. Beier, *Masterless Men: The Vagrancy Problem in England, 1560–1640* (London: Methuen, 1985), 93. For further examples of the rosary's continued use, see McClain, *Lest We Be Damned*, 86–87, and J. Scarisbrick, *Reformation*, 141.

12. Louis Montrose describes this as a "comically idolatrous episode" in *Subject of Elizabeth*, 108. The rosary references in the masque are also discussed in Hackett, *Virgin Mother*, 92.

13. T. Cutwode [Tailboys Dymoke], *Caltha Poetarum* (London: Thomas Creede for Richard Olive, 1599), 70.

14. Ibid., 116.

15. Frances E. Dolan, "Gender and the 'Lost' Spaces of Catholicism," *Journal of Interdisciplinary History* 32, no. 4 (Spring 2002): 641, 644.

16. Diana Scarisbrick, *Tudor and Jacobean Jewellery* (London: Tate, 1995), 41.

17. Alexandra Walsham, "'Domme Preachers'? Post-Reformation English Catholicism and the Culture of Print," *Past and Present* 168 (August 2000): 80. A&R list 932 Catholic books printed in English and 1,619 in Latin and Continental languages.

18. Ceri Sullivan, *Dismembered Rhetoric: English Recusant Writing, 1580–1603* (London: Associated University Presses, 1995), 13.

19. Dillon, "Praying by Number."

20. Nathan D. Mitchell, *The Mystery of the Rosary: Marian Devotion and the Reinvention of Catholicism* (New York: New York University Press, 2009), 8.

21. Dillon, "Praying by Number," 453, 463–70. Dillon's article underlines that both Dominican and Carthusian versions of the rosary were popular in England in the Middle Ages. However, the Dominican rosary dominated in Reformation England, as it was the version used by the Jesuit mission.

22. Ibid., 465.

23. For the rosary's association with military symbolism, see Warner, *Alone*, 308.

24. McClain, *Lest We Be Damned*, 99, 96–107.

25. Henry Garnet, *The Societie of the Rosary, Newly Augmented* (London[?]: Henry Garnet's secret press, [1596 or 1597]).

26. Ibid., sigs. *2r, *3r.

27. Ibid., sigs. *4r, *5r.

28. Richard Smith, *An Elizabethan Recusant House, 1609*, ed. A. C. Southern (1609; repr., London: Sands, 1954), is an evocative firsthand account of the house of Lady Magdalen Montague, a woman from a prominent Catholic family who blended power with piety. Lady Montague's life and entourage are discussed by Michael Questier in *Catholicism and Community in Early Modern England* (Cambridge: Cambridge University Press, 2006), 211–32.

29. Bucke's and I. M.'s texts should be distinguished from Garnet's, as they do not encourage their readers to join a confraternity. See Dillon, "Praying by Number," 463.

30. A&R list I. M., conjecturally, as the Carthusian John Mitchell, 546.

31. Discussions of Loyolan methods can be found in N. Mitchell, *Mystery of the Rosary*, 19, 56, 115, and Miola, *Early Modern Catholicism*, 289–96.

32. M. J. Rodriguez-Salgado, "Suárez de Figueroa [Dormer], Jane, Duchess of Feria in the Spanish Nobility (1538–1612)," in *ODNB*.

33. Obvious printer's errors have here been silently corrected.

34. Norman Tanner, ed., *Decrees of the Ecumenical Councils*, 2 vols. (Washington, DC: Georgetown University Press, 1990), 1:774–76.

35. Gaspar Loarte, *Meditations, of the Life and Passion of our Lord and Saviour Jesus Christ*, trans. Anon (London: Fr. Garnet's Second Press, 1596–98), sig. A7v.

36. A discussion of this method can be found in Sullivan, *Dismembered Rhetoric*, 82–83.

37. *Denounced* here has the meaning of "proclaimed" or "announced."

38. Chambers, *Garden*, 134.

39. Gerard Kilroy discusses Harington's allegiances to Catholic families in *Edmund Campion: Memory and Transcription* (Aldershot: Ashgate, 2005), 89–96. *Leicester's Commonwealth* was a ferociously satirical pamphlet written by a group of disaffected Catholic ex-courtiers: it was a capital offense merely to own it. In a manuscript of it now held at Exeter College Oxford, the last part is written entirely in Harington's hand. I am grateful to Gerard Kilroy for alerting me to the existence of this manuscript.

40. For Harington's enthusiasm for metrical psalms, and for an analysis of his own translations of psalms, see Steven W. May, *The Elizabethan Courtier Poets* (Columbia: University of Missouri Press, 1992), 211–14. Harington describes himself as a "protesting Catholic Puritan" in *An Apologie* (London: Richard Field, 1596), sig. P8v, and *A Tract on the Succession to the Crown*, ed. Clements R. Markham (1602; repr., London: Roxburghe Club, 1880), 3.

41. Sir John Harington, *The Epigrams of Sir John Harington*, ed. Gerard Kilroy (Surrey: Ashgate, 2009), 185. Further citations are to page numbers in this edition and are given parenthetically in the text.

42. May, *Courtier Poets*, includes a more detailed dating of the *Epigrams*, 142.

43. Recipients of gift-books by Harington included Lucy, Countess of Bedford, who was a lady of the bedchamber of Queen Anna, as well as Tobie Matthew, Archbishop of York. The significance of these recipients is discussed by Jason Scott-Warren in *Sir John Harington and the Book as Gift* (Oxford: Oxford University Press, 2001). For a discussion of manuscript gift-books and

their relationship with patronage, see H. R. Woudhuysen, *Sir Philip Sidney and the Circulation of Manuscripts* (Oxford: Clarendon Press, 1996), 90–92.

44. The gift-book is now in the Folger Shakespeare library and forms the basis of Gerard Kilroy's edited edition. See Harington, *Epigrams*, ed. Kilroy, 96. For the book to Henry as a way of influencing James, see Scott-Warren, *Book as Gift*, 204, and Kilroy, *Campion*, 98.

45. May, *Courtier Poets*, 150.

46. Although the poems are not, strictly speaking, all epigrams, I term them in this way in this chapter because Harington clearly wanted them to be viewed as such. The use of the titular *Epigrams* refers to the collection in its entirety, as ordered and presented to King James and Prince Henry.

47. The epigrams themselves owe a debt to Martial. See May, *Courtier Poets*, 143.

48. Scott-Warren, *Book as Gift*, chap. 5. The manuscript of the first gift-book, *A Newyeares Guift Sent to the Kings Majestie of Scotland, Anno 1602*, is now lost.

49. Alan Stewart, *The Cradle King: A Life of James I* (London: Chatto and Windus, 2003), 249.

50. Harington, *Epigrams*, ed. Kilroy, 43.

51. These overwritings and emendations are discussed in detail by Kilroy in *Campion*, 105.

52. T. G. A. Nelson, "Death, Dung and the Devil, and Worldly Delights," *Studies in Philology* 76, no. 3 (Summer 1979): 272–74.

53. Jason Scott-Warren, "The Privy Politics of Sir John Harington's *New Discourse of a Stale Subject, Called the Metamorphosis of Ajax*," *Studies in Philology* 93, no. 4 (Autumn 1996): 412–42.

54. Robert Burton, *The Anatomy of Melancholy* (Oxford: John Lichfield and James Short for Henry Cripps, 1621), 21; Curione, *Pasquine*, sig. R3v. For anti-Catholic uses of the word *mumbled* to denote Latin prayers, see Lake and Questier, *Antichrist's Lewd Hat*, 245–46, and Wilkins, *Rose-Garden Game*, 64–79.

55. Dolan, "Gender," 641–65.

56. *The Arundel Manuscript of Tudor Poetry*, ed. Ruth Hughey, 2 vols. (Columbus: Ohio State University Press, 1960), 1:66–67.

57. Ibid., 105.

58. Ibid., 106. Gerard Kilroy sees the presence of the poem as evidence of Harington's lifelong fascination with Edmund Campion; *Campion*, 67–71.

59. Joshua Eckhardt, *Manuscript Verse Collectors and the Politics of Anti-Courtly Love Poetry* (Oxford: Oxford University Press, 2009), 10–11.

60. Marotti, "Marian Verse," 37.

61. Ceri Sullivan, "Constable." Harington recorded twenty-one of Constable's secular sonnets in the Arundel-Harington manuscript. Hughey, *Arundel Manuscript*, 1:244–52.

62. The English translation is headed in Harington's own autograph; Kilroy, *Campion*, 97. See also May, *Courtier Poets*, 213.

63. May, *Courtier Poets*, 202.

64. Harington's poem on Mary Queen of Scots, "A tragicall Epigram" (185), draws comparisons between Mary Queen of Scots and Elizabeth as a Queen "without an head." Its unfavorable presentation of Elizabeth is described by Alison Shell as a poem that "strains at the boundaries of loyalism"; *Catholicism, Controversy*, 120.

65. Debora Shuger, "A Protesting Catholic Puritan in Elizabethan England," *Journal of British Studies* 48 (July 2009): 595, 597, 630.

CHAPTER 7. THE ASSUMPTION AND CORONATION IN
THE POETRY OF ROBERT SOUTHWELL

Sections of an earlier draft of this chapter appear in the article "No Tombe but Throne," in "Readings of Love and Death," ed. Jessica Dyson, Niamh Cooney, and Jana Pridalova, special issue 24, *Early Modern Literary Studies*, 2015, https://extra.shu.ac.uk/emls/journal/index.php/emls/issue/view/13.

1. An account of Southwell's trial and execution is given in "Leake's Relation of the Martyrdom of Father Southwell," reproduced in *Unpublished Documents Relating to the English Martyrs*, Catholic Record Society, ed. John Hungerford Pollen, 2 vols. (London: Burns and Oates, 1891), 1:333–36. An Italian letter written by Henry Garnet on the event is cited in detail in Janelle, *Robert Southwell the Writer*, 86–91. The Jesuit friend in the crowd who received the rosary from Southwell was possibly Garnet himself. See Philip Caraman, *Henry Garnet, 1555–1606, and the Gunpowder Plot* (London: Longmans, 1964), 198–99.

2. BM. Landsdown MS 72, fol. 113, "Burghley Papers, 1592," reproduced in Christobel Hood, *The Book of Robert Southwell: Priest, Poet, Prisoner* (Oxford: Basil Blackwell, 1926), 48.

3. *As You Like It*, 2.7.149.

4. "Epistle" from "The Sequence of Poems from the 'Waldegrave' Manuscript (Stonyhurst MS A.v.27)," included in Southwell, *Collected Poems*, ed. Davidson and Sweeney, 1. Further citations to Southwell's poetry are to page numbers in this edition and are given parenthetically in the text.

5. Anne Sweeney, *Robert Southwell, Snow in Arcadia: Redrawing the English Landscape, 1586–95* (Manchester: Manchester University Press, 2006), 8.

6. Emil Villaret, *An Abridged History of the Sodality of Our Lady* (St. Louis, MO: Queens Work, 1957), 37.

7. Foley, *Records*, 1:319.

8. Elizabethan sanctions toward Jesuits and recusants are outlined in Robert Hutchinson, *Elizabeth's Spy Master: Francis Walsingham and the Secret War That Saved England* (London: Phoenix, 2006), 53–144.

9. For a discussion of the lines between treason and religion, see also Lake and Questier, *Antichrist's Lewd Hat*, 233.

10. Pollen, *Unpublished Documents*, 1:313.

11. Geoffrey Hill, *The Lords of Limit: Essays on Literature and Ideas* (London: André Deutsch, 1984), 20.

12. Nancy Pollard Brown, "Paperchase: The Dissemination of Catholic Texts in Elizabethan England," in *English Manuscript Studies, 1100–1700*, ed. Peter Beal and Jeremy Griffiths (Oxford: Basil Blackwell, 1989), 120–43. See also *Southwell: Collected Poems*, ed. Davidson and Sweeney, xii–xiii. Southwell's poems feature prominently, for example, in Constance Aston Fowler's verse miscellany of the 1630s and in the Catholic verse miscellany Bodleian MS Eng. poet. b. 5. See Helen Hackett, "Women and Catholic Manuscript Networks in Seventeenth-Century England," *Renaissance Quarterly* 65, no. 4 (Winter 2012): 1094–1124, and Cedric C. Brown, "Recusant Community and Jesuit Mission in Parliament Days: Bodleian MS Eng. poet. b. 5," *Yearbook of English Studies* 33 (January 2003): 290–315.

13. Philip Caraman, *A Study in Friendship: Saint Robert Southwell and Henry Garnet* (Saint Louis, MO: Institute of Jesuit Sources, 1995), 68 and passim.

14. Robert S. Miola, "Publishing the Word: Robert Southwell's Sacred Poetry," *Review of English Studies* 64, no. 265 (2013): 410–32.

15. Robert Southwell, *The Poems and Prose Writings of Robert Southwell SJ*, ed. James H. McDonald (Oxford: Roxburghe Club, 1937), 67–101.

16. Cummings, *Literary Culture*, 330.

17. The final two poems from Southwell's sequence, "The Death of Our Ladie" and "The Assumption of Our Lady," were omitted from the first printed editions of Southwell's poetry and were not published until 1856. See F. W. Brownlow, *Robert Southwell* (New York: Twayne, 1996), 104.

18. Shell, *Catholicism, Controversy*, 61; Scott R. Pilarz, *Robert Southwell and the Mission of Literature, 1561–1595: Writing Reconciliation* (Aldershot: Ashgate, 2004), xxi.

19. Christobel Hood's 1926 edition of the poetry of the "sweet Elizabethan singer" gives an example of the kind of language often used; *Book of*

Robert Southwell, 1. See also Rose Anita Morton, *An Appreciation of Robert Southwell* (Philadelphia: University of Pennsylvania Press, 1929), and D. H. Moseley, *Blessed Robert Southwell* (New York: Sheed and Ward, 1957).

20. Janelle, *Robert Southwell the Writer,* 153.

21. Joseph D. Scallon, *The Poetry of Robert Southwell S.J.* (Salzburg: Institut fur Englische Sprache und Literatur, 1975), vii and passim; Anthony Raspa, *The Emotive Image: Jesuit Poetics in the English Renaissance* (Austin: Texas University Press, 1983); Peter Davidson, *The Universal Baroque* (Manchester: Manchester University Press, 2007).

22. Brownlow, *Robert Southwell,* x.

23. Martz, *Poetry of Meditation,* 179–210.

24. Brownlow, *Robert Southwell,* 127, 134; Shell, *Catholicism, Controversy,* 2.

25. Shell, *Catholicism, Controversy,* 63. Brownlow argues that Southwell was a "born poet who in normal circumstances might have produced a body of work comparable to any in his period"; *Robert Southwell,* 134.

26. Shell, *Catholicism, Controversy,* 70–80. See also Christopher Devlin, *The Life of Robert Southwell, Poet and Martyr* (London: Longmans), 222–23.

27. Ben Jonson, *Conversations with William Drummond of Hawthornden,* ed. R. F. Patterson (1619; repr., London: Blackie and Son, 1923), 17.

28. The line appears in verses from "The Author to the Reader" at the opening of *Saint Peters Complaynt.* See Southwell, *Collected Poems,* ed. Davidson and Sweeney, 63. The dedication appeared in a 1616 edition of *Saint Peters Complaynt* published in St. Omer's Jesuit press. The hypothesis that this referred to Shakespeare was first presented in 1868 by the Protestant minister A. B. Grosart in Robert Southwell, *Complete Poems of Robert Southwell,* ed. A. B. Grosart (London: Robson and Sons, 1868), lxxxix–xcii.

29. Richard Wilson's conclusion—that Southwell had read *Venus and Adonis* in manuscript and wrote his dedication to Shakespeare as a result—is a daring leap of faith. See *Secret Shakespeare,* 126–43. John Klause takes the more measured view that Southwell was probably part of Shakespeare's "Catholic reading," positing that Shakespeare seemed "both consciously and unconsciously to have welcomed a Jesuit into his mind." See "New Sources for Shakespeare's *King John*: The Writings of Robert Southwell," *Studies in Philology* 98, no. 4 (Autumn 2001): 403. See also John Klause, *Shakespeare, the Earl and the Jesuit* (Madison, WI: Fairleigh Dickinson University Press, 2008), 19. In *Shakespeare and Religion,* Alison Shell realistically suggests that both writers may in fact have been drawing on similar contemporary commonplaces, but she does not dismiss entirely the notion that Southwell was criticizing Shakespeare's erotic verse. See 85–91 and 256n33.

30. Stonyhurst MS A.vii.1, dated from Rome, October 20, 1580, reproduced in Southwell, *Collected Poems*, ed. Davidson and Sweeney, 118. I am grateful to Tristan Franklinos for the translations of Southwell's Latin verse that appear in this chapter.

31. Raspa, *Emotive Image*, 54.

32. Villaret, *Abridged History*, 38; Pilarz, *Robert Southwell*, 221.

33. Sweeney, *Robert Southwell*, 38.

34. The poem is preserved in the "Autograph" manuscript (Stonyhurst A.v.4) and is reproduced in Southwell, *Collected Poems*, ed. Davidson and Sweeney, 88. Davidson and Sweeney observe that it was written with a readership in mind that was well versed in post-Tridentine theology (140). For manuscripts of Southwell's work still in existence, see Peter Beal, *Index of English Literary Manuscripts*, 4 vols. (London: Mansell, 1980) vol. 1, pt. 2: 495–522, and Southwell, *Poems and Prose Writings*, ed. McDonald, 9–65.

35. Davidson, *Universal Baroque*, 49.

36. Southwell, *Collected Poems*, ed. Davidson and Sweeney, xv. For the importance of theatricals in Jesuit schools, see John W. O'Malley, *The First Jesuits* (Cambridge, MA: Harvard University Press, 1993), 242, and Davidson, *Universal Baroque*, 50–51.

37. Sweeney, *Robert Southwell*, 38–39.

38. Janelle comments that the Virgin's assumption is "disposed of in a couple of prosaic lines," seeing the poem as a flawed juvenile college exercise. See *Robert Southwell the Writer*, 127–31.

39. For the use of syphilis as a powerful symbolic signifier linking disease with desire and pleasure, see Margaret Healy, *Fictions of Disease in Early Modern England* (Basingstoke: Palgrave, 2001), 172.

40. Bale, *Image of Both Churches*, in Bale, *Select Works*, ed. Christmas, 498.

41. In "Loves Servile Lott" (52), Southwell again uses the metaphor of "bait" for earthly beauty, describing a beautiful woman as one who "letteth fall some luring baytes," 25.

42. Peter denies knowing Christ to a servant girl in both Luke 22:54–57 and Mark 14:69–70.

43. Villaret refers to the Sodalists as "knights of our lady" in *Abridged History*, 24–27. See also Devlin, *Life of Robert Southwell*, 10.

44. Although Henry Constable professed his Catholic faith in passionate terms, he was publicly hostile to the Jesuit mission. However, in renouncing secular for sacred verse, and criticizing secular love poetry, he ironically espoused many of Southwell's poetic theories.

45. It is also significant that Southwell here diverts considerably from the source of his poem, Luigi Tansillo's *Le lagrime di San Pietro*, which only alludes

to Christ's glance toward Peter. See Janelle, *Robert Southwell the Writer*, 216. Tansillo's poem as Southwell's source is discussed by Mario Praz in "Robert Southwell's *Saint Peter's Complaint* and Its Italian Source," *Modern Language Review*, 19, no. 3 (July 1924): 273–90.

46. Devlin, *Life of Robert Southwell*, 30; Pilarz, *Robert Southwell*, 117–33.

47. The poems were preserved in the "Waldegrave" manuscript (Stonyhurst MS A.v.27), dating from between 1590 and 1609. Davidson and Sweeney observe that they were written with the beleaguered Catholic community of late Elizabethan England as their intended audience; Southwell, *Collected Poems*, ed. Davidson and Sweeney, xi, 148.

48. Waller, *Virgin Mary*, 150. A similar argument can be found in Brownlow, *Robert Southwell*, 109.

49. Pilarz, *Robert Southwell*, 227.

50. Martz, *Poetry of Meditation*, 101–7. Scallon concludes differently, arguing that the sequence does not concur with the numerical nature of the rosary; *Poetry of Robert Southwell*, 97.

51. This view is discussed by Caraman in *Study in Friendship*, 68, and Sweeney, *Robert Southwell*, 109.

52. Scallon gives a detailed exploration of the epigrammatic nature of the sequence as a whole in *Poetry of Robert Southwell*, 100.

53. In "The prodigall chylds soule wracke," for example, Southwell's sinful speaker bewails the inadequacy of his "dazeled eyes" (38).

54. Robert Southwell, *The Poems of Robert Southwell, S.J.*, ed. James H. McDonald and Nancy Pollard Brown (Oxford: Clarendon Press, 1967), 123.

55. Waller, *Virgin Mary*, 119.

56. Anthony D. Cousins, *The Catholic Religious Poets, from Southwell to Crashaw* (London: Sheed and Ward, 1991), 71.

57. Brownlow, *Robert Southwell*, 120.

58. Visscher, "Marian Devotion," 182.

59. Warner, *Alone*, 221–23.

60. Anne Dillon, *The Construction of Martyrdom in the English Catholic Community* (Aldershot: Ashgate, 2002), 112.

61. Robert Southwell, *An Epistle of Comfort* (Paris[?], 1587–88), 133.

62. Cummings, *Literary Culture*, 331.

63. Davidson, *Universal Baroque*, 177–78.

64. Pollen, *Unpublished Documents*, 1:334.

65. Hill, *Lords of Limit*, 19. Susannah Monta discusses how Southwell's work presents a challenge to Protestant martyrologies in *Martyrdom and Literature*, 128–31.

66. Brownlow, *Robert Southwell*, 23.

67. Dillon, *Construction of Martyrdom*, 113.

68. Shell, *Oral Culture and Catholicism*, 114–48, and Marotti, *Religious Ideology*, 66–94. For the transition from oral accounts of executions to manuscript circulation, see Dillon, *Construction of Martyrdom*, 77.

69. Circignani's paintings were subsequently published in plate form by Giovanni Baptista de Cavelleriis in *Ecclesiae Anglicanae Trophaea* (Rome: Ex Officina Bartholomaei Grassi, 1584), plate 33. See also Miola, *Early Modern Catholicism*, 131–32. The use of Roman dress in Renaissance images of martyrdom and its relation to the persecution of early Christians in Rome is discussed by Anne Dillon in *Michelangelo and the English Martyrs* (Farnham: Ashgate, 2012), 40.

70. Thomas S. Freeman, "*Imitatio Christi* with a Vengeance: The Politicisation of Martyrdom in Early Modern England," in *Martyrs and Martyrdom in England, c. 1400–1700*, ed. Thomas S. Freeman and Thomas F. Mayer (Woodbridge: Boydell Press, 2007), 37. See also Alice Dailey, *The English Martyr from Reformation to Revolution* (Notre Dame, IN: University of Notre Dame Press, 2012), 100. The significance of the *ars moriendi* is discussed by Lake and Questier in *Antichrist's Lewd Hat*, 241.

71. Pilarz, *Robert Southwell*, 85–194; Dillon, *Construction of Martyrdom*, 225.

72. Guiney, *Recusant Poets*, 178.

73. Monta gives a reading of this poem and discusses its relationship with Campion's own famed eloquence in *Martyrdom and Literature*, 26–27.

74. Executed Catholics including John Short, William Filbie, Cuthbert Maine, and Mary Queen of Scots reportedly used this prayer at the point of their death. See Craig Monson, "Byrd, the Catholics and the Motet: The Hearing Reopened," in *Hearing the Motet: Essays on the Motet of the Middle Ages and Renaissance*, ed. Dolores Pesce (Oxford: Oxford University Press, 1997), 370.

75. Foley, *Records*, 374. The main manuscript source for this is Stonyhurst, Anglia A.ii.1., a manuscript by an eyewitness that was copied by Richard Verstegan in 1595. See Devlin, *Life of Robert Southwell*, 323 and 358, note i.

76. For the speech at the scaffold as a way of fostering Catholic communities, see McLain, *Lest We Be Damned*, 148–52.

77. McCarthy, *Liturgy and Contemplation*, 45–59 and 64–69. William Byrd also set select, noncontroversial verses from Walpole's poem "Why do I use my paper, inke and penne." See Kilroy, *Edmund Campion*, 64–65.

78. The scholarship of Joseph Kerman has been seminal in conflating Byrd's motets with occluded references to the plight of English Catholics. See

Joseph Kerman, *The Masses and Motets of William Byrd* (London: Faber and Faber, 1981). Kerman's research was furthered by Craig Monson in an excellent essay arguing that Byrd's familiarity with both Southwell and Garnet was a driving force behind the unusual wording of "In Manus Tuas." See "Byrd, the Catholics," 348–74.

79. Arthur Marotti, "Southwell's Remains," in *Religious Ideology*, 9–31.

80. Caraman, *Study in Friendship*, 11.

81. Southwell, *Epistle of Comfort*, 191–92.

82. Gerard Kilroy makes the same observation about Campion's life in *Edmund Campion*, 7.

Epilogue

1. Got Questions Ministries, "Who Is the Queen of Heaven?," n.d., accessed May 11, 2017, http://www.gotquestions.org/Queen-of-Heaven.html.

2. Charlotte Spretnak, *Missing Mary: The Queen of Heaven and Her Re-emergence in the Modern Church* (New York: Palgrave Macmillan, 2004), 1. The Second Vatican Council (1962–65) introduced a range of changes that shaped the Catholic Church's role in a modern world.

3. Ibid., 1.

4. Ibid., 9.

5. Ayo, *Hail Mary*, 1.

6. Ibid., 3.

7. N. Mitchell, *Mystery of the Rosary*, 234.

8. See Michael Yelton, *Alfred Hope Patten and the Shrine of Our Lady of Walsingham* (Norwich: Canterbury Press, 2006), and William Strange, *The Shrine of Our Lady of Walsingham* (Boston, Lincs: W. H. Smith and Son, 1924).

9. In the Middle Ages, Norfolk was a rich and thriving county and to a great extent rivaled Westminster as a religious center. For changes of the geographical and political landscape, see Stella A. Singer, "Walsingham's Local Genius: Norfolk's 'Newe Nazareth,'" in Janes and Waller, *Walsingham*, 23–34.

10. The Anglican Shrine of Our Lady of Walsingham, "Why Pilgrimage?," n.d., accessed May 25, 2017, https://www.walsinghamanglican.org.uk/the-shrine/why-pilgrimage.

11. Simon Coleman and John Elsner, "Pilgrimage to Walsingham and the Re-invention of the Middle Ages," in *Pilgrimage Explored*, ed. J. Stopford (Woodbridge: York Medieval Press, 1999), 209.

BIBLIOGRAPHY

PRIMARY WORKS

Aldegonde, Marnix van St. *The Bee Hive of the Romishe Church a Commentarie Upon the Sixe Principall Pointes of Master Gentian Hervet*. Translated by George Gylpen. London: Thomas Dawson, 1579.

Allison, A. F., and D. M. Rogers. *The Contemporary Printed Literature of the English Counter-Reformation between 1558 and 1640*. Vol. 2. *Works in English*. Aldershot: Scolar Press, 1994.

Armstrong, Brian G., and Vivienne Larminie. "Du Moulin, Pierre (1568–1658)." In *ODNB*.

Arnauld, Antoine. *Le Franc Discours, Faithfully Englished*. London: James Roberts, 1602.

Aylmer, John. *An Harborowe for Faithfull and Trewe Subjectes Agaynst the Late Blowne Blaste, Concerninge the Governme[n]t of Wemen*. London: John Day, 1559.

Bale, John. *Select Works of John Bale, D.D*. Edited by Henry Christmas. 1545[?] Reprint, Cambridge: Cambridge University Press, 1849.

Barrow, Henry. *A Brief Discoverie Of The False Church*. Dort[?], 1590[?].

Beadle, Richard, ed. *The York Plays: A Critical Edition of the York Corpus Christi Play as Recorded in British Library Additional MS 35290*. 2 vols. Oxford: Oxford University Press, 2009 and 2013.

Becon, Thomas. *The Catechism of Thomas Becon: With Other Pieces Written by Him in the Reign of King Edward the Sixth*. 1564. Reprint, Cambridge: Cambridge University Press for the Parker Society, 1844.

Bell, Thomas. *The Woefull Crie of Rome Containing a Defiance to Popery*. London: T[homas] C[reed] for William Welby, 1605.

Benson, George. *A Sermon Preached at Paules Crosse the Seventh of May, M.DC.IX*. London: H. L[owns] for Richard Moore, 1609.

Bisse, James. *Two Sermons Preached, the One at Paules Crosse the Eighth of Januarie 1580. The Other, at Christe Churche in London on the Same Day in the After Noone.* London: Thomas Woodcocke, 1581.

Black, Joseph L., ed. *The Martin Marprelate Tracts: A Modernised and Annotated Edition.* Cambridge: Cambridge University Press, 2008.

Boys, John. *An Exposition of the Dominical Epistles and Gospels Used in our English Liturgie Throughout The Whole Yeare.* London: Felix Kyngston for William Apsley, 1610.

Bridges, John. *The Supremacie of Christian Princes Over all Persons Throughout Their Dominions.* London: Henrie Bynneman, for Humfrey Toye, 1573.

Bucke, John. *Instructions for the Use of the Beades, Conteining Many Matters of Meditation.* Louvain, 1589.

Burton, Robert. *The Anatomy of Melancholy.* Oxford: John Lichfield and James Short for Henry Cripps, 1621.

Calvin, Jean. *A Harmonie Upon the Three Evangelists, Matthew Mark and Luke.* Translated by E. P. London: Thomas Dawson, 1584.

———. *Tracts and Treatises on the Reformation of the Church.* Translated by Henry Beveridge. 7 vols. Edinburgh: Oliver and Boyd, 1844.

Cavelleriis, Giovanni Baptista de. *Ecclesiae Anglicanae Trophae.* Rome: Ex Officina Bartholomaei Grassi, 1584.

Chambers, Sabine. *The Garden of our B. Lady. Or a Devout manner, How to Serve Her in Her Rosary.* [St. Omer], 1619.

Charke, William. *An Answeare for the Time, unto that foule, and wicked Defence of the censure, that was giuen vpon M. Charkes booke.* London: Thomas Dawson and Tobie Smith, 1583.

Cleaver, Robert. *A Godlie Forme of Householde Government for the Ordering of Private Families, According to the Direction of Gods Word.* London: Felix Kingston for Thomas Man, 1598.

Clinton, Elizabeth. *The Countesse of Lincolnes Nurserie.* Oxford: John Lichfield and James Short, 1622.

Constable, Henry. *Diana: The Sonnets and Other Poems.* Edited by William Carew Hazlitt. London: Basil Montagu Pickering, 1859.

———. *The Poems of Henry Constable.* Edited by Joan Grundy. Liverpool: Liverpool University Press, 1960.

Crashaw, Richard. *The Complete Poetry of Richard Crashaw.* Edited by George Walton Williams. New York: New York University Press, 1972.

Crashaw, William. *The Jesuites Gospel.* London: E. A. for Leonard Becket, 1610.

Cummings, Brian, ed. *The Book of Common Prayer.* Oxford: Oxford University Press, 2011.

Curione, Celio Secundo. *Pasquine in a Traunce a Christian and Learned Dialogue (Contayning Wonderfull and Most Strange Newes Out of Heaven, Purgatorie and Hell).* Translated by W. P. London: Wyliam Seres, 1566[?].

Cutwode, T. [Tailboys Dymoke]. *Caltha Poetarum: or The Bumble Bee.* London: Thomas Creede for Richard Olive, 1599.

Donne, John. *Sermons.* Edited by G. R. Potter and E. M. Simpson. 10 vols. Berkeley: University of California Press, 1953–62.

Downame, George. *A Treatise Concerning Antichrist Divided into Two Bookes.* London: Cuthbert Burbie, 1603.

Du Moulin, Pierre. *Father Cotton a Jesuite.* London: John Barnes, 1614.

Elisabeth of Schönau. *The Complete Works.* Translated and introduced by Anne L. Clark. Preface by Barbara Newman. New York: Paulist Press, 2000.

Erasmus, Desiderius. *Colloquies.* Translated by N. Bailey. 2 vols. 1526. Reprint, London: Reeves and Turner, 1878.

Foley, Henry. *Records of the English Province of the Society of Jesus.* 7 vols. London: Burns and Oates, 1877.

Freud, Sigmund. *The Interpretation of Dreams.* Translated by James Strachey. London: George Allen and Unwin, 1954.

Fulke, William. *A Defense of the Sincere and True Translations of the Holie Scriptures into the English Tong.* London: Henrie Bynneman for George Bishop, 1583.

Garnet, Henry. *The Societie of the Rosary.* London[?]: Henry Garnet's secret press, [1593 or 1594].

———. *The Societie of the Rosary, Newly Augmented.* London[?]: Henry Garnet's secret press, [1596 or 1597].

———. *A Treatise of Christian Renunciation.* London: Fr. Garnet's First Press, 1593.

The Geneva Bible. Introduced by Lloyd E. Berry. Facsimile of 1560 edition. 1969. Reprint, Peabody: Hendrickson, 2007.

Gerard, John. *The Autobiography of an Elizabethan.* Translated by Philip Caraman. 1951. Reprint, London: Longmans, Green, 1965.

Geveren, Sheltco à. *Of the End of This World, and Second Coming of Christ.* Translated by Thomas Rogers. London: Henry Middleton, for Andrew Maunsell, 1582.

Greenwood, Henry. *The Race Celestial, or, A Direct Path to Heaven.* London: N. O. for Henry Bell, 1609.

Griffiths, John, ed. *Book of Homilies.* 1560. Reprint, Vancouver: Regent College, 2008. Facsimile of the 1859 Oxford University Press edition of *The Two Books of Homilies Appointed to Be Read in Churches.*

Guiney, Louise Imogen, ed. *Recusant Poets.* Vol. 1. *St Thomas More to Ben Jonson.* London: Sheed and Ward, 1938.

Harington, Sir John. *An Apologie.* London: Richard Field, 1596.

———. *The Epigrams of Sir John Harington.* Edited by Gerard Kilroy. Farnham: Ashgate, 2009.

———. *A Tract on the Succession to the Crown.* Edited by Clements R. Markham. 1602. Reprint, London: Roxburghe Club, 1880.

Herbert, George. *The English Poems of George Herbert.* Edited by C. A. Patrides. London: Dent, 1974.

Hughey, Ruth, ed. *The Arundel Manuscript of Tudor Poetry.* 2 vols. Columbus: Ohio State University Press, 1960.

I. M. *A Breefe Directory, and Playne Way Howe to Say the Rosary of Our Blessed Lady.* Bruges Flandrorum: excudebat Hu. Holost [i.e., London, W. Carter and J. Lion], 1576.

Jackson, Thomas. *Judah Must into Captivitie.* London: I. Haviland, 1622.

Jewel, John. *Certaine Sermons Preached before the Queenes Majestie, and at Paule's Crosse.* London: Christopher Barker, 1583.

———. *A Defence of the Apologie of the Churche of Englande, Conteininge an Answeare to a certaine Booke lately set foorthe by M. Hardinge.* London: Henry Wykes, 1567.

Jonson, Ben. *Conversations with William Drummond of Hawthornden.* Edited by R. F. Patterson. 1619. Reprint, London: Blackie, 1923.

Knell, Thomas. *A Declaration of Such Tempestuous, and Outrageous Fluddes.* London: William How, 1571.

Knox, John. *The First Blast of the Trumpet Against The Monstruous Regiment of Women.* Geneva: J. Poullain and A. Rebul, 1558.

Lanyer, Aemilia. *The Poems of Aemilia Lanyer, Salve Deus Rex Judaeorum.* Edited by Susanne Woods. Oxford: Oxford University Press, 1993.

Latimer, Hugh. *Sermons.* Edited by George Elwes Corrie. Cambridge: Cambridge University Press, 1845.

Leigh, Dorothy. *The Mothers Blessing.* London: John Budge, 1616.

Loarte, Gaspare. *Meditations, of the Life and Passion of Our Lord and Saviour Jesus Christ.* Translated by Anon. London: Fr. Garnet's Second Press, 1596–98.

Luther, Martin. *Works.* 55 vols. Edited by Jaroslav Pelikan and Helmut T. Lehmann. Saint Louis, MO: Concordia Publishing House, 1956.

Mason, Thomas. *Christs Victorie Over Sathans Tyrannie.* London: George Eld and Ralph Blower, 1615.

Miola, Robert S., ed. *Early Modern Catholicism: An Anthology of Primary Sources.* Oxford: Oxford University Press, 2007.

Mirk, John. *Festial.* 2 vols. Edited by Susan Powell from British Library MS Cotton Claudius A.11. Oxford: Oxford University Press, 2011.

Munday, Antony. *A Second and Third Blast of Retrait from Plaies and Theaters.* London: Henrie Denham, 1580.

Norbrook, David, and H. R. Woudhuysen, eds. *The Penguin Book of Renaissance Verse.* 1992. Reprint, London: Penguin, 2005.

Perkins, William. *The Combat Betweene Christ and the Divell Displayed: or A Commentarie Upon the Temptations of Christ.* London: Melchisedech Bradwood for E. E[dgar], 1606.

———. *An Exposition of the Symbole or Creed of the Apostles According to the Tenour of the Scriptures.* Cambridge: John Legate, 1595.

———. *A Golden Chaine: or The Description of Theologie Containing the Order Of The Causes of Salvation and Damnation.* Cambridge: John Legate, 1600.

———. *Of the Right Knowledge of Christ Crucified.* Cambridge: John Legate, 1596.

———. *A Reformed Catholike.* Cambridge: John Legate, 1598.

———. *Satans Sophistrie Answered by our Saviour Christ and in Divers Sermons Further Manifested.* London: Richard Field for E. E., 1604.

———. *A Warning Against the Idolatrie of the Last Times.* Cambridge: John Legate, 1601.

Platter, Thomas. *Thomas Platter's Travels in England, 1599.* Translated by Clare Williams. London: Jonathan Cape, 1937.

Pollen, John Hungerford, ed. *The Catholic Record Society: Unpublished Documents Relating to the English Martyrs.* 2 vols. London: Burns and Oates, 1891.

Raynalde, Thomas. *The Birth of Mankind, Otherwise Named, The Woman's Book.* Edited by Elaine Hobby. 1560. Reprint, Farnham: Ashgate, 2009.

Sander, Nicholas. *Rise and Growth of the Anglican Schism.* Translated by David Lewis. 1585. Reprint, London: Burns and Oates, 1877.

Saward, John, John Morrill, and Michael Tomko, eds. *Firmly I Believe and Truly: The Spiritual Tradition of Catholic England.* Oxford: Oxford University Press, 2011.

Shakespeare, William. *The Complete Works.* Edited by Gary Taylor, Stanley Wells, John Jowett, and William Montgomery. Oxford: Clarendon Press, 1986.

Sidney, Sir Philip. *The Major Works.* Edited by Katherine Duncan-Jones. 1989. Reprint, Oxford: Oxford University Press, 2002.

Smith, Henry. *A Preparative to Marriage.* London: Thomas Orwin for Thomas Man, 1591.

Smith, Richard. *An Elizabethan Recusant House.* Edited by A. C. Southern. 1609. Reprint, London: Sands, 1954.

Southern, A. C., ed. *Recusant Prose, 1559–1582.* London: Sands, 1950.

Southwell, Robert. *Collected Poems.* Edited by Peter Davidson and Anne Sweeney. Manchester: Carcanet Press, 2007.

———. *Complete Poems of Robert Southwell.* Edited by A. B. Grosart. London: Robson and Sons, 1868.

———. *An Epistle of Comfort.* Paris[?], 1587–88.

———. *The Poems and Prose Writings of Robert Southwell S.J.* Edited by James H. McDonald. Oxford: Roxburghe Club, 1937.

———. *The Poems of Robert Southwell, S.J.* Edited by James H. McDonald and Nancy Pollard-Brown. Oxford: Clarendon Press, 1967.

Spector, Stephen, ed. *The N-Town Play. Cotton MS Vespasian D. 8.* 2 vols. Oxford: Oxford University Press, 1991.

Spenser, Edmund. *The Faerie Queene.* Edited by A. C. Hamilton, Hiroshi Yamashita, and Toshiyuki Suzuki. 2nd ed. Harlow: Pearson Education, 2007.

Spenser, Edmund, and Gabriel Harvey. *Three Proper, and Wittie, Familiar Letters: Lately Passed Betweene two Universitie Men.* London: H. Bynneman, 1580.

Swetnam, Joseph. *The Arraignment of Lewde, Idle, Froward, and Unconstant Women.* London: George Purslowe for Thomas Archer, 1615.

Swift, Edgar, and Angela M. Kinney, eds. *The Vulgate Bible, Douay-Rheims Translation.* 6 vols. Cambridge, MA: Harvard University Press, 2011.

Tanner, Norman, ed. *Decrees of the Ecumenical Councils.* 2 vols. Washington, DC: Georgetown University Press, 1990.

Tuke, Thomas. *New Essayes: Meditations, and Vowes Including In Them The Chiefe Duties Of A Christian.* London: N[icholas] O[kes], 1614.

Tyndale, William, *The Obedience of a Christen Man.* Antwerp: Hans Luft [Hoochstraten], 1528.

Vives, Juan Luis. *The Instruction of a Christen Woman.* Translated by Richard Hyrde, edited by Virginia Walcott Beauchamp, Elizabeth H. Hageman, and Margaret Mikesell. 1529. Reprint, Urbana: University of Illinois Press, 2002.

Voragine, Jacobus de. *The Golden Legend.* Translated by William Granger Ryan, with an introduction by Eamon Duffy. 1993. Reprint, Princeton, NJ: Princeton University Press, 2012.

Whately, William. *A Bride Bush or Wedding Sermon.* London: William Jaggard for Nicholas Bourne, 1619.

Willet, Andrew. *Synopsis Papismi.* London: Thomas Orwin for Thomas Man, 1592.

Williamson, Magnus, ed. *The Eton Choirbook Facsimile and Introductory Study*. Oxford: DIAMM [Digital Image Archive of Medieval Music], 2010.

Worthington, Thomas. *Rosarie of Our Ladie, Otherwise Called Our Ladies Psalter*. Antwerp: Joannem Keerbergium, 1600.

SECONDARY WORKS

Ackerman, Susan. "'And the Women Knead Dough': The Worship of the Queen of Heaven in Sixth Century Judah." In *Gender and Difference in Ancient Israel*, edited by Peggy L. Day, 109–24. Minneapolis: Fortress Press, 1987.

Allinson, David J. "The Rhetoric of Devotion: Some Neglected Elements in the Context of the Early Tudor Votive Antiphon." PhD diss., University of Exeter, 1998.

Amussen, Susan D. *An Ordered Society: Gender and Class in Early Modern England*. New York: Basil Blackwell, 1988.

Ashe, Geoffrey. *The Virgin: Mary's Cult and the Re-emergence of the Goddess*. 1976. Reprint, Reading, PA: Arkana, 1988.

Asquith, Clare. *Shadowplay: The Hidden Beliefs and Coded Politics of William Shakespeare*. New York: Public Affairs, 2005.

Aston, Margaret. *England's Iconoclasts*. Oxford: Oxford University Press, 1988.

———. *Faith and Fire: Popular and Unpopular Religion, 1350–1600*. London: Hambledon Press, 1993.

———. *Lollards and Reformers: Images and Literacy in Late Medieval Religion*. London: Hambledon Press, 1984.

Atkinson, Clarissa W. *The Oldest Vocation: Christian Motherhood in the Middle Ages*. Ithaca, NY: Cornell University Press, 1991.

Ayo, Nicholas. *The Hail Mary: A Verbal Icon of Mary*. Notre Dame, IN: University of Notre Dame Press, 1994.

Barrol, Leeds. "Looking for Patrons." In Grossman, *Aemilia Lanyer*, 29–48.

Bass, Marissa. "Justus Lipsius and His Silver Pen." *Journal of the Warburg and Courtauld Institutes* 70 (2007): 157–94.

Bates, Catherine. *The Rhetoric of Courtship in Elizabethan Language and Literature*. Cambridge: Cambridge University Press, 1992.

Beal, Peter. *Index of English Literary Manuscripts*. 4 vols. London: Mansell, 1980.

Beattie, Tina. *Eve's Pilgrimage: A Woman's Quest for the City of God*. London: Burns and Oates, 2002.

———. "Mary in Patristic Theology." In Boss, *Mary*, 75–105.

Beier, A. L. *Masterless Men: The Vagrancy Problem in England, 1560–1640.* London: Methuen, 1985.

Beilin, Elaine. *Redeeming Eve: Women Writers of the English Renaissance.* Princeton, NJ: Princeton University Press, 1987.

Bell, Ilona. *Elizabethan Women and the Poetry of Courtship.* Cambridge: Cambridge University Press, 1998.

Belting, Hans. *Likeness and Presence: A History of the Image before the Era of Art.* Translated by Edmund Jephcott. Chicago: University of Chicago Press, 1994.

Bennett, Lyn. *Women Writing of Divinest Things: Rhetoric and the Poetry of Pembroke, Wroth and Lanyer.* Pittsburgh, PA: Duquesne University Press, 2004.

Berger, Harry. *The Allegorical Temper: Vision and Reality in Book II of Spenser's "Faerie Queene."* New Haven, CT: Yale University Press, 1957.

Berry, Philippa. *Of Chastity and Power: Elizabethan Literature and the Unmarried Queen.* London: Routledge, 1989.

Bevington, David. "A. L. Rowse's Dark Lady." In Grossman, *Aemilia Lanyer,* 10–28.

Blench, John Wheatley. *Preaching in England in the Late Fifteenth and Sixteenth Centuries: A Study of English Sermons, 1450–c.1600.* Oxford: Basil Blackwell, 1964.

Boase, Roger. *The Origin and Meaning of Courtly Love: A Critical Study of European Scholarship.* Manchester: Manchester University Press, 1977.

Boose, Lynda E. "Scolding Brides and Bridling Scolds: Taming the Woman's Unruly Member." *Shakespeare Quarterly* 42, no. 2 (Summer 1991): 179–213.

Boss, Sarah Jane. "The Development of the Virgin's Cult in the High Middle Ages." In Boss, *Mary,* 149–72.

———. *Empress and Handmaid: Nature and Gender in the Cult of the Virgin Mary.* London: Cassell, 2000.

———, ed. *Mary: The Complete Resource.* Oxford: Oxford University Press, 2007.

Bossy, John. "À Propos of Henry Constable." *Recusant History* 6 (1962): 228–37.

———. *The English Catholic Community, 1570–1850.* London: Longman and Todd, 1975.

Brown, Cedric C. "Recusant Community and Jesuit Mission in Parliament Days: Bodleian MS Eng. poet. b. 5." *Yearbook of English Studies* 33 (January 2003): 290–315.

Brown, Nancy Pollard. "Paperchase: The Dissemination of Catholic Texts in Elizabethan England." In *English Manuscript Studies, 1100–1700,* edited by Peter Beal and Jeremy Griffiths, 120–43. Oxford: Basil Blackwell, 1989.

Brown, Raymond E., Karl P. Donfried, Joseph A. Fitzmyer, and John Reumann, eds. *Mary in the New Testament.* Philadelphia: Fortress Press, 1978.

Brownlow, F. W. *Robert Southwell.* New York: Twayne, 1996.

Buccola, Regina, and Lisa Hopkins, eds. *Marian Moments in Early Modern British Drama.* Aldershot: Ashgate, 2007.

Bynum, Caroline Walker. *Fragmentation and Redemption: Essays on Gender and the Human Body in Medieval Religion.* New York: Zone Books, 1991.

———. *Jesus as Mother: Studies in the Spirituality of the High Middle Ages.* Berkeley: University of California Press, 1982.

Cameron, Averil. "The Cult of the Virgin in Late Antiquity: Religious Development and Myth Making." In Swanson, *Church and Mary*, 1–21.

Caraman, Philip. *Henry Garnet, 1555–1606, and the Gunpowder Plot.* London: Longmans, 1964.

———. *A Study in Friendship: Saint Robert Southwell and Henry Garnet.* Saint Louis, MO: Institute of Jesuit Sources, 1995.

Carey, John. *John Donne: Life, Mind and Art.* London: Faber and Faber, 1981.

Carroll, Michael P. *The Cult of the Virgin Mary: Psychological Origins.* Princeton, NJ: Princeton University Press, 1986.

———. *Madonnas That Maim: Popular Catholicism in Italy since the Fifteenth Century.* Baltimore: John Hopkins University Press, 1992.

———. "Pilgrimage at Walsingham on the Eve of the Reformation: Speculations on a 'Splendid Diversity' Only Dimly Perceived." In Janes and Waller, *Walsingham in Literature*, 35–48.

Catty, Jocelyn. "Leigh, Dorothy (*d.* in or before 1616)." In *ODNB*.

Chedgzoy, Kate, Melanie Hansen, and Suzanne Trill, eds. *Voicing Women: Gender and Sexuality in Early Modern Writing.* Pittsburgh, PA: Duquesne University Press, 1996

Clark, Stuart. *Vanities of the Eye: Vision in Early Modern European Culture.* Oxford: Oxford University Press, 2007.

Clarke, Danielle. "The Iconography of the Blush: Marian Literature of the 1630s." In Chedgzoy, Hansen, and Trill, *Voicing Women*, 111–28.

Clarke, Elizabeth. *Politics, Religion and the Song of Songs in Seventeenth-Century England.* Basingstoke: Palgrave Macmillan, 2011.

Claydon, Tony. "The Sermon, the 'Public Sphere' and the Political Culture of Late Seventeenth-Century England." In *The English Sermon Revised: Religion, Literature and History, 1600–1750*, edited by Lori Anne Ferrell and Peter McCullough, 208–34. Manchester: Manchester University Press, 2000.

Clayton, Mary. *The Apocryphal Gospels of Mary in Anglo-Saxon England.* Cambridge: Cambridge University Press, 1998.

Coch, Christine. "'Mother of My Contreye': Elizabeth I and Tudor Constructions of Motherhood.'" *English Literary Renaissance* 26, no. 3 (1996):
423–50.

Coleman, Simon. "Mary: Images and Objects." In Boss, *Mary*, 395–410.

Coleman, Simon, and John Elsner. "Pilgrimage to Walsingham and the Re-
invention of the Middle Ages." In *Pilgrimage Explored*, edited by J. Stopford, 189–214. Woodbridge: York Medieval Press, 1999.

Collinson, Patrick. "Barrow, Henry (c. 1550–1593)." In *ODNB*.

———. "Biblical Rhetoric: The English Nation and National Sentiment in the
Prophetic Mode." In *Religion and Culture in Renaissance England*, edited by Claire McEachern and Debora Shuger, 15–45. Cambridge: Cambridge University Press, 1997.

———. *The Birthpangs of Protestant England: Religious and Cultural Change
in the Sixteenth and Seventeenth Centuries.* Basingstoke: Macmillan, 1988.

———. *From Cranmer to Sancroft.* New York: Hambledon Continuum, 2006.

———. *The Religion of Protestants: The Church in English Society, 1559–1625.*
Oxford: Oxford University Press, 1982.

Collinson, Patrick, Arnold Hunt, and Alexandra Walsham. "Religious Publish-
ing in England, 1557–1640." In *The Cambridge History of the Book in
Britain*, vol. 4, *1557–1695*, edited by John Barnard and D. F. McKenzie with
Maureen Bell, 29–66. Cambridge: Cambridge University Press, 2002.

Cook, Timothy. "Gabriel Harvey, 'Pasquill,' Spenser's Lost 'Dreames,' and
The Faerie Queene." *Yearbook of English Studies* 7 (1977): 75–80.

Cousins, Anthony D. *The Catholic Religious Poets, from Southwell to Crashaw.* London: Sheed and Ward, 1991.

Craig, John. "Jewel, John (1522–1571)." In *ODNB*.

———. "Sermon Reception." In McCullough, Adlington, and Rhatigan, *Oxford Handbook*, 178–97.

Crawford, Katherine. "Catherine de Medicis and the Performance of Political
Motherhood." *Sixteenth Century Journal* 31, no. 3 (2000): 643–73.

Crockett, Bryan. *The Play of Paradox: Stage and Sermon in Renaissance England.* Philadelphia: University of Pennsylvania Press, 1995.

Cross, Claire. "Excising the Virgin Mary from the Civic Life of Tudor York."
Northern History 39 (2002): 279–84.

Cummings, Brian. *The Literary Culture of the Reformation: Grammar and
Grace.* Oxford: Oxford University Press, 2002.

———. *Mortal Thoughts: Religion, Secularity and Identity in Shakespeare
and Early Modern Culture.* Oxford: Oxford University Press, 2013.

Cummings, Brian, and James Simpson, eds. *Cultural Reformations: Medieval
and Renaissance in Literary History.* Oxford: Oxford University Press, 2010.

Cunneen, Sally. *In Search of Mary: The Woman and the Symbol.* New York: Ballantine Books, 1996.

Dailey, Alice. *The English Martyr from Reformation to Revolution.* Notre Dame, IN: University of Notre Dame Press, 2012.

Davidson, Peter. *The Universal Baroque.* Manchester: Manchester University Press, 2007.

Davis, David J. *Seeing Faith, Printing Pictures: Religious Identity during the English Reformation.* Leiden: Brill, 2013.

Dent, Robert William. *Proverbial Language in English Drama Exclusive of Shakespeare, 1495–1616: An Index.* Berkeley: University of California Press, 1984.

Devlin, Christopher. *The Life of Robert Southwell, Poet and Martyr.* London: Longmans, 1956.

Dickens, A. G. *The English Reformation.* 2nd ed. London: B. T. Batsford, 1989.

Dickinson, J. C. *The Shrine of Our Lady of Walsingham.* Cambridge: Cambridge University Press, 1956.

Diehl, Huston. *Staging Reform, Reforming the Stage: Protestantism and Popular Theater in Early Modern England.* Ithaca, NY: Cornell University Press, 1997.

Dillon, Anne. *The Construction of Martyrdom in the English Catholic Community.* Aldershot: Ashgate, 2002.

———. *Michelangelo and the English Martyrs.* Farnham: Ashgate, 2012.

———. "Praying by Number: The Confraternity of the Rosary and the English Catholic Community, c. 1580–1700." *History* 88, no. 291 (July 2003): 451–71.

DiPasquale, Theresa M. *Refiguring the Sacred Feminine: The Poems of John Donne, Aemilia Lanyer, and John Milton.* Pittsburgh, PA: Duquesne University Press, 2008.

Dolan, Frances E. "Gender and the 'Lost' Spaces of Catholicism." *Journal of Interdisciplinary History* 32, no. 4 (Spring 2002): 641–65.

———. *Whores of Babylon: Catholicism, Gender, and Seventeenth-Century Print Culture.* Ithaca, NY: Cornell University Press, 1999.

Doran, Susan. "Why Did Elizabeth Not Marry?" In Walker, *Dissing Elizabeth*, 30–59.

Dubrow, Heather. *Echoes of Desire: English Petrarchism and Its Counterdiscourses.* Ithaca, NY: Cornell University Press, 1995.

Duffy, Eamon. *Fires of Faith: Catholic England under Mary Tudor.* New Haven, CT: Yale University Press, 2009.

———. *The Stripping of the Altars: Traditional Religion in England, c. 1400–c. 1580.* 2nd ed. New Haven, CT: Yale University Press, 2005.

Dunn-Hensley, Susan. "Return of the Sacred Virgin." In Janes and Waller, *Walsingham in Literature*, 185–97.

Dutka, Joanna. *Music in the English Mystery Plays*. Early Drama, Art and Music Series. Kalamazoo, MI: Medieval Institute Publications, 1980.

Dutton, Richard, Alison Findlay, and Richard Wilson, eds. *Lancastrian Shakespeare*. Vol. 1. *Region, Religion and Patronage*. Manchester: Manchester University Press, 2003.

———. *Lancastrian Shakespeare*. Vol. 2. *Theatre and Religion*. Manchester: Manchester University Press, 2003.

Dymond, D., and C. Paine. *The Spoil of Long Melford Church: The Reformation in a Suffolk Parish*. Ipswich: Salient, 1992.

Eckhardt, Joseph. *Manuscript Verse Collectors and the Politics of Anti-Courtly Love*. Oxford: Oxford University Press, 2009.

Eggert, Katherine. *Showing Like a Queen: Female Authority and Literary Experiment in Spenser, Shakespeare and Milton*. Philadelphia: University of Pennsylvania Press, 2000.

Ellington, Donna Spivey. *From Sacred Body to Angelic Soul: Understanding Mary in Late Medieval and Early Modern Europe*. Washington, DC: Catholic University of America Press, 2001.

Elliot, J. K. "Mary in the Apocryphal New Testament." In *The Origins of the Cult of the Virgin Mary*, edited by Chris Maunder, 57–70. London: Burns and Oates, 2008.

Espinosa, Ruben. *Masculinity and Marian Efficacy in Shakespeare's England*. Farnham: Ashgate, 2011.

Ferrell, Lori Anne, and Peter McCullough, eds. *The English Sermon Revised: Religion, Literature and History, 1600–1750*. Manchester: Manchester University Press, 2000.

———. *Government by Polemic: James I, the King's Preachers, and the Rhetorics of Conformity*. Stanford, CA: Stanford University Press, 1998.

Ford, Judy Ann. *John Mirk's "Festial": Orthodoxy, Lollardy and the Common People in Fourteenth-Century England*. Cambridge: D. S. Brewer Press, 2006.

Foster, Leonard. *The Icy Fire: Five Studies in European Petrarchism*. Cambridge: Cambridge University Press, 1969.

Franssen, Paul J. C. M. "Donne's Jealous God and the Concept of Sacred Parody." In Wilcox, Todd, and MacDonald, *Sacred and Profane*, 150–62.

Freeman, Thomas S. "*Imitatio Christi* with a Vengeance: The Politicisation of Martyrdom in Early Modern England." In *Martyrs and Martyrdom in England, c. 1400–1700*, edited by Thomas S. Freeman and Thomas F. Mayer, 35–69. Woodbridge: Boydell Press, 2007.

Frieda, Leonie. *Catherine de Medici.* London: Phoenix, 2003.

Gibson, Gail McMurray. *The Theatre of Devotion: East Anglian Drama and Society in the Late Middle Ages.* Chicago: University of Chicago Press, 1989.

Gibson, Kenneth. "Downham [Downame], George (d. 1634)." In *ODNB.*

Gilman, Ernest B. *Iconoclasm and Poetry in the English Reformation.* Chicago: University of Chicago Press, 1986.

Graef, Hilda. *Mary: A History of Doctrine and Devotion.* Rev. ed. Notre Dame, IN: Ave Maria Press, 2009.

Gray, Catherine. "Feeding on the Seed of the Woman: Dorothy Leigh and the Figure of Maternal Dissent." *English Literary History* 68, no. 3 (Fall 2001): 563–92.

Greaves, Richard L. "Charke, William (d. 1617)." In *ODNB.*

Green, Ian. "Preaching in the Parishes." In McCullough, Adlington, and Rhatigan, *Oxford Handbook,* 137–54.

———. *Print and Protestantism in Early Modern England.* Oxford: Oxford University Press, 2000.

Greenblatt, Stephen. *Hamlet in Purgatory.* Princeton, NJ: Princeton University Press, 2001.

———. *Shakespearean Negotiations.* Oxford: Oxford University Press, 1988.

Greenfield, Sayre N. *The Ends of Allegory.* Newark: University of Delaware Press, 1998.

Grindlay, Lilla. "No Tombe but Throne." In "Readings of Love and Death," edited by Jessica Dyson, Niamh Cooney, and Jana Pridalova, special issue 24, *Early Modern Literary Studies,* 2015. https://extra.shu.ac.uk/emls/journal/index.php/emls/issue/view/13.

Grogan, Jane. *The Persian Empire in English Renaissance Writing, 1549–1622.* Basingstoke: Palgrave Macmillan, 2014.

Grossman, Marshall, ed. *Aemilia Lanyer: Gender, Genre and the Canon.* Lexington: University Press of Kentucky, 1998.

Guibbory, Achsah. "The Gospel According to Aemilia: Women and the Sacred." In Grossman, *Aemilia Lanyer,* 191–211.

Hackett, Helen. "The Art of Blasphemy? Interfusions of the Erotic and the Sacred in the Poetry of Donne, Barnes and Constable." *Renaissance and Reformation/Renaissance et Réforme* 28, no. 3 (2004): 27–51.

———. "The Rhetoric of (In)fertility: Shifting Responses to Elizabeth I's Childlessness." In *Rhetoric, Women and Politics in Early Modern England,* edited by J. Richards and A. Thorne, 149–71. New York: Routledge, 2007.

———. *Virgin Mother, Maiden Queen: Elizabeth I and the Cult of the Virgin Mary.* Basingstoke: Palgrave, 1995.

———. "Women and Catholic Manuscript Networks in Seventeenth-Century England." *Renaissance Quarterly* 65, no. 4 (Winter 2012): 1094–1124.

Hadfield, Andrew. *Edmund Spenser: A Life.* Oxford: Oxford University Press, 2012.

Haigh, Christopher. "The Continuity of Catholicism in the English Reformation." *Past and Present* 93 (1981): 37–69.

———. *Reformation and Resistance in Tudor Lancashire.* Cambridge: Cambridge University Press, 1975.

Haller, William, and Malleville Haller. "The Puritan Art of Love." *Huntington Library Quarterly* 5, no. 2 (January 1942): 235–72.

Hamrick, Stephen. *The Catholic Imaginary and the Cults of Elizabeth, 1558–1582.* Burlington, VT: Ashgate, 2009.

Hankins, John E. "Spenser and the Revelation of St John." *PMLA* 60 (1945): 364–81.

Heal, Bridget. *The Cult of the Virgin Mary in Early Modern Germany.* Cambridge: Cambridge University Press, 2007.

———. "Marian Devotion and Confessional Identity in Sixteenth-Century Germany." In Swanson, *Church and Mary,* 218–27.

Healy, Margaret. *Fictions of Disease in Early Modern England.* Basingstoke: Palgrave, 2001.

Henderson, Katherine Usher, and Barbara F. McManus, eds. *Half Humankind: Contexts and Texts of the Controversy about Women in England, 1540–1640.* Urbana: University of Illinois Press, 1985.

Hill, Geoffrey. *The Lords of Limit: Essays on Literature and Ideas.* London: André Deutsch, 1984.

Hindson, Bethan. "Attitudes towards Menstruation and Menstrual Blood in Elizabethan England." *Journal of Social History* 43, no. 1 (Autumn 2009): 89–114.

Hood, Christobel M. *The Book of Robert Southwell: Priest, Poet, Prisoner.* Oxford: Basil Blackwell, 1926.

Houlbrooke, Ralph. *Church Courts and the People during the English Reformation, 1520–70.* Oxford: Oxford University Press, 1979.

Hughes, Peter. "Curione, Celio Secondo." In *Dictionary of Unitarian and Universalist Biography,* edited by Unitarian Universalist History and Heritage Society. http://uudb.org/articles/celiosecondocurione.html.

Huizinga, J. J. *The Waning of the Middle Ages.* 1924. Reprint, New York: Anchor Books, 1954.

Hull, Suzanne W. *Chaste, Silent and Obedient: English Books for Women, 1475–1640.* San Marino, CA: Huntington Library, 1982.

Hume, Anthea. *Edmund Spenser, Protestant Poet.* Cambridge: Cambridge University Press, 1984.

Hunt, Arnold. *The Art of Hearing: English Preachers and Their Audiences.* Cambridge: Cambridge University Press, 2010.

Hutchinson, Robert. *Elizabeth's Spy Master: Francis Walsingham and the Secret War That Saved England.* London: Phoenix, 2006.

Janelle, Pierre. *Robert Southwell the Writer: A Study in Religious Inspiration.* Clermont-Ferrand: Vallier; New York: Sheed and Ward, 1935.

Janes, Dominic, and Gary Waller, eds. *Walsingham in Literature and Culture from the Middle Ages to Modernity.* Farnham: Ashgate, 2010.

Jardine, Lisa. *Still Harping on Daughters: Women and Drama in the Age of Shakespeare.* Brighton: Harvester Press, 1983.

Johnson, Trevor. "Mary in Early Modern Europe." In Boss, *Mary*, 363–84.

Jones, Ann Rosalind. *The Currency of Eros: Women's Love Lyric in Europe, 1540–1620.* Indianapolis: Indiana University Press, 1990.

Jones, Ann Rosalind, and Peter Stallybrass. "The Politics of *Astrophil and Stella.*" *Studies in English Literature, 1500–1900* 24, no. 1 (1984: Winter): 53–68.

Kastan, David Scott. *A Will to Believe: Shakespeare and Religion.* Oxford: Oxford University Press, 2014.

Kelso, Ruth. *Doctrine for the Lady of the Renaissance.* Urbana: University of Illinois Press, 1956.

Kerman, Joseph. *The Masses and Motets of William Byrd.* London: Faber and Faber, 1981.

Kessler, Herbert L., and Johanna Zacharias. *Rome 1300: On the Path of the Pilgrim.* New Haven, CT: Yale University Press, 2000.

Kilroy, Gerard. *Edmund Campion: Memory and Transcription.* Aldershot: Ashgate, 2005.

King, John N. *Spenser's Poetry and the Reformation Tradition.* Princeton, NJ: Princeton University Press, 1990.

———. *Tudor Royal Iconography: Literature and Art in an Age of Religious Crisis.* Princeton, NJ: Princeton University Press, 1989.

Klause, John. "New Sources for Shakespeare's *King John*: The Writings of Robert Southwell." *Studies in Philology* 98, no. 4 (Autumn 2001): 401–27.

———. *Shakespeare, the Earl, and the Jesuit.* Madison, WI: Fairleigh Dickinson University Press, 2008.

Knapp, Jeffrey. *Shakespeare's Tribe: Church, Nation, and Theater in Renaissance England.* Chicago: University of Chicago Press, 2002.

Knox, Francesca Bugliani, and David Lonsdale, eds. *Poetry and the Religious Imagination: The Power of the Word.* Farnham: Ashgate, 2015.

Kreitzer, Beth. *Reforming Mary: Changing Images of the Virgin Mary in Lutheran Sermons of the Sixteenth Century.* Oxford: Oxford University Press, 2004.

Krier, Theresa M. *Gazing on Secret Sights: Spenser, Classical Imitation, and the Decorums of Vision.* Ithaca, NY: Cornell University Press, 1990.

Kristeva, Julia. "Stabat Mater." In *The Female Body in Western Culture: Contemporary Perspectives,* edited by Susan Rubin Suleiman, 99–118. Cambridge, MA: Harvard University Press, 1986.

Kuchar, Gary. "Aemilia Lanyer and the Virgin's Swoon: Theology and Iconography in *Salve Deus Rex Judaeorum.*" *English Literary Renaissance* 37, no. 1 (December 2007): 47–73.

———. "Henry Constable and the Question of Catholic Poetics: Affective Piety and Erotic Identification in the Spiritual Sonnets." *Philological Quarterly* 85, nos. 1–2 (Winter 2006): 69–90.

Lake, Peter. "Anti-Popery." In *Conflict in Early Stuart England,* edited by Richard Cust and Ann Hughes, 72–106. London: Longman, 1989.

Lake, Peter, and Michael Questier. *The Antichrist's Lewd Hat: Protestants, Papists and Players in Post-Reformation England.* New Haven, CT: Yale University Press, 2002.

Lee, Christopher. *1603: A Turning Point in British History.* London: Headline, 2003.

Levering, Matthew. *Mary's Bodily Assumption.* Notre Dame, IN: University of Notre Dame Press, 2015.

Levin, Carole. "'We Shall Never Have a Merry World While the Queene Lyveth': Gender, Monarchy, and the Power of Seditious Words." In Walker, *Dissing Elizabeth,* 77–95.

Lewalski, Barbara Kiefer. "Of God and Good Women: The Poems of Aemilia Lanyer." In *Silent but for the Word: Tudor Women as Patrons, Translators and Writers of Religious Works,* edited by Margaret Patterson Hannay, 203–24. Kent, OH: Kent State University Press, 1985.

———. *Writing Women in Jacobean England.* Cambridge, MA: Harvard University Press, 1993.

Loomis, Catherine. *The Death of Elizabeth I: Remembering and Reconstructing the Virgin Queen.* Basingstoke: Palgrave Macmillan, 2010.

Lupton, Julia Reinhard. *Afterlives of the Saints: Hagiography, Typography and Renaissance Literature.* Stanford, CA: Stanford University Press, 1996.

Luria, Keith P. "Popular Catholicism and the Catholic Reformation." In *Early Modern Catholicism: Essays in Honour of J. W. O'Malley, S.J.,* edited by Kathleen M. Comerford and Hilmar M. Pabel, 114–31. Toronto: University of Toronto Press, 2002.

MacCulloch, Diarmaid. *A History of Christianity*. London: Penguin, 2009.

———. "Mary and Sixteenth-Century Protestants." In Swanson, *Church and Mary*, 191–217.

MacDonald, A. A. "Contrafacta and the *Gude and Godlie Ballatis*." In Wilcox, Todd, and MacDonald, *Sacred and Profane*, 33–44.

Mack, Peter. *Elizabethan Rhetoric: Theory and Practice*. Cambridge: Cambridge University Press, 2002.

MacLure, Millar. *The Paul's Cross Sermons, 1534–1641: An Introductory Survey*. Toronto: University of Toronto Press, 1958.

Marotti, Arthur F., ed. *Catholicism and Anti-Catholicism in Early Modern English Texts*. Basingstoke: Macmillan Press, 1999.

———. "'Love Is Not Love': Elizabethan Sonnet Sequences and the Social Order." *English Literary History* 49, no. 2 (Summer 1982): 396–428.

———. "Marian Verse as Politically Oppositional Poetry in Elizabethan England." In *Religious Diversity and Early Modern English Texts: Catholic, Judaic, Feminist, and Secular Dimensions*, edited by Arthur F. Marotti and Chanita Goodblatt, 25–54. Detroit, MI: Wayne State University Press, 2013.

———. *Religious Ideology and Cultural Fantasy: Catholic and Anti-Catholic Discourses in Early Modern England*. Notre Dame, IN: University of Notre Dame Press, 2005.

Martz, Louis L. *The Poetry of Meditation*. Rev. ed. New Haven, CT: Yale University Press, 1962.

Matter, E. Ann. *The Voice of My Beloved: The Song of Songs in Western Medieval Christianity*. Philadelphia: University of Pennsylvania Press, 1990.

Maunder, Chris. "Mary in the New Testament and Apocrypha." In Boss, *Mary*, 11–46.

May, Steven W. *The Elizabethan Courtier Poets: The Poems and Their Contexts*. Columbia: University of Missouri Press, 1992.

Mayr-Harting, Henry. "The Idea of the Assumption of Mary in the West, 800–1200." In Swanson, *Church and Mary*, 86–111.

Mazzola, Elizabeth. *The Pathology of the English Renaissance: Sacred Remains and Holy Ghosts*. Studies in the History of Christian Thought 86. Leiden: Brill, 1998.

McCarthy, Kerry. *Liturgy and Contemplation in Byrd's Gradualia*. New York: Routledge, 2007.

McClain, Lisa. *Lest We Be Damned: Practical Innovation and Lived Experience among Catholics in Protestant England, 1559–1642*. New York: Routledge, 2004.

McCoog, Thomas M. "Martin, Gregory (1542?–1582)." In *ODNB*.

McCullough, Peter. *Sermons at Court: Politics and Religion in Elizabethan and Jacobean Preaching.* Cambridge: Cambridge University Press, 1998.

McCullough, Peter, Hugh Adlington, and Emma Rhatigan, eds. *The Oxford Handbook of the Early Modern Sermon.* Oxford: Oxford University Press, 2011.

McDannell, Colleen, and Bernhard Lang. *Heaven, a History.* New Haven, CT: Yale University Press, 1988.

McEachern, Claire. *The Poetics of English Nationhood, 1590–1612.* Cambridge: Cambridge University Press, 1996.

McGiffert, Michael. "God's Controversy with Jacobean England." *American Historical Review* 88 (1983): 1151–76.

McGinn, Bernard. "Teste David cum Sibylla: The Significance of the Sibylline Tradition in the Middle Ages." In *Women of the Medieval World: Essays in Honour of John H. Mundy,* edited by Julius Kirshner and Suzanne Wemple, 6–35. Oxford: Basil Blackwell, 1985.

McGrath, Lynette. *Subjectivity and Women's Poetry in Early Modern England.* Burlington: Ashgate, 2002.

McGrath, Patrick. *Papists and Puritans under Elizabeth I.* London: Blandford Press, 1967.

McGuckin, John. "The Early Cult of Mary and Inter-Religious Contexts in the Fifth-Century Church." In *The Origins of the Cult of the Virgin Mary,* edited by Chris Maunder, 1–22. London: Burns and Oates, 2008.

Meikle, Maureen M. "A Meddlesome Princess: Anna of Denmark and Scottish Court Politics, 1589–1603." In *The Reign of James VI,* edited by Julian Goodare and Michael Lynch, 126–40. East Lothian: Tuckwell, 2000.

Merritt, J. F. "Tuke, Thomas (1580/81–1657)." In *ODNB.*

Mikesell, Margaret. "The Place of Vives's Instruction of a Christen Woman in Early Modern English Domestic Book Literature." In *Contextualizing the Renaissance: Returns to History: Selected Proceedings from the 28th Annual CEMERS Conference,* edited by Albert H. Tricomi, 105–18. Turnhout: Brepols, 1999.

Miles, Margaret. *A Complex Delight: The Secularization of the Breast, 1350–1750.* Berkeley: University of California Press, 2008.

———. *Image as Insight: Visual Understanding in Western Christianity and Secular Culture.* Boston: Beacon, 1985.

Miller, David Lee. *The Poem's Two Bodies: The Poetics of the 1590 "Faerie Queene".* Princeton, NJ: Princeton University Press 1988.

Miller, Naomi J. "(M)other Tongues: Maternity and Subjectivity." In Grossman, *Aemilia Lanyer,* 141–66.

Milton, Anthony. *Catholic and Reformed.* Cambridge: Cambridge University Press, 1995.

Milward, Peter. *The Catholicism of Shakespeare's Plays.* Southampton: Saint Austin Press, 1997.

———. *Shakespeare's Religious Background.* London: Sidgwick and Jackson, 1973.

Miola, Robert S. *Early Modern Catholicism.* Oxford: Oxford University Press, 2007.

———. "Publishing the Word: Robert Southwell's Sacred Poetry." *Review of English Studies* 64 (2013): 410–32.

Mitchell, Nathan D. *The Mystery of the Rosary: Marian Devotion and the Re-invention of Catholicism.* New York: New York University Press, 2009.

Mitchell, William Fraser. *English Pulpit Oratory from Andrewes to Tillotson.* London: S. P. C. K., 1932.

Monson, Craig. "Byrd, the Catholics and the Motet: The Hearing Re-opened." In *Hearing the Motet: Essays on the Motet of the Middle Ages and Renaissance,* edited by Dolores Pesce, 348–74. Oxford: Oxford University Press, 1997.

Monta, Susannah Brietz. *Martyrdom and Literature in Early Modern England.* Cambridge: Cambridge University Press, 2005.

Montrose, Louis. "Celebration and Insinuation: Sir Philip Sidney and the Motives of Elizabethan Courtship." *Renaissance Drama* 8 (1977): 3–35.

———. "*Eliza, Queen of Shepheardes* and the Pastoral of Power." *English Literary Renaissance* 10 (1980): 153–82.

———. "The Purpose of Playing: Reflections on a Shakespearean Anthropology." *Helios* 7 (1980): 51–74.

———. "Shaping Fantasies: Figurations of Gender and Power in Elizabethan Culture." *Representations* 2 (Spring 1983): 61–94.

———. *The Subject of Elizabeth: Authority, Gender and Representation.* Chicago: University of Chicago Press, 2006.

Morrison, Susan Signe. *Women Pilgrims in Late Medieval England.* London: Routledge, 2000.

Morrissey, Mary. "Elect Nations and Prophetic Preaching: Types and Examples in the Paul's Cross Jeremiad." In *The English Sermon Revised: Religion, Literature and History, 1600–1750,* edited by Lori Anne Ferrell and Peter McCullough, 43–58. Manchester: Manchester University Press, 2000.

Morton, Rose Anita. *An Appreciation of Robert Southwell.* Philadelphia: University of Pennsylvania Press, 1929.

Moseley, D. H. *Blessed Robert Southwell.* New York: Sheed and Ward, 1957.

Mudan, Kavita. "'A Queen in Jest': Queenship and Historical Subversion in Shakespeare's *3 Henry VI* and *Richard III.*" In *Representations of Elizabeth I in Early Modern Culture*, edited by Alessandra Petrina and Laura Tosi, 244–56. Basingstoke: Palgrave Macmillan, 2011.

Mueller, Janet. "The Feminist Poetics of *Salve Deus Rex Judaeorum.*" In Grossman, *Aemilia Lanyer*, 99–127.

Nelson, T. G. A. "Death, Dung and the Devil, and Worldly Delights: A Metaphysical Conceit in Harington, Donne and Herbert." *Studies in Philology* 76, no. 3 (Summer 1979): 272–87.

Null, Ashley. "Official Tudor Homilies." In McCullough, Adlington, and Rhatigan, *Oxford Handbook*, 348–65.

O'Connell, Michael. *The Idolatrous Eye: Iconoclasm and Theatre in Early Modern England.* Oxford: Oxford University Press, 2000.

———. *Mirror and Veil: The Historical Dimension of Spenser's "Faerie Queene."* Chapel Hill: University of North Carolina Press, 1977.

O'Malley, John W. *The First Jesuits.* Cambridge, MA: Harvard University Press, 1993.

Orlin, Lena Cowen. "The Fictional Families of Elizabeth I." In *Political Rhetoric, Power, and Renaissance Women*, edited by Carole Levin and Patricia A. Sullivan, 84–110. Albany: State University of New York Press, 1995.

Osherow, Michelle. *Biblical Women's Voices in Early Modern England.* Farnham: Ashgate, 2009.

Overell, Anne. *Italian Reform and English Reformations, c.1535–1585.* Aldershot: Ashgate, 2008.

Oxford Dictionary of National Biography Online. http://www.oxforddnb.com.

Panizza, Letizia. "Pasquino among Anglican Reformers: The Two Editions in English (1566 and 1584) of Celio Secondo Curione's *Pasquino in Estasi.*" In *Ex Marmore: Pasquini, Pasquinisti, Pasquinate nell'Europa moderna. Atti del colloquio internazionale, Lecce-Otranto, 17–19 novembre 2005*, edited by Chrysa Damianaki, Paulo Procaccioli, and Angelo Romano, 407–28. Rome: Vecchiareli Editore, 2006.

Paster, Gail Kern. *The Body Embarrassed: Drama and the Disciplines of Shame in Early Modern England.* Ithaca, NY: Cornell University Press, 1993.

Pearson, Jacqueline. "Women Writers and Women Readers: The Case of Aemilia Lanyer." In Chedgzoy, Hansen, and Trill, *Voicing Women*, 45–54.

Pelikan, Jaroslav. *Mary through the Centuries.* New Haven, CT: Yale University Press, 1996.

Peters, Christine. *Patterns of Piety: Women, Gender and Religion in Late Medieval and Reformation England.* Cambridge: Cambridge University Press, 2003.

Pettegree, Andrew. *Reformation and the Culture of Persuasion.* Cambridge: Cambridge University Press, 2005.

Phillips, James Emerson. *Images of a Queen: Mary Stuart in Sixteenth-Century Literature.* Berkeley: University of California Press, 1964.

Phillips, John. *The Reformation of Images: Destruction of Art in England, 1535–1660.* Berkeley: University of California Press, 1973.

Pilarz, Scott R. *Robert Southwell and the Mission of Literature, 1561–1595: Writing Reconciliation.* Aldershot: Ashgate, 2004.

Praz, Mario. "Robert Southwell's *Saint Peter's Complaint* and Its Italian Source." *Modern Language Review* 19, no. 3 (July 1924): 273–90.

Price, Richard. "Theotokos: The Title and Its Significance in Doctrine and Devotion." In Boss, *Mary,* 56–74.

Pritchard, Arnold. *Catholic Loyalism in Elizabethan England.* London: Scolar Press, 1979.

Questier, Michael. *Catholicism and Community in Early Modern England.* Cambridge: Cambridge University Press, 2006.

Raber, Karen. *Dramatic Difference: Gender, Class, and Genre in the Early Modern Closet Drama.* Newark: University of Delaware Press, 2001.

Raspa, Anthony. *The Emotive Image: Jesuit Poetics in the English Renaissance.* Fort Worth: Texas University Press, 1983.

Rastall, Richard. *The Heaven Singing: Music in Early English Religious Drama.* 2 vols. Cambridge: D. S. Brewer, 1996.

Ray, Sid. *Mother Queens and Princely Sons: Rogue Madonnas in the Age of Shakespeare.* New York: Palgrave Macmillan, 2012.

Read, Sophie. *Eucharist and the Poetic Imagination in Early Modern England.* Cambridge: Cambridge University Press, 2013.

Rendle-Short, Morwenna, and John Rendle-Short. *The Father of Child Care: Life of William Cadogan (1711–1797).* Bristol: John Wright, 1966.

Rhatigan, Emma. "Preaching Venues: Architecture and Auditories." In McCullough, Adlington, and Rhatigan, *Oxford Handbook,* 87–119.

Richardson, William. "Boys, John (*bap.* 1571, *d.* 1625)." In *ODNB.*

Rigney, James. "Sermons into Print." In McCullough, Adlington, and Rhatigan, *Oxford Handbook,* 198–212.

Rodriguez-Salgado, M. J. "Suárez de Figueroa [Dormer], Jane, Duchess of Feria in the Spanish Nobility (1538–1612)." In *ODNB.*

Rouse, Clive E. *Medieval Wall Paintings.* 1968. Reprint, Princes Risborough: Shire, 1991.

Rowlands, Mary B. "Recusant Women, 1560–1640." In *Women in English Society, 1500–1800,* edited by Mary Prior, 149–80. London: Methuen, 1985.

Rubin, Miri. *Mother of God: A History of the Virgin Mary.* London: Penguin, 2009.

Ryan, Salvador. "The Persuasive Power of a Mother's Breast: The Most Desperate Act of the Virgin Mary's Advocacy." *Studia Hibernica* 32 (2002–3): 59–74.

Santi, Angelo de. "Litany of Loreto." In *The Catholic Encyclopedia.* New York: Robert Appleton Company, 1910.

Scallon, Joseph D. *The Poetry of Robert Southwell S.J.* Salzburg: Institut fur Englische Sprache und Literatur, 1975.

Scarisbrick, Diana. *Tudor and Jacobean Jewellery.* London: Tate, 1995.

Scarisbrick, J. J. *The Reformation and the English People.* Oxford: Basil Blackwell, 1984.

Scott-Warren, Jason. "The Privy Politics of Sir John Harington's *New Discourse of a Stale Subject, Called the Metamorphosis of Ajax.*" *Studies in Philology* 93, no. 4 (1996): 412–42.

———. *Sir John Harington and the Book as Gift.* Oxford: Oxford University Press, 2001.

Shami, Jeanne. "Women and Sermons." In McCullough, Adlington, and Rhatigan, *Oxford Handbook,* 155–77.

Shell, Alison. *Catholicism, Controversy and the English Literary Imagination, 1558–1660.* Cambridge: Cambridge University Press, 1999.

———. *Oral Culture and Catholicism in Early Modern England.* Cambridge: Cambridge University Press, 2007.

———. *Shakespeare and Religion.* London: Arden, 2010.

Shoemaker, Stephen J. *Ancient Traditions of the Virgin Mary's Dormition and Assumption.* Oxford: Oxford University Press, 2002.

———. "Marian Liturgies and Devotion in Early Christianity." In Boss, *Mary,* 130–45.

Shuger, Debora. "A Protesting Catholic Puritan in Elizabethan England." *Journal of British Studies* 48 (July 2009): 587–630.

Siemon, James R. *Shakespearean Iconoclasm.* Berkeley: University of California Press, 1985.

Singer, Stella A. "Walsingham's Local Genius: Norfolk's 'Newe Nazareth.'" In Janes and Waller, *Walsingham in Literature,* 23–34.

Spaeth, John W., Jr. "Martial and the Pasquinade." *Transactions and Proceedings of the American Philological Association* 70 (1939): 242–55.

Spiller, Michael R. G. *The Development of the Sonnet: An Introduction.* London: Routledge, 1992.

Spretnak, Charlotte. *Missing Mary: The Queen of Heaven and Her Re-emergence in the Modern Church.* New York: Palgrave Macmillan, 2004.

Spurr, Barry. *See the Virgin Blest: The Virgin Mary in English Poetry*. Basingstoke: Palgrave Macmillan, 2007.

Stallybrass, Peter. "Patriarchal Territories: The Body Enclosed." In *Rewriting the Renaissance: The Discourses of Sexual Difference in Early Modern Europe*, edited by Margaret W. Ferguson, Maureen Quilligan, and Nancy J. Vickers, 123–42. Chicago: University of Chicago Press, 1986.

Stevens, John. "The Music of Play XLV: The Assumption of the Virgin." In *The York Plays*, edited by Richard Beadle, 465–74. London: Edward Arnold, 1982.

Stewart, Alan. *The Cradle King: A Life of James I*. London: Chatto and Windus, 2003.

Stone, Lawrence. *The Family, Sex and Marriage in England, 1500–1800*. London: Penguin, 1977.

Strange, William. *The Shrine of Our Lady of Walsingham*. Boston, Lincs: W. H. Smith and Son, 1924.

Stringer, Gary A. "Some Sacred and Profane Contexts of John Donne's 'Batter My Hart.'" In Wilcox, Todd, and MacDonald, *Sacred and Profane*, 173–83. Amsterdam: VU University Press, 1996.

Strong, Roy. *Gloriana: The Portraits of Queen Elizabeth I*. London: Thames and Hudson, 1987.

Sullivan, Ceri. "Constable, Henry (1562–1613)." In *ODNB*.

———. *Dismembered Rhetoric: English Recusant Writing, 1580–1603*. London: Associated University Presses, 1995.

Swanson, R. N., ed. *The Church and Mary: Papers Read at the 2001 Summer Meeting and the 2002 Winter Meeting of the Ecclesiastical History Society*. Woodbridge: Ecclesiastical History Society, 2004.

Sweeney, Anne. *Robert Southwell, Snow in Arcadia: Redrawing the English Landscape, 1586–95*. Manchester: Manchester University Press, 1988.

Tennenhouse, Leonard. "Sir Walter Ralegh and the Literature of Clientage." In *Patronage in the Renaissance*, edited by Guy Fitch Lytle and Stephen Orgel, 235–58. Princeton, NJ: Princeton University Press, 1981.

Tillyard, Jeane-Marie R. "The Marian Issues." In *Studying Mary: Reflections on the Virgin Mary in Anglican and Roman Catholic Theology and Devotion*, edited by Adelbert Denaux and Nicholas Sagovsky, 4–11. London: Continuum, 2007.

Todd, Margo. *Christian Humanism and the Puritan Social Order*. Cambridge: Cambridge University Press, 1987.

Tolhurst, J. B. L. "The Hammer-Beam Figures of the Nave Roof of St. Mary's Church, Bury St. Edmunds." *Journal of the British Archaeological Association*, 3rd ser., 25 (1962): 66–70.

Turner, Victor, and Edith Turner. *Image and Pilgrimage in Christian Culture*: *Anthropological Perspectives.* Oxford: Basil Blackwell, 1978.

Tyacke, Nicholas, ed. *England's Long Reformation, 1500–1800.* London: UCL Press, 1998.

Underdown, David. "The Taming of the Scold: The Enforcement of Patriarchal Authority in Early Modern England." In *Order and Disorder in Early Modern England*, edited by Anthony Fletcher and John Stevenson, 116–36. Cambridge: Cambridge University Press, 1985.

———. "Yellow Ruffs and Poisoned Possets: Placing Women in Early Stuart Political Debate." In *Attending to Early Modern Women*, edited by Susan D. Amussen and Adele F. Seeff, 230–43. Cranbury: Associated University Press, 1998.

Veevers, Erica. *Images of Love and Religion: Queen Henrietta Maria and Court Entertainments.* Cambridge: Cambridge University Press, 1989.

Villaret, Emil. *An Abridged History of the Sodality of Our Lady.* St. Louis: Queens Work, 1957.

Visscher, Eva de. "Marian Devotion in the Latin West in the Late Middle Ages." In Boss, *Mary*, 177–201.

Wabuda, Susan. *Preaching during the English Reformation.* Cambridge: Cambridge University Press, 2002.

Walker, Julia M., ed. *Dissing Elizabeth: Negative Representations of Gloriana.* Durham, NC: Duke University Press, 1998.

Wall, Wendy. *The Imprint of Gender: Authorship and Publication in the English Renaissance.* Ithaca, NY: Cornell University Press, 1993.

Waller, Gary. *A Cultural Study of Mary and the Annunciation: From Luke to the Enlightenment.* London: Pickering and Chatto, 2015.

———. *The Virgin Mary in Late Medieval and Early Modern English Literature and Popular Culture.* Cambridge: Cambridge University Press, 2011.

———. "The Virgin's 'Pryvytes:' Walsingham and the Late Medieval Sexualisation of the Virgin." In Janes and Waller, *Walsingham in Literature*, 113–29.

———. *Walsingham and the English Imagination.* Farnham: Ashgate, 2011.

Walsham, Alexandra. "Bell, Thomas (*b. c.*1551, *d.* in or after 1610)." In *ODNB*.

———. *Church Papists: Catholicism, Conformity and Confessional Polemic in Early Modern England.* Woodbridge: Boydell Press, 1999.

———. "'Domme Preachers'? Post-Reformation English Catholicism and the Culture of Print." *Past and Present* 168 (2000): 77–123.

———. *Providence in Early Modern England.* Oxford: Oxford University Press, 1999.

———, ed. *Relics and Remains. Past and Present.* Suppl. 5. Oxford: Oxford University Press, 2010.

Warner, Marina. *Alone of All Her Sex: The Myth and the Cult of the Virgin Mary*. 1976. Reprint, New York: Vintage, 1983.

Watt, Tessa. *Cheap Print and Popular Piety, 1550–1640*. Cambridge: Cambridge University Press, 1991.

Wells, Robin Headlam. *Spenser's "Faerie Queene" and the Cult of Elizabeth*. London: Croom Helm, 1983.

Whitelock, Anna. *Mary Tudor: England's First Queen*. London: Bloomsbury, 2009.

Wiesner-Hanks, Merry E. "Luther and Women: The Death of Two Marys." In *Disciplines of Faith: Studies in Religion, Politics and Patriarchy*, edited by Jim Obelkevich, Lyndal Roper, and Raphael Samuel, 295–308. London: Routledge and Kegan Paul, 1987.

———. *Women and Gender in Early Modern Europe*. Cambridge: Cambridge University Press, 2008.

Wilcox, Helen, Richard Todd, and Alasdair MacDonald, eds. *Sacred and Profane: Secular and Devotional Interplay in Early Modern British Literature*. Amsterdam: VU University Press, 1996.

Wilkins, Eithne. *The Rose-Garden Game: The Symbolic Background to the European Prayer Beads*. London: Victor Gollancz, 1969.

Williams, Paul. "The English Reformers and the Blessed Virgin Mary." In Boss, *Mary*, 238–55.

Williams, Rowan. *Ponder These Things: Praying with Icons of the Virgin*. Norwich: Canterbury Press, 2002.

Wilson, Richard. *Secret Shakespeare: Studies in Theatre, Religion and Resistance*. Manchester: Manchester University Press, 2004.

Woods, Gillian. *Shakespeare's Unreformed Fictions*. Oxford: Oxford University Press, 2013.

Woods, Susanne. *Lanyer: A Renaissance Woman Poet*. Oxford: Oxford University Press, 1999.

Woudhuysen, H. R. *Sir Philip Sidney and the Circulation of Manuscripts*. Oxford: Clarendon Press, 1996.

Yalom, Marilyn. *A History of the Breast*. London: Harper Collins, 1997.

Yates, Frances A. "Queen Elizabeth as Astraea." *Journal of the Warburg Institute* 10 (1947): 27–82.

Yelton, Michael. *Alfred Hope Patten and the Shrine of Our Lady of Walsingham*. Norwich: Canterbury Press, 2006.

Zlatar, Antoinina Bevan. *Reformation Fictions: Polemical Protestant Dialogues in Elizabethan England*. Oxford: Oxford University Press, 2011.

INDEX

Adam, 124, 195
Aldegonde, Marnix van St., 79–80
Allinson, David, 33
ancilla Domini, 4, 13, 44, 63–67, 82,
  107–9, 112, 127
  and godly Protestant woman,
  108–12
  separation from *Regina Coeli*,
  35–36, 66–69, 73, 79–80, 131,
  132, 217–18
  See also Magnificat; silence
Angel Gabriel, 18, 31, 112, 127–29,
  161, 186, 195–96, 245n.45
Anna of Denmark, 9, 53, 122,
  234n.38, 250n.48
Annunciation, 4, 18, 31, 37–38, 43,
  126–29, 161, 168, 173, 178, 220,
  245n.45
apostasy, 117, 134–35, 137–39
apostles, 18, 27–29, 146, 176–77,
  209
  John the Evangelist, 23, 28–29
  Peter, 18, 199–201, 259n.42
  Thomas, 30
Arnauld, Antoine, 151–52
Arundel-Harington manuscript,
  182–84, 256n.61

Assumption, history of
  belief in bodily assumption,
  17–18, 20–22, 26, 28, 38,
  176–77
  Feast of the Assumption, 18,
  24–26, 31, 33, 37–38
  patristic history and early
  narratives, 16–18
Aston, Margaret, 72, 76
Aylmer, John, 54, 235n.45
Ayo, Nicholas, 219, 245n.47

Bale, John, 35, 74, 98, 198
Baroque aesthetic, 130, 193,
  196, 201, 213, 215. *See also*
  Counter-Reformation
Barrow, Henry, 59–60, 236n.61
Battle of Lepanto, 168
Beattie, Tina, 8
Becon, Thomas, 108–9
Beilin, Elaine, 109
Bell, Thomas, 65–67
Belting, Hans, 25
Berger, Harry, 93
Bernard of Clairvaux, 24, 28,
  207–8
Bèze, Théodore de, 79, 185

LILLA GRINDLAY

is the head of the English faculty at

Sutton Valence School in Kent, England.

CPSIA information can be obtained
at www.ICGtesting.com
Printed in the USA
FFHW021303120219
50532095-55803FF

9 780268 104108